THE NATURE OF THE WORLD

THE NATURE
OF THE WORLD

*An Essay
in Phenomenalist Metaphysics*

BY

Walter Terrance

W. T. STACE
III

GREENWOOD PRESS, PUBLISHERS
NEW YORK

Originally published in 1940
by Princeton University Press

First Greenwood Reprinting, 1969

Library of Congress Catalogue Card Number 69-14093

SBN 8371-1039-4

PRINTED IN UNITED STATES OF AMERICA

PREFACE

ABOUT the beginning of this century realism displaced idealism as the dominant philosophy of England and America. I should perhaps go beyond the truth if I were to suggest that phenomenalism is now displacing realism. If I were to say that our grandfathers were idealists, our fathers realists, and we of this generation phenomenalists—those of us who are not nihilists—I should be uttering a pleasant exaggeration. But at least I shall not overstate my case if I say that there are signs in many quarters, both among philosophers and men of science, of a drift away from realism towards phenomenalism. I count myself among those who wish to forward this movement.

But phenomenalism, so far, has no metaphysic. It is a kind of spirit or flavour which appears sporadically in the treatment of detached problems, mostly in epistemology and the philosophy of science. Hence this attempt to found a phenomenalistic metaphysic. Not that I expect other phenomenalists to agree with my specific views. But I shall perhaps be able to make some suggestions which will give my philosophical friends—and enemies—material for discussion.

The remark in a preface that one has learned most from those from whom one differs most is indeed trite. And yet I cannot forbear to repeat it. The type of philosophy with which I am most palpably in disagreement is realism. Yet it is to the British realists, Russell, Broad, Alexander, Price—but above all G. E. Moore—that I am most indebted. And I believe that they have contributed elements of lasting value to philosophy. I find that Professor Dawes Hicks, in his book "Critical Realism," expresses a view of consciousness which has strong

*points of resemblance, in certain respects, to mine. But I had
not read his book until after my own was completed.*

*Among older writers, I am most indebted to Hume and
Berkeley.*

W. T. S.

PRINCETON UNIVERSITY
20 JANUARY, 1940

CONTENTS

THE NATURE OF THE WORLD

CHAPTER I

Metaphysics and Empiricism

1

METAPHYSICS is the search for the real. It follows that the notion of reality is not the same as the notion of mere being or existence, for if the real were simply identified with whatever has being, there would be no occasion to search for it. A man, to find the real, would need only to open his eyes. Hence an explanation of the notion of reality is due. How is it to be distinguished from that existence which is not real?

There are two possible conceptions of the real. The first is that which distinguishes it from mere appearance. The second distinguishes it from mere abstraction. On the first view the problem of metaphysics is to find reality within, beyond, or behind appearance. This is, subject to the qualification of the next paragraph, the prevailing view of Bradley. According to the second view the problem of metaphysics is to search for the concrete, and to distinguish it from the merely abstract. This, on the whole, is the view of Whitehead.[1]

Sometimes the two notions are combined. Thus the real, for Bradley, is opposed both to the apparent and the abstract. It is the concrete as well as that which lies behind appearance. But he puts the emphasis on reality as distinguished from appearance.

I reject the distinction between appearance and reality in this sense. It implies that the universe has two layers or strata,

---

[1] Whitehead, however, uses the term "actual." The term "reality" has in his writings a wider sense.

one of the real, the other of the merely apparent. The merely apparent, however, is identical with the world of "phenomena," that is, the experiencible world. Hence reality is conceived as being outside and beyond all possible experience. But according to the empirical principle, which I accept, the notion of a being beyond all possible experience has no meaning. We cannot, therefore, admit this hidden and inaccessible layer. This means that the distinction between appearance and reality is rejected. All existence is on one plane, the plane of possible experience. In our metaphysic the world must be conceived as having only one layer. The real is to be discovered, if anywhere, in what was in earlier times called "the phenomenal world," the everyday world of which we are aware through our intellects and senses. The real, if it has any meaning at all, means the concrete.

It is true that those who preach the distinction of reality from appearance might, with some show of reason, protest against the interpretation of their views just given. We do not teach, they would say, this sharp division between reality and appearance. We do not place them on two opposite sides of a fence. Reality is not merely behind appearance, hidden from all view, totally invisible. Appearance is taken up into reality and included in it. It is the real which appears. The placing of reality in a world beyond the world is the very thing against which we protest.[2]

True, but is this position intelligible? I believe it is not. It is this which leads to all the endless contradictions with which readers of Bradley (for example) are so familiar. The world in space and time is both real and not real. It is mere appearance and yet it is "taken up" into reality. Time, for example, is mere appearance. But yet it cannot be excluded from the real, for the real is the whole and so must include everything. Time, as being mere appearance, is certainly *not* in the Absolute. The Absolute is not temporal. Yet time must be in the Absolute since everything is. How can this be? Is it

[2] See, for example, Bradley, *Appearance and Reality*, Book I, Chap. XII.

not a flat contradiction? No. For what is meant is that although time is in the Absolute, it is not time *as such*. Time, when it enters into the bosom of the Absolute, is transfigured. But the contradiction is not thus to be exorcized. It breaks out again. For this transfigured time, which is in the Absolute, is it really time at all, or is it something quite different? If it is really time, for example if it is *successive*, then it has not been transfigured and cannot be in the Absolute. But if it is really transformed, so as no longer to be successive, then it is no longer in any sense time. And in that case time is not taken up into the Absolute. The suggestion that all these contradictions must be resolved "somehow, we know not how"[3] in the Absolute, gives little consolation and less light.

Thus the distinction between appearance and reality leads to one of two results. Either we shall have a two-layer world, with reality cut off altogether from all possible experience. And this is forbidden by the empirical principle. Or we shall have an attempt to conceive a mere appearance which is yet not a mere appearance but a part of reality. And this leads to utter self-contradiction. Thus the distinction of appearance from reality must be abandoned.

2

WE are left with the suggestion that the real is the concrete. But it will be well to reflect a little further on the rejection of a two-layer world, and to observe that this already "places" us and decides our sympathies and dis-sympathies in regard to many of the most vital problems of philosophy and religion. For just as there are two-layer and one-layer philosophies, so there are two-layer and one-layer religions. And it will help us to consider them. One-layer religions are theistic, two-layer religions pantheistic. The former are European, the latter Indian—not necessarily, I mean, in their origins, but in their spirit. Hinduism is the typical two-layer religion. The absolute being is not for it *before* the beginning of the world in time,

[3] This phrase constantly appears in Bradley's book.

but *behind* the world. Time itself is a veil which hides the inscrutable being. This being is not in the stream of time. As a waterfall flows over an unchanging wall of perpendicular rock, blotting it out from view, so does the stream of time fall over and hide the changeless face of God.

Christianity is the typical one-layer religion. God for it is not behind the world, but before the beginning of it. Go back in time far enough and you come to the act of creation, and then before that there was God in awful loneliness. It is true that learned theologians reject this view of a time before creation and substitute more complicated ideas. God created time as part of the world. But these are the refinements of highly sophisticated minds, philosophically educated men, men who imported into Christianity alien ideas from Greece and from the Asiatic hinterland far beyond Palestine. The pure and essential Christianity is and always has been a religion of plain and simple men, fisher-folk and artisans, a popular religion. It was founded by simple and uneducated men, and it has been kept alive by such men to this day, not by theologizing intellectuals. It is of this Christianity that I speak. And whatever He may be for the learned, God is for the masses of Christians essentially a person among other persons, greater than they, lasting throughout all time, while they last only a few brief years. He existed for all time before the world, and then at a certain moment in his beginningless life created the world.

It is for this reason that Christianity is a one-layer religion. There is the layer of time, with the stream of phenomena in time. God is in this world, part of it. He belongs to the same layer as do all other existences. Hence there is no other layer.

We find two utterly different conceptions of the coming into being of the world. In Christianity it is by an act of *creation*. In Hinduism the world is a *manifestation*. Creation implies an act in time, and a time before which there was no world. It implies that God was *before* the world, and that the world flows in time from Him as source. Manifestation means that God timelessly thrusts the world outwards from Himself as

[6]

centre. He supports the world from behind, shining through it as the light of a lamp shines through a translucent screen.

With the pantheistic two-layer religions go the pantheistic two-layer philosophies, such as those of Spinoza, Schelling, Schopenhauer, Bradley. They are Indian in their fundamental conception. With the theistic one-layer religions go the theistic one-layer philosophies, such as those of Descartes, Berkeley, and Leibniz. They are essentially European philosophies. The most typical of these is the system of Berkeley. Berkeley's God is simply a person among other persons. He is one of ourselves in the sense that, although the supreme creator, although supposed to be "infinite," He is yet in reality simply *another* mind. His existence is "proved" by Berkeley by the same argument by which—it is supposed—we prove the existence of each other's minds, the analogy from behaviour. He is certainly along with us in the same layer of being. There is no suggestion of another layer. Berkeley's world, like that of any good empiricist, is all surface. And God is part of the surface. The fact that He created the other parts does not alter this.

One-layer philosophies can believe in a personal God, but such a conception is repugnant to a two-layer system. A person necessarily exists in time, for he cannot be conceived except as a stream of consciousness. Hence a God who lies outside the stream of time cannot be a person. Attempts to reconcile in one idea a timeless God and a God who is a person are mere metaphysical acrobatics.

The considerations of this section may seem to constitute a digression from our topic. But I hold them to be important. They indicate from the start to which of the two great types of world-conceptions, the Indian and the European, this metaphysic will give its adherence. It will evidently belong to the European type. And on its religious side, it will be theistic, not pantheistic. All this is determined from the outset by the initial rejection of the distinction of appearance from reality, by the rejection, that is, of a two-layer universe.

WE are committed to the conception of the real as being identical with the concrete. What is meant by the concrete? If there are two entities, *A* and *B*, which are elements in a whole, *X*; and if *A* is in its nature such that it cannot exist without *B*, nor *B* without *A*, then in our terminology *A* and *B* will be called "abstractions." Whether the whole, *X*, is a concrete, cannot be determined until it is known whether it can exist by itself. If *X* in its turn cannot exist apart from its junction with *Y*, then it is still not fully concrete. It is conceivable that, as some philosophers have supposed, nothing less than the whole universe is genuinely concrete. But I find no evidence for this view. According to this metaphysic there are many concretes. This metaphysic is pluralistic.

The metaphysical hypothesis to be unfolded here is that the ultimate constituents of the universe are what will be termed metaphysical "cells." Cells alone are concrete. All conceivable abstractions arise from separating out in thought the elements of cells which are in fact inseparable from one another. The universe is a multitude of cells. But the hypothesis is monistic in the sense that it admits only one kind of reality. It does not admit, for example, that minds are concrete, and that matter is concrete, and that they are two different kinds of concrete. Cells or concretes, though various in qualitative character, are all structurally of one kind.

The following will illustrate the notions of concrete and abstract. In the visual world colour cannot exist without surface, nor surface without colour. Visual surface and colour are therefore abstractions. Whether the compound, coloured surface, is a concrete, or is still an abstraction from some fuller concrete, need not at present be considered.

Another example is afforded by Berkeley's argument against the objectivity of primary qualities. He urged that primary and secondary qualities must have the same *locus* since they cannot be separated or exist apart from one another. This was a mode of expressing the belief that each set of qualities, taken alone, is an abstraction.

The notion of the concrete takes the place, in this metaphysic, of the older notion of "substance." There have been various conceptions of substance. The various conceptions, however, have not usually been kept apart in philosophical discussions, but have tended to melt into one another. The two most important may be distinguished. First, a substance is a hidden substratum supporting qualities. Second, a substance is that which can exist by itself without the aid of anything else. The first notion is, of course, rejected here as being forbidden by the empirical principle. The second notion practically makes substantiality identical with concreteness. It is philosophically unobjectionable. The current outcry against substances is aimed at the first conception because of its non-empirical character. There would be no objection to calling cells substances, provided this does not import an unchanging entity underneath, which yet somehow carries change on its surface. There is nothing in the cells which is not in constant process. I shall not use the word substance because of its associations. I shall call the cells reals or concretes.

It is very fashionable to talk about "events" and to contrast them with substances to the disadvantage of the latter. This is part of the campaign against substances conceived as permanent substrata. But it may be asked what is the relation between events and concretes. At present I can only say that there is no opposition between the notions of event and concrete. Presumably if you hold that the constituents of the world are events, then you must conceive events as concretes. There is no objection against regarding the metaphysical cells of this philosophy as being essentially streams of events.

The enterprise in which we are engaged, the discovery of concretes, is no new adventure. It has generally been the leading aim of metaphysics. The philosophy of Aristotle was concerned with it. Descartes found two, or rather three, kinds of concretes, Berkeley only one, which he called "spirits." Leibniz's monads are his concretes. The modern realist believes that bits of matter, such as atoms or stars, can exist in the absence of minds or any other thing. That is, he believes them to be concretes. If anyone thinks, to the contrary, that matter cannot exist without mind, nor mind without matter, then he thinks that both mind and matter are abstractions, not concretes. Thus the question what is concrete has always been a main problem of metaphysics.

4

THE empirical principle has two parts:

(1) Every concept is either the concept of a datum, or of patterns of data, such that every datum has actually occurred in the direct experience of the mind which has the concept; or it is analysable into component concepts each of which is the concept of a datum or of patterns of data, such that every datum has actually occurred in the direct experience of the mind which has the concept.

(2) Every image is either the image of a datum, or of patterns of data, such that every datum has actually occurred in the direct experience of the mind which contemplates the image; or it is analysable into component images each of which is the image of a datum, or of patterns of data, such that every datum has actually occurred in the direct experience of the mind which contemplates the image.

It should be remembered that data include given relations. For instance, the concept of the relation "to the left of" is the concept of a given or datal relation, and so conforms to the principle.

The essence of the principle is that every concept or image must be founded on data. And if the data cannot be found in which an alleged concept or image is founded, it is a pseudo-concept or there is no such image. The principle, as above worded, is merely a restatement of the principle established by Hume. It contains the essence of empiricism.

The more important part of the principle for us is the first part, which refers to concepts. It is this which we shall mostly have in mind in speaking of the empirical principle. But the second part is also important. For instance, it is this which is at issue in Hume's question whether we could conjure up the image of a shade of blue which we have never seen.

It is of the utmost importance to keep clear the distinction between concepts and images. Many philosophers—one is tempted to say most philosophers—either confuse them or at least have a tendency to confuse them at times. James habitually confused them.[4] Berkeley in effect denied the existence of concepts, and admitted only images. He supposed that all thinking is imaging, and his argument against abstract ideas is based on this mistake. Kant exhibits the same confusion when he distinguishes between sensuous and non-sensuous or pure concepts. For all concepts are non-sensuous or pure. But Kant mistakenly supposed that the concept "green" is, or contains, sensuous greenness, i.e. imagery.

The image of green is green. The concept of green is not. It has no colour. The image of a square is square. The concept "square" has no shape or other spatial character. This is what was dimly perceived by those philosophers who have said that "ideas" and mental processes generally have no shape, size, or position in space, and that the mind has none either. This is correct because cognition—as will be shown later—consists solely of concepts or conceptual processes. Images, which may have shape, are not part of it. They stand over against the mind, part of the not-self, objective.

Concepts are subjective, images objective. Images have the same status and relation to the mind as sense-data, which are objective. The word "idea," as used in common speech, includes both concepts and images. It is thus thoroughly misleading, since it lumps together things of utterly different status, and implies that images, as well as concepts, are mental.

4 See, for example, Sections III and VI of "Does Consciousness Exist?" in *Essays in Radical Empiricism.*

[11]

It has been doubted whether concepts, as distinguished from images, have actual psychological existence. This is not the same as the question, also often debated, whether there is imageless thinking. There is probably no imageless thinking, for the mind's conceptual processes are always *accompanied by* images, even if only the auditory images of words. But that concepts are always, in the stream of consciousness, accompanied by images, does not mean that the concept, in itself, is sensuous or is any kind of imagery. The non-sensuous concept and the sensuous image may be factually inseparable, but the concept is completely non-sensuous for all that. You cannot have colour without spatial expanse, but colour is nevertheless not the same thing as spatial expanse. Similarly with the relation between concepts and images. They are radically distinct kinds of entity, but they are inseparable.

The actual psychological existence of concepts is proved by the fact that we understand general meanings. The meaning *is* the concept. All attempts to reduce concepts to particular images fail. Berkeley thinks the concept is merely a particular image which *represents* all the other members of a class. But in this notion of "representation" the concept is smuggled in again. How can this image represent others except by being the vehicle of a general meaning? A similar criticism applies to Mr. Russell's doctrine in *The Analysis of Mind.* No doubt we sometimes seem to think with nothing but words. But it is the words *as having meaning* which function, not the words as mere noises. When I hear a sentence in which the word "man" occurs, I very likely experience no image of a man. But I do not merely experience the noise "man." This noise is the vehicle of the meaning or concept "man." The very fact that we can think with no images except those of words proves the presence of non-sensuous concepts.

A concept may be analysable into component concepts some of which obey the empirical principle while others do not. Thus the point of Hume's analysis of causality (whether correct or not) was that it is analysable into two sub-concepts,

(1) sequence, and (2) power; and that the first of these passes the test of the empirical principle since it is the concept of patterns of data actually found in experience, while the second does not pass the test since no data can be found for it. Thus, according to Hume, the second sub-concept is a pseudo-concept.

5

THE empirical principle does not preclude the existence in the mind of *a priori* concepts in the manner supposed by Kant. Certain concepts might possibly be given by the mind in the sense that the possibility of their exemplification in experience might depend upon the structure of the mind rather than on the structure of that which is presented to it. It does not really concern the empirical principle whether this is so or not, although misunderstanding on the matter is probably rife among empiricists themselves. All that the principle lays down is that we cannot think a concept unless its elements have exemplification in direct experience. Agree, for the sake of argument, that the concept of causality is *a priori* in Kant's sense. Yet it is, as a matter of fact, exemplified in experience, at any rate in so far as it means only sequence. And what the empirical principle asserts is that if it, or its elements, were not so exemplified, we should have no consciousness of it and could not think the concept. We should have been unconscious of the concept, notwithstanding that it might have been in some sense a potentiality of the mind awaiting the touch of experience to bring it into actuality.

There are some points in the formula of the principle given above which need elucidation. Firstly, it will be noted that the word "experience" is qualified by the adjective "direct." A direct experience is a *datum*. Hence the exemplification of the elements of the concept must be found in the form of data.[5] I doubt whether any satisfactory definition of data can be

---

[5] By the "elements" of a concept I mean the simple component concepts or sub-concepts into which it is analysable, if it is not itself a simple concept.

given. It seems to be, in some sense, an ultimate notion, indefinable. But I hope that something may be done in the sequel to clarify it.

That the elements of the concept must be identifiable as originating from data means merely that to think about, or reason about, or feel emotions about something is not to experience it in the sense required. Thus I may think about a new colour, say ultraviolet colour, in the sense that I may speculate as to whether the eyes of some insect may be sensitive to ultraviolet rays and whether he may perceive them as a colour sensation wholly unimaginable to me. But for me to *think about* ultraviolet colour in this way is not to experience it. The insect may have experienced it, but I cannot. On the other hand I have experienced red colour. For there are red data in my world.' *To experience, as the word is used in the empirical principle, means to have direct apprehension of something as a datum.*

But if I can "think about" ultraviolet colour—as when I ask whether it is a datum to some insect—although it has never been a datum to me, does not this fact glaringly contradict the empirical principle? When I talk about ultraviolet colour in this way, it will not be contended[6] that my words are meaningless, are mere empty noises. I must have some notion of what I mean by ultraviolet colour if I am able thus to speak intelligently about it. Yet it is admitted that I have no datum, no experience of ultraviolet colour. How can this be possible if the empirical principle is correct?

But the principle does not assert that every concept must have its counterpart in direct experience. It asserts that the *elements* of the concept must apply to data found in experience. The data may be put together by the mind in patterns in which they have never been found in experience. Thus I can have the notion of a centaur, although I have never experienced centaurs. For all the ele-

---

[6] Except by irresponsible philosophers.

ments of the notion are the concepts of colours, shapes, etc., which have been experienced.

The elements of a concept are, strictly speaking, the concepts of the ultimate unanalysable data which enter into it. One may analyse the notion of centaur into the notions of "horse," "man," etc. One might sometimes speak of "horse," "man," etc., as the elements of the concept of centaur. But they are only relatively more elementary than the compound concept of centaur. They are themselves further analysable. Ultimately we shall come down to colours, sounds, etc., which cannot be further analysed. These are the true "elements." And the empirical principle says only that the elements of a concept must be concepts of data found in experience, not that their combination in some whole must be.

Now if we apply this conception to our notion of ultraviolet colour we shall not find that there is in principle any difficulty. If it is said that we have no "idea" of ultraviolet colour, what is meant is that we have no image of it. But we have a concept of it, as is shown by the fact that we can converse intelligently about it. We might describe our concept roughly in some such terms as this—"a colour sensation never sensed by us, which nevertheless might be sensed by us if our retinas were sensitive to radiations of a certain periodicity." We have here analysed our concept into a great number of parts, or sub-concepts, such as "colour," "unsensed by us," "radiations," "retina," "periodicity," and the like. Each of these can be further analysed till we reach concepts of unanalysable data. The complete analysis would, of course, be enormously complicated. But we should ultimately reach elements all of which would be concepts of data found in our own experience. *These data would not include the datum of ultraviolet colour.* This is why, in accordance with the second part of the empirical principle, we cannot image it. But when we use the words "ultraviolet colour" our minds are not blank. We have a concept. This concept is knowledge by description, and it is a perfectly true concept so far as it goes, though it may be inade-

[15]

quate. It is wholly based upon data which are found in our own experience, although these do not include the datum of the colour itself. With this the empirical principle is satisfied, and the apparent contradiction is cleared up.

I return then to the point that for the empirical principle "experience" means only the direct experience of data, and does not include thinking, reasoning, and the like. This is important because some writers insist that thinking and reasoning are forms of experiencing. They are entitled to their own terminology which may well be justified having regard to the special purposes to which they apply it. But it is essential to understand that the term "experience," *as used in the empirical principle,* refers to nothing save the immediate apprehension of data. Utter confusion results from neglect of this.

6

To illustrate such confusions I shall consider here the meaning of certain phrases, such as "emotional experience," and "religious experience." Some philosophers are fond of telling us that philosophy must take account of esthetic experience or religious experience as much as of sense-experience. What do such statements *mean*?

It will be convenient to begin with emotional experience, although as a rule no special claim is made on behalf of this. I do not doubt the propriety of such a phrase as an expression for what happens when we live through an emotion. But we must be careful that we are not misled. What actually is an emotional experience? Suppose that I am frightened at seeing a tiger before me. Experience, in the sense in which the empirical principle uses the term, refers only to the apprehending of data. The only data present in seeing and being frightened of a tiger would seem to be the tiger-data, his colour, shape, etc. I experience these. But this is a cognitive experience, not an emotional one. But then in addition to being cognitively aware of the tiger-data, I am frightened of them. Is this emotion of fear an "experience"? Not unless it is the apprehension of a datum. But there is no datum not included in the sense-data already. There is therefore no such thing as an emotional experience. Of course, in addition to being frightened I may be aware that I am frightened. I may, more or less consciously, introspect my fear. In that case the fear becomes an introspective datum to my consciousness. But this is then again a cognitive experience. It is a conscious awareness of a certain datum, namely my own emotion. The fact is that in the sense in which empiricism uses the word experience, all experiences are cognitive, and there is no such thing as an emotional experience at all.

The only way of avoiding this conclusion will be to assert that an emotion is as a matter of fact the cognitive awareness of a peculiar non-sensuous datum, for example, that the tiger has the objective quality of fearfulness just as he has the quality of being yellow. In that case there will be a genuine emotional experience in addition to sensuous and introspective experiences. This is, of course, a possible view, though in my opinion a very implausible one. But the point is that either there is no such thing as an emotional experience at all; or there must be these objective emotional qualities in things, such as fearfulness, which are capable of becoming data to us. Whoever talks about emotional experience, and asserts that a genuine empiricism ought to take account of it, is either talking about something which has no existence, or he is committing himself to the view that there are objective emotional data, such as fearfulness. If he realized this, he might be more careful to think out what he means.

Again there is a great deal of vague talk about "religious experience," and it is said that philosophy ought to take account of it in constructing its view of the world. I do not deny that this is true. But we ought first to understand what it means, and only then to ask whether it is true. It is said that God's reality is witnessed to us by religious experience. Well and good. But what actual experience do we have here? A man goes to church and is deeply moved by the prayers, the music, the solemn ritual, the dim light, the architecture. A highly complicated emotional tension is set up. The man feels elevated. All this is apt to be called "religious experience." But what are the *data* which the man has experienced? There are the sense-data, the colours, sounds, and the like. If this is all, then the religious experience is nothing but an experience of sense-data. We have, of course, left out the feelings of love, worship, elevation, the general emotional tension. But we have just seen that to live through an emotional state is not to have an experience at all, and that—save on the basis of a very special and doubtful theory of emotional data—there is no such thing as an emotional experience. Is there nothing else? The worshipper may have, of course, introspective data by being aware of his own emotions. But that will not help. And if this is a complete analysis of the contents of the man's mind, it has to be said that he has no religious experience at all, and that there is in fact no such thing.

But this may not be a complete analysis. Perhaps the most important thing has been left out. It is possible that, in addition to having sense-data and introspective data of his own emotions, the man may have a direct experience of God. If so, God has become for his consciousness a datum. I am far from denying that this may be the case. It is, I think, the meaning of the claim put forward by mystics that in certain states of illumination they find themselves in the immediate presence of God. They *see* God. This must mean that God has become for them a datum, and not a mere thought.

Now it may be that there really are God-data sometimes directly presented to the minds of religious men. If so, there is such a thing as religious experience, and metaphysics must take account of it. But I am sure that many people talk glibly about having religious experience without in the least understanding the tremendous claim which this implies. It implies that they claim to apprehend God-data. I am also sure that many people mean by religious experience nothing but their own emotional introspective data. Further, assuming that there really are God-data, it is probably extremely difficult to distinguish them from other kinds of data, and there is grave danger of mistaking other data—such as introspective data of one's own feelings of elevation—for God-data. For a man to be sure of his claims of being the possessor of religious experience he ought to be able to distinguish God-data from other data as easily as he distinguishes red from green, or colours from sounds. If we are to accept their testimony, the great mystics are apparently able to do this. But how many ordinary men can?

The point, however, is this. Unless God is a datum, there is no such thing as religious experience in any sense of which philosophy need take account as evidence for its constructions. Most people who chatter about their "religious experience" are certainly entirely muddle-headed and have no clear idea of what it means. Most people mean by it whatever they happen to feel when they go to church or say their prayers. And their confusion is due to the fact that they have not analysed the meaning of "experience," and have not perceived that, if any experience is to be taken as evidence of anything, if it is to be admitted as a basis for philosophical construction, it must be confined to the direct experience of data.

7

THE empirical principle requires that data correspond to the elements of every concept. If not, it declares that there is no concept. It says nothing, however, as to what *kinds* of data may exist. It does not restrict them to sense-data. If there exist introspective data, then such data fulfil the requirements of the principle and constitute good experience which may be the basis of concepts. For example, if there is such a thing as the concept of the concept, this must be because concepts in the stream of consciousness have been introspectively examined and have been treated as data to the examining mind. Nor are data necessarily confined to the two kinds just mentioned. There may be God-data, and conceivably many other kinds of non-sensuous data as well. The empirical principle makes no pronouncement and is entirely neutral in regard to the question whether a particular kind of datum, claimed to exist, does actually exist. This is a pure question of fact, to be settled by the ordinary rules of evidence, by the same rules which govern the questions whether there exist tigers, ghosts, or men in Mars. It cannot be settled by the empirical principle.

It is quite certain that this is not usually understood by empiricists themselves. They seem to think that empiricism lays some special emphasis on sense-data, or even excludes other data from having their claims considered. Empiricism may even be found *defined* in dictionaries as the view that all knowledge is based upon sense-experience. But the hostility of most empiricists to non-sensuous data is not based upon their empiricism, although they themselves may believe that it is. They then lay themselves open to the suspicion that they are influenced by some secret or avowed materialistic bias, or by the grossness of their own perceptions. Those who claim that a genuinely empirical philosophy ought to take account of religious experience are right, if there really do exist God-data. On the other hand, if by religious experience they merely mean their emotional feelings of reverence, compassion, awe, love, wonder, and the like, then they are sham empiricists.

8

THE empirical principle enables us to solve certain difficulties in the theory of meaning. The modern theory of meaning exhibits itself in three historical stages—the operational theory, the verificational theory, and the empirical theory.

1. *The operational theory* was propounded by Professor Bridgman in his *Logic of Modern Physics*. Its formula is: *the meaning of a concept is a set of operations*. If there is no set of operations there is no meaning. Thus the concept of length is definable in terms of the operation of measuring with a measuring rod. The concept of the simultaneity of two distant events is definable in terms of the operation of sending

light signals from the events to an observer, placed at the middle point between the events, who is to observe whether they reach him at the same moment.

This theory suffered from the limitation that it was conceived too exclusively in terms of the concepts of physics. It needed to be generalized so as to make it readily applicable to all meanings, including those of everyday discourse. So to generalize it was the work of the verificational theory.

2. *The Verificational Theory.* This theory simply substitutes "method of verification" for "operation." Its formula is: *the meaning of a statement is identical with the method of its verification.* The method of verifying the statement that the cat's eyes are blue is to look at them and see whether one experiences blue sense-data. Hence the meaning of the statement is that if one looks at them one will experience blue sense-data. Similarly the meaning of the statement that the table is made of wood is that, if one taps it, it will give out a woody sound, that if one scratches off the varnish, one will experience a whitish fibrous appearance, that if one burns it, it will turn charcoaly black, that if one applies certain chemical tests, one will perceive certain changes, etc.

This is simply the operational theory generalized. For a method of verification is always an operation. Looking at the cat is an operation. So is scratching the table with a penknife. Hence the operational and verificational theories may be criticized together, for they are essentially the same theory.

The *reductio ad absurdum* of these theories is that they involve the consequence that all statements about the past are meaningless. For since we cannot travel backwards in time, we cannot experience or verify anything in the past. Thus the statement "Caesar's hat was red" is meaningless because we cannot verify this redness.

Verification of the present effects of past events does not help, since this also verifies only the present.

It is also idle to modify the theory by introducing the notion of indirect verification. This involves a gross confusion of thought. When one says that the blueness of the cat's eyes is verified by looking at the cat, the phrase "to verify" means simply to experience. But indirect verification is verification in a totally different sense. It means proving by argument or inferring. It is only if verification is interpreted as meaning directly experiencing that the theory can be regarded as an application of the principles of empiricism—which is certainly its claim. If the theory is taken to mean that a statement has meaning if there is a method of proving it by logical argument, then it is a totally different theory, which has nothing to do with empiricism.

The so-called logical positivists, who invented the theory, appear now to have abandoned it or at least modified it out of all recognition. But their subsequent work does not appear to the present writer to be helpful. The correct modification of the verificational theory seems to be contained in the empirical theory.

3. *The Empirical theory.* The formula of this theory is: *A meaning or concept is always a concept of patterns of data, or is analysable into concepts which are concepts of patterns of data.* This is directly deducible from the empirical principle, or rather it simply is that principle.[7]

Consider the meaning of "horse." A particular horse is a certain pattern of sense-data (possibly with the addition of non-sensuous data). The meaning of the general term "horse" is the concept of such patterns.

Again, a particular consciousness is a pattern of introspective data. The meaning of the term "consciousness" is the concept of such patterns.

A pattern of data may be more simple or more complex. The limiting pattern in the direction of simplicity is a single datum. Thus the meaning of "red" is the concept of patterns each of which consists of a single red sense-datum.

[7] The theory, though not in the words of this formula, was suggested by me in an article called *Metaphysics and Meaning* in *Mind*, XLIV., N.S., 176. A fuller discussion than is here possible will be found in that article.

The essence of the theory lies in its insistence that all meanings are definable in terms of *data*—not in terms of operations or verifications. Thus the analysis of a concept consists in exhibiting in detail all the data on which it is based. If there are no data, there is no concept, no meaning. It was for this reason that, on Hume's analysis, such terms as causal "power," substratal "substance," were declared to be meaningless.

The condition of the meaningfulness of a term or set of terms is, not the possibility of an operation or of verification, but simply that the data which make up the pattern referred to in the concept should be discoverable somewhere in the past experience of the subject. Thus the word "red" has meaning for me because red data have appeared in my past experience. To a man congenitally blind the word may still have meaning, though not quite the same meaning as for me. The meaning for him will be based on data in *his* experience (Section 5).

The enormous difference of the empirical from the verificational theory may now be pointed out. The mistake of the latter theory is that it implies that every time a term, say "red," is mentioned, it is necessary for meaningfulness that *that particular instance* of redness should be experiencible (verifiable). Whereas, according to the true theory, redness need only have been experienced once, whereupon the term becomes intelligible in all future instances.

Thus if we have a set of statements "*A* is red," "*B* was red," "*C* will be red," "*D* is red" . . . "*N* is red," in order that these statements may have meaning it is necessary, on the verificational theory, that *in each separate case* it should be in principle possible to verify (experience) the particular instance of redness referred to. Thus "my hat is red" has meaning because I can look at my hat and verify *its* redness. But "Caesar's hat was red" has no meaning because I cannot verify that particular instance of redness. If this interpretation be doubted, take the case of consciousness. According to the former doctrine of the logical positivists, which we are considering, "I am conscious" might have meaning, but "Smith is conscious" could have no meaning except a behaviouristic one. Obviously the principle was that I could experience my own consciousness, but not Smith's.

But on the empirical theory "red" has meaning for me in all instances once I have experienced redness. I then know what the word means. And I know what it means in the statement "Caesar's hat was red" just as well as in the statement "my hat is red." So also "Smith is conscious" has meaning for me because, although I cannot experience Smith's consciousness, I have experienced *a* consciousness, namely my own.

The empirical theory thus cures the paradoxes and absurdities which flow from the operational and verificational theories.

9

PROFESSOR WHITEHEAD, who does not accept the empirical principle, makes much of a famous admission by Hume, who is the father of empiricism. Hume wrote: "Suppose, therefore, a person to have enjoyed his sight for thirty years, and to have become perfectly well acquainted with colours of all kinds, excepting one particular shade of blue. . . . Let all the different shades of that colour, except that single one, be placed before him, descending gradually from the deepest to the lightest . . . he will perceive a blank, where that shade is wanting. . . . I ask whether it is possible for him, from his own imagination, to supply this deficiency, and to raise up to himself the idea of that particular shade, though it had never been conveyed to him by his senses. I believe there are few but will be of opinion that he can."[8]

Professor Whitehead considers that this admission is fatal to empiricism. For if there is a single exception to the principle that there can be no concept or image in the mind the elements of which are not exemplified in experience, the principle fails of universality, and so falls to the ground. Also if there is one exception, there may be many others.[9]

[8] *Treatise on Human Nature,* Book I, Part I, Sec. 1.
[9] *Process and Reality,* Part II, Chap. III, Sec. 1, and Part II, Chap. V, Sec. 1.

But it is by no means certain that Hume was right to have made this admission. I am not convinced that the mind could supply the missing shade of blue. And I know of no way of settling the question. It is possible that a psychologist—if he could be induced to take any interest in the matter—might devise a crucial experiment, although it seems to me that the attempt would be beset with almost insuperable difficulties. But since we are not in a position to disprove the correctness of Hume's admission, let us grant, for the sake of argument, that it is correct. Does it really, as Whitehead supposes, destroy the empirical principle, or even seriously embarrass it?

It will be noted, in the first place, that if the mind really has the power to originate the image of a completely novel shade of blue, it is very strange that it cannot originate the images of invisible colours, such as ultraviolet and infrared. Of course the human retina is presumably sensitive to the missing shade of blue, but not to ultraviolet and infrared. But this has no bearing on the matter. There would be no plausibility in the suggestion that the mind can originate colours to the rays of which the retina is sensitive, even though those rays happen never to have impinged upon it, while it cannot originate colours to the rays of which the retina is not sensitive. For in the first case the mind must have originated the colour without any cooperation of the retina, and the fact that the retina, if stimulated, *could* have given a sensation of the colour, can have nothing to do with it. And if the mind can create the image of the missing shade of blue without the help of the senses, why cannot it originate the image of ultraviolet without the aid of the senses and even though the retina is not sensitive to the rays of that colour?

My suggestion is that in the case of the missing shade of blue the man has already in his mind the image-elements which, when fused together, will yield the required shade of blue, and that he has gathered these elements from the experience of other colours which he has actually seen; whereas in the case of the invisible colours he has not received from sight-experience the necessary visual data. Suppose we place the blues in a series with the darkest shades at the bottom and the lightest shades at the top. And somewhere in the middle of this scale let there be a blank space where the missing shade would come. Now ask the man who has never experienced this shade to try to conjure up the image of it before his mind. Anyone faced with this challenge would note, I think, that the darkest blues tend towards black, the lightest shades towards white; and that a darker shade appears to have, as it were, more blackness in it, a lighter shade more whiteness. (Whether this is an entirely correct account of the matter physically does not matter. For we are speaking of the man's impressions.) To get the missing shade the man would try to image a slightly blacker shade than that which adjoins the top boundary of the gap or a slightly whiter shade than that which adjoins the lower boundary. That is, he would add a little more black or a little more white to the shades he has actually before him. These impressions of darkness and lightness he has already received from previous experience. Thus his image of the missing shade is manufactured out of the given shades of blue and previously received impressions of darkness and lightness. It is entirely made up of ingredients which have been given to him as data. If this is anything like a correct account of the manner in which a person actually faced with this problem would attempt to fill up the gap, no exception to the empirical principle is involved.

There is involved, however, the principle that the mind has not only the power to juxtapose sensory images in new spatial patterns, as in the cases of the centaur and the golden mountain—a capacity which has never been doubted; but also the power to *fuse* images of sensations, as red and white are fused in pink. And whether this is so or not should be a question of great interest to psychology. On it depends the question whether Hume was right in admitting the possibility of imaging the missing shade of blue.

The difference between invisible colours and visible colours is fairly presumed to be a difference of *kind,* like the difference between green and red. But the difference between the experienced shades of blue and the missing shade is only a difference of *degree* within the same kind. We have with all the shades of blue only one fundamental kind of sensory stuff, namely blueness; only we have, so to speak, more or less of it with the different shades. We cannot in our minds create a new kind of sensory stuff. But we can imaginatively increase or decrease the degree of a known kind. And this is all that we have to do to get the missing shade.

It seems to me that Professor Whitehead's argument against empiricism is a failure.

10

THE debate whether metaphysics is possible has been revived of late by the school of the so-called logical positivists. This school holds that all metaphysical propositions are meaningless. To prove it they rely upon the empirical principle, or at least upon their version of it. They derive, as does all modern empiricism, from Hume. But—except in the sphere of pure logic—they have added not a jot to what Hume has already said, but have only, by twisting and straining his principle, sought to deduce from it all manner of extreme and absurd conclusions; whereby they bring undeserved discredit upon empiricism. Their attack upon metaphysics is based upon the belief that it is concerned with entities which lie beyond all possible experience. It follows from the empirical principle that we cannot have any concept of that which lies beyond all possible experience. Metaphysical propositions therefore do not express concepts and are consequently without any meaning.

This criticism would only be valid if metaphysic placed its reality completely beyond experience and entirely cut off from it. Even a two-layer metaphysic does not do this, and hence the proper criticism of it is not that it is meaningless, but

[27]

that it is self-contradictory (Chapter I, Section 2). In any case the attack has force only against a two-layer metaphysic. There is nothing in the empirical principle which forbids one-layer metaphysical doctrines such as those of Berkeley, Leibniz, Descartes. Descartes' doctrine of substance as substratum is, of course, rendered untenable by the empirical principle. So is Berkeley's conception of the nature of spirit-substance. But I can think of nothing else in these writers which is destroyed by it. Their main conceptions stand. For instance, in Berkeley's philosophy the universe consists of minds and their ideas. Among them is the mind of God which created all the rest. There are doubtless many objections to such a scheme. But an infringement of the empirical principle is not one of them. If this philosophy seems to some empiricists to violate their principles, this is because they have injected into the pure empirical principle some bias, or at least some opinion of their own, which, whether true or false, has nothing to do with empiricism and is not justified by the empirical principle. For instance, denial of the existence of introspective data will lead to the denial that the notion of consciousness or mind has any meaning when not behaviouristically interpreted. This, of course, will destroy Berkeley's belief in minds as the only concretes and also his belief in the supreme mind of God. It will thus destroy his whole philosophy. Such an attack might be justified. But the point is that it is not by the empirical principle that it is justified. It has nothing to do with this principle. For as we have seen in Section 7 the rejection of introspective data cannot be based upon empiricism. It must be based upon an examination of the alleged evidence for the existence of introspective data.

As already stated Berkeley's world is all surface, and the mind of God is part of the surface. This means that it satisfies the empirical principle. For the principle is that the surface of experience is what alone has meaning for us, and that we can have no concept of an entity not conceivable in terms of that surface. Berkeley's philosophy contains no such entity. Hence unless we are prepared to argue that his philosophy is not metaphysics, we must conclude that, so far as empiricism is concerned, metaphysics is possible. Conceivably it might be repudiated on other grounds, but not on the grounds alleged by the logical positivists.

11

THE method of metaphysics is the method of hypothesis. An hypothesis is put forward regarding the nature of the concrete. An attempt is then made to show that this hypothesis "explains" the known facts about the world. Finally, reasons are given why this hypothesis should be preferred to others which equally explain the facts. This is all that any metaphysician can do.

Explanation, as the term is here used, does not consist in giving any "reason" for things, nor in answering the question "why?" In the last analysis no reason for anything can be given. The world simply is what it is. The metaphysical hypothesis only explains the facts of the world in the sense that it is, or hopes to be, a true generalization about the nature of the real, such that every known fact can be shown to be an example of it. It explains only in the sense in which the law of gravitation explains the falling of stones to the ground, the rise and fall of tides, the orbits of the planets. The law of gravitation gives no reason why any of the facts are what they are. It is simply a generalization which covers them all. It states as a fact that all material particles have gravitational properties, regarding which it gives quantitative details for purposes of calculation. Or it states that space-time has a certain geometrical character. Why these should be the facts no one knows. Or rather it has no meaning to ask why. Any further information which could be given would simply consist in more facts.

Professor Whitehead appears still to labour in the belief that metaphysics can give reasons. But in the end his own philosophy is simply a statement that the essential nature of the world is thus and thus. No reason is or can be given for this. Nor, if his particular hypothesis were true, would it constitute a reason for anything. The difficulty appears clearly in what he calls the "ontological principle." "The reasons for things," he writes, "are always to be found in the composite nature of definite actual entities. . . . The ontological principle can be summarized as: no actual entity, then no reason."[10] This is to assert that *things* (conceived in a certain way) are reasons, and moreover that they are the only reasons which can exist for anything. But a thing is simply a thing, that is, a fact. It cannot be a reason. Hegel, who believed he could give a reason for everything in the universe, at least conceived his reasons as logical principles, not as solid things. One can understand how he could think that a logical principle might be a reason why things are as they are. For the principles of logic are the principles of reason. As an example, if it were true that *being* logically implies *becoming,* then it would follow that any existence whatever must of necessity be impermanent, and thus a logical reason might be given why the world is in universal flux. Hegel's principle of explanation is invalid because it is not true, as he thought, that a logical form can produce its own content out of itself. But the notion that particular entities can constitute reasons is from the first unthinkable.

That Whitehead's universe is in the end nothing but a brute fact universe is also indicated by what he says of induction. He criticizes positivism on the ground that it can show no reason why the future should resemble the past, e.g. why the sun should rise tomorrow as it has in the past.[11] And what reason can Whitehead give? The reason is that the universe has a certain character, that of the involvement ("objectification") of everything in everything else. Hence everything influences everything else, and the past influences the future.

[10] *Process and Reality,* Part I, Chap. II, Sec. 1. There are numerous other similar passages.
[11] *Adventures of Ideas,* Chap. VIII, Sec. 6.

Also natural laws are immanent in the very natures of the objects which come under them. Hence things cannot continue to be what they are and yet change their laws. If the laws changed, the things would not be the same things. If the sun did not rise tomorrow, it would simply not be the sun. Thus the reason given for the uniform behaviour of things is that *the universe has a certain character,* that of the universal involvement of everything in everything else.[12] But in the first place, that the universe has this character is a brute fact for which no reason is or can be given. And secondly, how does it solve the problem of induction? I know the sun will rise tomorrow because the universe has this character. But how do I know that the universe will continue to have this character tomorrow? But, you say, this is the fundamental metaphysical character of being, and it is absurd to suggest that it might change. Then why should we not say at once that it is the fundamental character of being to observe the principle of the uniformity of nature, and that it is absurd to suggest that that character might change? One might as well posit straightway the fundamentally orderly and uniform character of the world and leave it at that. One gains nothing, so far as the justification of induction is concerned, by positing some other character as the ground for this. If one might change, so might the other.

Metaphysics can give no reasons why the world is as it is. It can only state *what* the world is. Explanation, whether in science or philosophy, can only mean the exhibiting of every detail of the world as an example of some principle. This is Whitehead's own view of explanation.[13] But he adds to it the untenable notion of giving reasons.

12 The following are some of the passages which explain Whitehead's view of induction: *Process and Reality,* Part II, Chap. IX, Secs. 5 and 6; *Adventures of Ideas,* Chap. VII, Sec. 5; *Science and the Modern World,* pp. 62-4 and 75 (American edition).

13 For example, see *Process and Reality,* Book I, Chap. I, Sec. 1.

IT is not possible to "prove" a metaphysical hypothesis, nor in any manner to attain to certainty that it is true. All such hopes must be finally abandoned by human beings. Doubt and perplexity will remain with us always. If we insist upon absolute certainty, there is only one possible metaphysical position for us to adopt, that of the "solipsism of the present moment." This is the inescapable lesson of Professor Santayana's *Scepticism and Animal Faith*. Such solipsism is, of course, completely barren. Therefore we have the choice between this barren futility on the one hand and a philosophy based upon a bold spirit of intellectual adventure on the other. This, however, is not peculiar to philosophy. It is equally true of science and even of common sense. Atoms and electrons are very uncertain hypotheses. The so-called "common-sense view of the world" is also an hypothesis. Moreover, it is a metaphysic. It is an elaborate and highly speculative adventure in philosophy.

The belief that it ought to be possible to prove with certainty the truth of a metaphysical idea is due to a mistake about the nature and function of logic. As a matter of fact there is no proposition in the world, whether metaphysical or other, which logic can with certainty validate—except formal propositions which carry no material information. For the most rigorous logical argument only shows that *if* p is true, q must be true also. It shows that it is inconsistent to maintain both p and not-q. One of them must be false. But which of them is true, which false, logic alone is unable to inform us. When this is effectively realized, the whole notions of "proof" and "certainty"—except for the certainty of immediate data, which however are validated by themselves and not by logic—are seen to crumble to nothing.

In the absence of proof the means by which a metaphysical hypothesis can be recommended are the following. First, it can be shown that it hangs together, that it is self-consistent;

secondly, that it explains the known facts, that no fact falls outside it or is inconsistent with it. But it will be found that there are a number of hypotheses which fulfil these conditions. How are we to choose among them?

All one can do is to marshal the points for and against each hypothesis and make one's choice. One has to weigh the evidence—evidence which, in the nature of things, can never be conclusive. And the process will not depend on a mechanical weighing. For one man will attach more importance to one set of considerations, another to another. It is here that the imponderable elements of good sense and good judgment make themselves felt. The only *method* which can be prescribed is that of trying to show, by whatever considerations are relevant, that the chosen hypothesis is superior to others which equally explain the facts and are equally self-consistent.

CHAPTER II

The Theory of Cells

1

THE hypothesis is that the universe is a plurality of cells, all cells being of the same fundamental structure, though apart from structure they vary indefinitely. Thus there is only one kind of concrete in the world, and from this point of view the theory is a monism. For the universe not only contains cells, but is exclusively composed of them. Nothing save cells exists.

The word "cell," used as a name for the concrete constituents of reality, is clearly no more than a biological metaphor. There is no word in language which expresses the actual meaning required. Roundabout phrases might be used, but it is desirable to have a single word for the notion, and I choose the word "cell." The terms "atom" and "monad" might naturally suggest themselves. The first would correctly describe the absolute indivisibility of the concrete unit. But it would suggest the material concretes of Democritus and the modern physicists, whereas the theory of cells denies that matter is concrete. Moreover the traditional atoms exist in a void of space and time, whereas metaphysical cells are not, in this sense, spatial and temporal at all. They have space and time, or at least the basic elements out of which space and time are constructed, within them as abstract elements of themselves. But there is no space or time outside them or between them, nor containing them; nor, if they be looked at from the outside, would they exhibit lapse or expanse. Strictly speaking it is nonsense to talk of looking at them from the outside. For they have no outsides. They have only interiors. But each cell has, of course, that which is external to it, namely other cells—though the externality is not spatial. Altogether the suggestion of atoms and the void is impertinent to the nature of the cell. The term "monad" on the other hand, would be equally misleading, though for opposite reasons. It would suggest the spiritual concretes of Leibniz, whereas the theory of cells denies that spirits are concrete.

Even the term "cell" is misleading unless precautions are taken to point out wherein it fits and wherein it fails to fit the metaphysical units of existence. It fails to fit exactly, because the biological cell has not the absolute indivisibility which characterizes the metaphysical cell. The splitting of the metaphysical cell, if it could occur, would cause its total disappearance out of the universe and the disappearance of every one of its abstract elements. This is in fact the meaning of the term "concrete." And from this point of view the theory of cells is at one with atomism. For it is the attempt to discover the smallest possible indivisible parts of the universe. But the biological cell is divisible into its component molecules and atoms, and to this extent is an unsuitable metaphor for our purposes. But the point which makes the analogy between biological and metaphysical cells valuable is the fact that if the biological cell is split up, although there remains dead matter, at least one element of its reality does totally disappear, namely its life. Considered as a living being the cell is gone. In the metaphysical cell all the elements, and thus the whole cell, would disappear if it could be divided. Thus the principle of the disappearance of the elements on splitting, which is partial in the biological cell, is extended till it becomes absolute in the metaphysical cell. If both the strength and weakness of the analogy be remembered, the metaphor of the cell should not be misleading. It yields the nearest possible approach to an accurate term, unless some barbarous neologism be introduced.

A CELL is not the same thing as a mind or a subject. It is not the same thing as a spirit. Nor are such phrases as "selves," "centres of experience," "centres of sentience" suitable synonyms for the cell. They all suggest a subjectivist or idealist metaphysic, which is here rejected. A mind or consciousness or self is not a concrete. It is an abstract element within the cell, nor is it even the predominant element. It is not the cause, foundation, or ground of the cell. It has no special preeminence in the universe. It cannot exist by itself. It would be correct to say that the cell is a "private world," provided that this phrase too is emptied of all subjectivistic associations.

' The structure of every cell in the universe is correctly described if we say that it consists of two essential abstract elements or parts, namely consciousness and datum. Consciousness is not abstract cognition, but includes valuation. Both parts, consciousness and datum, are necessary to constitute any existence at all. If one disappears, the other disappears also. Cells vary in the quantitative and qualitative characters of their data. They also vary in valuation and intensity of consciousness. But the twofold structure of consciousness and datum is universal.'

The question what *kinds* of data exist in the cells and how many kinds of data there are in the universe does not concern the structure of the cell, and is therefore not discussed here. But there is nothing in the cell-structure to restrict data to sensuous data. If in the course of the exposition sensuous data are mostly taken as examples, this is merely because they are the most easy to study. It is not to be taken as a sign of any preeminence being attached to sensuous data by the theory of cells. That theory is concerned with the generalized notion of data as such, and not with any particular species of data. Not only may there be non-sensuous data, but there may be many kinds of these. It is also possible that there may be cells in the universe which are destitute of any sensuous data, their objective sides being exclusively composed of non-sensuous data. It is not known whether any such cells exist or not, but the point is that the metaphysical structure of reality, which is cell-structure, does not forbid it. The theory insists that there must be consciousness and datum, but datum here means anything whatever which has a datal character.

The most intense consciousness known to us is found in those cells which are the private worlds of human beings. But the private world of an animal is also a cell. Probably cells can be ranged in order of intensity of consciousness and richness of data from man down to the private worlds of infusoria. The light of consciousness must here be very dim, so dim that it has almost flickered out into total darkness—the darkness in which nothing exists since all data have also disappeared. Whether there is such a thing as a plant's private world is unknown. If not, then plants are complexes of data within other cells. Some writers, such as Whitehead, postulate an unconscious "feeling," not only in plants, but even in inorganic matter. This suggestion is not followed by the theory of cells.

Although the theory of cells admits the possibility of different kinds of data, it does not admit the possibility of more than one kind of consciousness. No kind, save that which is known to us, is conceivable. There may indeed be many things in the universe which are not dreamed of in our philosophy, but they must fall on the side of data, not of consciousness. For if there be any such undreamt of things, they must be something *of* which we might be conscious, though we are not; that is, they must be possible data. Consciousnesses certainly differ very greatly from one another, but the difference is always one of degree, that is, of intensity, not of kind. Even the commonly accepted division of consciousness into layers or strata, such as the so-called mental acts of awareness, sensing, perceiving, thinking, is rejected here. But these matters must be left to be treated in their appropriate place.

As already explained, cells are not to be identified with selves, minds, centres of experience, and the like. A self is simply a consciousness which, taken alone, is an abstraction. It is a half of the concrete cell. The objection to all such phrases is their idealistic implication, just as the objection to the term atom, taken as the name of a concrete, is its materialistic implication. Idealism is the view that of the two halves of the cell, the conscious half has a superior ontological status. As against the datal half it is the more truly real, more fundamental to the universe. It creates the datal half, or is the ground of it, or is in some way prior to it. According to the theory of cells this view is entirely false. Consciousness has no such preeminence in the cell. Both elements, consciousness and datum, have equal ontological status and equal prestige. They are completely coordinate. Consciousness is no more fundamental, no more real, than datum. Nor is one prior to the other. The cell is subject-object, and is no more truly subject than it is truly object. Subject depends on object just as much as object depends on subject. Indeed the former dependency is far more obvious than the latter, which is the reason for the popularity of realism. Idealism and realism are both equally one-sided. Each takes an abstraction and sets it up as a real in its own right. The theory of cells attempts to insist on the concreteness of the real, and to do equal justice to both its elements.

Thus the data of the cell are not to be confused with the "ideas" of Berkeley, nor are they to be thought of as existing "in" a mind. The data are no more in the mind than the mind is in the data. But both are in the cell. Berkeley made two main mistakes. First, he regarded the objects of consciousness as mental, and this, or something like it, is a characteristic tenet of subjectivism. But this is utter confusion. "Mental" means appertaining to, or being part of, mind. And mind is the same as consciousness—at any rate in my view. But the datum is precisely that in the cell which does *not* appertain to, and is *not* a part of, consciousness. If the word "mind" is to have any meaning at all, the mind must be distinguished from *something*. And the something from which it is distinguished is precisely the datum. It must have taken human beings great labour of thought to have distinguished mind out of the universe. What is the use of first making this distinction, and giving mind a name for the express purpose of keeping it distinct from other things, and then, by splurging it over the whole universe, retracting and confounding the hardly won distinction? To make the distinction between consciousness and datum within the cell, and never again to confuse them, is the absolute prerequisite for any understanding of the theory of cells.[1] And this means that the datum must once and for all be recognized as *not* mental, as not in any way whatever of the nature of mind. This is the first way in which the data of the theory of cells are distinguished from the "ideas" of Berkeley.

The second mistake made by Berkeley is bound up with the first. He supposed that the "ideas" were *created* by minds. Real ideas (i.e. real things) were created by the mind of God, imaginary ideas by other minds. This power of creating ideas is supposed by Berkeley to be the essential character of the mind's activity.[2] Apart from his vague and very unclear references to what he called "notions," there is no evidence that he in any way understood the real nature of the activity of consciousness, or even recognized its existence as a being distinct from its data or objects. He seems to have thought that consciousness is actually composed of "ideas," that is, of smells, sounds, and the like; and the hidden spiritual substance creates these. This interpretation is in keeping with his denial of the existence of abstract ideas and his consequent belief that all thinking is imaging. If this is the correct view of his meaning, then the only entities the existence of which he recognized were (1) spiritual substances which are, of course, hidden from us, and (2) colours, sounds, and other "ideas." If this is so, he did not recognize the existence of consciousness as distinct from

---

[1] To have made clear this distinction for the first time in history was, in spite of subsequent criticism, one of the many great services to philosophy rendered by Professor G. E. Moore.

[2] *The Principles of Human Knowledge*, Sec. 28. "This making and unmaking of ideas doth very properly denominate the mind active."

data at all, though his references to "notions" perhaps show that he suspected it. The theory of cells does not accept the spiritual substances, but believes in (1) consciousness, and (2) data.

It is, however, with Berkeley's belief that minds create data that we are chiefly concerned. This is the essential mark of subjectivism, the notion of mind as creator and of data as creatures, of mind as prior and data as posterior, of mind as more eminent and data as inferior. This is what is specifically denied by the theory of cells. It is, of course, arguable that mind creates its data in reverie and free imaging. But apart from this exception—if it is a true exception at all—the data are no more created by the mind than the mind is created by the data. They both simply *are*. And they are indissolubly conjoined in the cell. They are indeed, in a sense, mutually dependent. For neither can exist without the other. But it would not be correct to express this by saying that the data create the consciousness while the consciousness at the same time creates the data. For creation is causal dependence. But the mutual dependence of consciousness and datum is not causal dependence. It is the mutual dependence of abstractions within a concrete. It is of the same order as the dependence of colour on visual extension and of visual extension on colour. No one would say that colour causes extension or that extension causes colour.

Thus the theory of cells is not an idealistic metaphysic. If it is necessary to have a label, it may be called phenomenalistic, since it holds that the only realities are what appears in experience, namely data and consciousness indissolubly joined.

3

THE study of valuation belongs to the theory of consciousness, which will be treated in Chapter V. But it is so vitally important that we should not make a false start by considering the mere abstraction of bare cognition to be the subjective side of the cell—since then we should mistake the abstract for the concrete from the very beginning—that it will be better to treat the subject of valuation very briefly at this point.

All consciousness includes valuation. This does not mean that we have two things, consciousness and valuation, always accompanying one another. It means that we have two inseparable aspects of one and the same process. We may for certain purposes separate out the cognitive side, but then it is an abstraction.

Every act of consciousness as such values or disvalues its data. Thus *what* is valued is always data. And what values is always consciousness. Data are the *objects* of valuation. We suppose that we value a thing or a person. But things are only complexes of data. And we value the red hue of the rose, the taste of the food, and so on. And in a person we value his gestures, his words, his smile, his voice, his actions. In what is called "instrumental" value we value something because it will lead to certain data beyond itself. It is these ulterior data that are in the end valued. And this value is intrinsic.

Valuation is the same thing as feeling. There are many different shades or forms of it, such as liking and disliking, desire, emotion, interest. Valuation is the *common element* in them all. With the precise psychological differences between them we are not concerned in metaphysics. It is enough for us that they are all forms of valuation, and that some form of valuation is an integral part of every conceivable act of consciousness.

But one mistake may be corrected. It used to be said that emotion is present in every state of mind. Of course it depends on how one uses the word emotion. Personally I should call anger, fear, jealousy, emotions. But I should not call my dislike of pepper an emotion, nor should I call thirst by this name. If we agree to use the word emotion for states such as anger and fear, but not for the dislike of pepper and the desire for drink, then it is not true that emotion is always present in the mind. It seems, for example, to be absent from the mind of the scientific observer, if he is observing as he should. But in his mind there must be some form of valuation, perhaps interest, perhaps desire—for instance, the desire to see. That there is a difference is witnessed by the fact that he does wish to eliminate emotion but does not wish to eliminate interest. The true doctrine is that valuation is the common element in all these forms, and that it is valuation in *some* form, not any particular form such as emotion, which is necessary to consciousness. There cannot be bare cognition of a datum. For without feeling of some kind the datum collapses and disappears. And if the datum collapses, the consciousness collapses. Without some kind of valuation, therefore, a datum cannot be held before consciousness at all.

Those psychologists who distinguish cognition from emotion (or as they should say from valuation) as two elements or functions of the mind do not go far enough. For though they admit their constant conjunction, they think of this as a mere external connection—as of one thing always accompanying another. The true relation may perhaps be illustrated by the relation of colour to light. Consciousness may be compared to a beam of light falling upon the datum. Valuation is then the colour of that light. A beam may be red or green or white. But it must have some colour. Red, green, and blue light are only different forms of light. So we may be angrily conscious of the object, or desiringly conscious, or hatingly conscious, or merely interestedly conscious. But our consciousness must have some shade of valuation. Perhaps the best way of expressing the difference between this and the common view is to say that the common view thinks of valuation as an entity to be represented in speech by a *noun*. On my view it can only be properly represented in speech by an adverb such as "angrily" or "hatingly" attached to the term "conscious"—though of course it is true that we are practically compelled to use such nouns as valuation and feeling if we are to avoid being pedantic.

The false view is reflected not only in the naïvely simple dichotomy of mind into cognition and emotion, but also in such distinctions as that between the "emotive" and the scientific use of words—as if these uses could possibly be separated.

Volition is not a distinct element of mind, nor a distinct form of consciousness. Consciousness as such, in its aspect of valuation, is an impulsion to act, because we try to attain what we value and avoid what we disvalue. Thus the eye shifts ceaselessly from point to point because consciousness is ceaselessly altering its valuations. One visual datum is brought momentarily into the focus of vision because it attracts, that is, because consciousness is at that moment valuing it highly. At the next instant consciousness devalues it, that is, loses interest in it, and transfers its valuation to another visual datum. Then the eye shifts. When conflicting emotions, desires, and interests—that is, conflicting shades of valuational consciousness—are struggling together for mastery, our actions are wavering and confused and tend to cancel each other out. When one valuation at length gains the upper hand, or when several blend and cease to conflict, there may ensue an apparently unhesitating departure of action along a straight line in a determinate direction towards a determinate goal. There is thus a point at which action seems suddenly to issue out of hesitancy. This point is what has been called the "fiat of the will." In this way the notion of volition arose. Hence mind is not divided into cognition, emotion, and will. It contains nothing except consciousness, which includes valuation. And the cell contains nothing except consciousness and datum.

Attention is the clear picking out by consciousness of the focal point of its immediate and momentary system of valuations. The concentration of the eye, or the convergence of muscular sets, upon this point, is not—as has sometimes been alleged—the essence of attention. These are only the physical actions which consciousness, as an impulsion to act, produces. Thus attention is an act of the mind, not of the body. Nor is it an act of will. There is no such thing as will.

It is sometimes disputed whether reason and thought can influence the will and produce action, or whether only desires and emotions can do this. It is suggested that our desires and feelings propel us into actions and that our reason looks impotently on. And then it is asked whether, if so, we can be free agents or are not rather the prey of blind impulses. But the question is founded upon a false division between cognition and feeling. Reason is thinking, and thinking is consciousness, —as we shall see later, it is the only form of consciousness— and consciousness carries valuation, and valuation impels to action. Therefore reason impels to action and is not impotent.

In the theory of cells valuation falls on the side of consciousness, not on the side of the datum. The datum is not as such valuable, but consciousness imparts value to the datum, as light imparts colour to that on which it shines. This implies that the theory of emotional data, mentioned in Chapter I, Section 6, is rejected. There is no objective fearfulness as a datum or character of data. Our view of valuation also involves the rejection of value-data, and the notion of value as a *quality* of the objective world. It may be thought to imply a subjective theory of value. This is not wholly untrue, but is very misleading. The theory of value maintained by the theory of cells cannot be labelled as subjectivist or objectivist in the ordinary senses of these terms. Or at least if it is called subjectivist, it must be understood that the usual implications of this term have no application. But the matter must be left for later discussion (Chapter VI).

4

SINCE cells constitute the whole of reality, there is nothing outside, beyond, or between them. Hence there is no space and no time outside them or between them. Hence that which divides them from one another, the *principium divisionis*, cannot be spatio-temporal. Each cell has its beginning and its ending, and yet it does not begin and end *in* time. But time begins and ends in it. Each cell has its own private time which begins and ends in its interior. And with the beginning and ending of its private time, the cell begins and ends. So also each cell has its own private space in its interior, and this space does not extend outside it. These internal spaces and times are not infinite, but finite.

The spaces and times appear as characters of the data within the cell. The data flow, as when I see a ball moving or colours changing. That is, my data have duration-spread. They arise and cease for me. The data—or some of them, for example, the colours—are also spatially extended. The interior of a cell may be compared to the interior of a hollow sphere, the interior walls of which are a kaleidoscope of changing colours. The interior may be brightly or dimly illuminated by the lamp of consciousness. In this figurative description, intended only to help the imagination, the colours have to be taken as symbolizing all kinds of sensuous and non-sensuous data.

This is the doctrine. If it appears paradoxical, this is because we approach it with sophisticated minds full of theories, whereas the doctrine is completely naïve, being nothing but a direct transcript of our actual experience. Rid ourselves in imagination of all sophistication and of all theories—admittedly a very difficult feat—and the doctrine will stand out in clear illumination as a simple statement of what we actually *find*.

For example, if we take a human private world as our example of a cell, it will no doubt be said that this private world has a beginning in time and an ending in time, since the human being is born and dies. My birth had a date in time, and time ran before I was born. Likewise time will run after I am dead.

But if we interrogate actual experience, we shall see that the time within which a cell thus appears to begin and end is always the time-series *of another cell*. My father may date my birth as having occurred in his fortieth year. Of course my beginning in the proper sense, that is the beginning of my own consciousness and my own data, never appeared in my father's time-series at all, since they are private to me. What he calls my birth means the appearance in his private world of certain of his private data which *correspond to* certain data in my world (see the principle of cellular correspondence, Section 9 of this chapter). Understanding the matter in this way, then, my birth occurred in the private time of my father, and in *his* time-series there was, of course, time before my birth. But there was no time for me, and *my* time-series began at my birth, and in that series there was, before my birth, nothing—not even time. Likewise my children will date what they will call my death, and for them there will be time after that event. But that will be *their* time, not mine. My time-series will have ended—unless the doctrine of survival is true. Thus all dating of events is in *someone's* time. An external time which is neutral and public is unknown to us. Public time is therefore a theory, not anything found in experience. Of course, it may possibly be a true theory. But that is not the point. The point is that it *is* a theory, and that it is this theory—whether true or false—which, because it is taken for granted, causes the theory of cells to appear paradoxical, although it is in fact simply a description of actual experience. In so far as the theory of cells merely states these facts, it is not really a *theory* at all. I hold that it is the views of other philosophers which are really theoretical.

The same point may be made in another way. The objector to our view took his cue from the facts of birth and death. But no man has ever experienced death (or birth). A man experiences his own consciousness up to its ceasing, that is, up to his death. But he cannot experience the actual ceasing of his consciousness, the fact that it *has* ceased. Thus he cannot experience his own death. Nor can any other man experience it. For another man cannot experience this man's consciousness at all, much less its ceasing. Thus no man has ever experienced death, either his own or that of another person, and there is no such thing as death to be found anywhere in human experience. Accordingly, the existence of death is a theory. This is doubtless why animals have no knowledge of death. For it is not within their experience, and they are not capable of theories. When therefore you object to the doctrine of cells because of the facts of birth and death, this is because you insist on introducing theories into what purports to be a simple description of experience.

But it will be objected that it is impossible to conceive of an end (or a beginning) without something beyond it. To conceive a limit is already to be beyond it in thought. I could not know what is meant by the end of a straight line unless I perceived or imaged the space beyond it. It is the same with time. Hence there cannot be, as supposed by the theory of cells, a private time which begins and ends but has no time before and after it. Likewise with private spaces.

Here is another theory with which we are to be confounded. Let us appeal once more to naïve experience. I look back in memory along the line of my own life. It becomes dimmer as I go back. Somewhere or other it happens that I cannot trace it any further. It does not end in a sharp point. It trails off into vagueness. But it does cease. And beyond its ceasing there is nothing. That has been my actual experience, theories or no theories.

The same point is perhaps more easily seen in the case of space. What I experience (to speak of visual experience only) is a visual field. There is a clear centre and a dim margin. The margin fades into nothingness. Thus I experience the spatial expanse coming to an end and having nothing beyond the end. Perhaps "end" is the wrong word. It seems to imply a sudden ceasing at a sharp boundary. Of course I do not experience any such sharp boundary. The visual field simply fades out. It can only be said to come to an end in the sense that it does not go on for ever. But if this may be called an ending, then I actually experience a finite visual field which ends and yet has nothing beyond the end. And if this is what I actually experience, how can any theory declare that it is "inconceivable"?

It may be urged that the question is not what I experience, but what can be—whether it is experienced or not. The argument is not that I do not experience a visual field with an end and no beyond, but that if I reflect I shall see that there must be a beyond, even if it lies outside my visual field. The fact that when I do not reflect, but simply look, I see no beyond proves nothing. It is logical thought, not experience, which shows that an end with no beyond is inconceivable.

But a thing cannot be logically inconceivable unless it is logically self-contradictory. Thus a circular square is inconceivable because contradictory propositions such as "it contains right angles" and "it contains no right angles" would have to be true of it. But if you say that an end with no beyond is in this way logically self-contradictory, then how is it that I can actually experience it? If anything is really self-contradictory, it not only cannot exist, but it cannot be experienced either. It would be impossible to experience a round square. But we do experience an end with no beyond. *Therefore the dogma that we cannot conceive a limit without anything beyond the limit must be false,* however great the authority which can be quoted for it.[1]

5

THE view that space and time must be infinite because it is impossible to conceive an end to them is rejected by the theory of cells. It rejects the existence of any infinite beings. When mathematicians talk about infinites, they are talking about ideas, not facts—whether they themselves admit this or not.

There cannot *be* any infinites, although it is true that we can operate with these ideas and that these operations may be important and useful. When it is said that there *is* an infinite number of numbers in the cardinal number series, this only means that theoretically there is nothing to stop a man going on adding ones to ones as long as he chooses. Death or dynamite may stop him. But there is nothing in the nature of arithmetic to make him pause. There is no law of the universe which, when a man comes to some very large number, would say "Stop. You cannot add another one." We can express this, if we like, by saying that there are an infinite number of numbers. But this cannot mean that these numbers *actually exist* somewhere waiting to be counted.

When it is said that space and time must be infinitely divisible, I take this to mean that there is nothing to stop a man going on dividing them. They are infinitely divis*ible,* but not infinitely divid*ed;* that is, they do not actually *have* an infinite number of parts.

There cannot be an infinite number of anything.'Hence there cannot be an infinite number of miles of space or years of time. The reason is that there must be as many miles as there are, no more, no less. That is, there must be a finite number. There cannot be an infinite number of sheep, or of horses, or of electrons, or of any actual entities anywhere in the world. However many there are, there must be exactly *that* number, and it must be possible to increase the number by adding one—which is a characteristic of finite numbers. If this is not true of the points in a line, this is because points are not actual entities. This means only that there is nothing to stop one dividing the line. The notion of infinity is not a *positive* idea at all. There is no such idea in the human mind. There is only the negative idea of the absence of an end to a process—such as dividing, adding, etc. The discovery of infinite numbers, and their successful use in mathematics, does not invalidate this reasoning.

There can be infinite numbers in mathematics, but there cannot be an infinite number of things in the world. That is, infinite numbers are fictitious in the sense that, although they can be successfully used mathematically, they do not apply to any empirical facts in the way in which the number 2 applies to two chairs. Numbers which are in this sense fictitious are common in mathematics. The readiest examples are minus numbers. Any child can operate with —2. But there cannot *be* minus two of anything in the world.'There cannot be min's two pounds of tea in a container, nor minus two strokes of a clock. Any number of actual things in the universe will always be a positive number. There is either a positive number of sheep in the field or there are none at all. You cannot ever set out to count any actual things which you find existing anywhere, and having counted them, turn to your neighbour and say "I find that there are minus two of these things." You can say that New York is minus three thousand miles east of London, but this only means that it is really three thousand miles west. This is a mere dodge.

If minus numbers can be thus fictitious and yet mathematically good conceptions, so can infinite numbers. Therefore the fact that mathematicians have discovered infinite numbers and operate with them successively does not prove that there could ever be an infinite number of things, for instance, an infinite number of miles of space. One might as well argue that when mathematicians discovered minus numbers this proved that there could be minus two pounds of tea in a can.

6

THE famous antinomies of space and time are insoluble so long as one sticks to a realist metaphysics, and this is in fact one of the strongest arguments against such a metaphysic. But the theory of cells offers a solution. According to that theory, there is no space and no time except the actually perceived finite expanses and durations within cells. Both are *plena.* Empty space and empty time are constructs. But once empty space has been invented, there is nothing to prevent it being extended for ever. For instance, visual space actually ends where the colours of the visual field end. But once one has conjured up the idea of an empty space beyond this end, there is nothing to stop its endless progress. This alone should be enough to convince us that empty space must be a construct, since infinite space leads to contradictions.

The solution of the antinomy is therefore that space and time are finite, not infinite. It is usually held, however, that this in turn leads to contradiction. This is because it is supposed that we cannot conceive a limit with nothing beyond the limit. It has already been shown that this must be false, since we actually *experience* an end with no beyond. But the same thing can be seen in other ways.

It is likely to be admitted (though not, of course, by all philosophers) that the notion of empty time is meaningless and impossible. The theory of cells holds that space and time are exactly on a par in this respect, and for the same reasons, and that empty space is as impossible as empty time. Even those philosophers who admit that empty time is impossible, since time is only meaningful if there is some kind of change or process of things going on, often stick to the notion of empty space. So I will take the case of time as the basis of my argument.

Let it be admitted, then, that there could be no empty time. It will follow that an end of time with no time beyond is conceivable and in no way self-contradictory.

For could it be argued that it is impossible to conceive of an end to the *filling* of time without there being more filling beyond that end? It could not. Picture this filling as, shall we say, a river of changing colours (any sensuous material which is changing will do). Does the fact that this stream of colours comes to an end at time *t* logically imply that beyond time *t* there must be more colours? Can the fact that I find colours here, on this side of a line, force me to believe that there must be more colours there, on that side of the line? Obviously not. For one particular fact, such as a colour in this place, cannot imply another particular fact, such as another colour in some other place. Then you will have to admit that it is not impossible to conceive of the *filling* of time coming to a limit without there being any filling beyond the limit. Thus the filling of time might come to an end. In that case either time itself must then come to an end, or there must be empty time beyond the end of the filling. Hence if we have admitted that there can be no empty time, we shall have to admit that time could come to an end. We either have to maintain the possibility of empty time (which seems meaningless) or we must admit that the dogma that there can be no limit without a beyond is false. And if it is false, there is no contradiction in the conception of finite time.

[51]

If this is admitted as regards time, the same possibility in regard to space is likely to be granted without further difficulty.

One further argument can be used. Suppose that there were only one mind in the universe, and that the rest of the universe were its dream—the oft-imagined world of the solipsist. That this is a fantastic supposal does not affect my argument. The important point is that this supposal is not logically self-contradictory. And it has usually been admitted that it is not.

Now if the dream-figures in this solipsist world moved and changed there would be time in it. Let it now be imagined that this mind should die, that its consciousness should cease, and therefore its dream disappear. There would be nothing left, no space, no time. If it is admitted that there is no self-contradiction here, it will follow that there cannot be any contradiction in the notion of a coming to an end of time with no time beyond.

7

OUTSIDE the cells and between them there is neither time nor space. Therefore that which separates them and makes them distinct from one another cannot be space or time. We have now to ask ourselves what is the *principium divisionis*. In order to answer this question we shall have to investigate the notion of *privacy*.

How and why have we been led to the conception of privacy? We need do no more than summarize the line of thought since it is an old and familiar story well understood by philosophers. The arguments are simple, though of course I do not mean that all philosophers will agree as to the conclusions to which they ought to lead us in regard to the question of privacy. When two persons, *A* and *B*, look at the "same" object, say a painted square piece of wood, they do not receive the "same" data. The datum of one is square, of the other some other shape. It follows that they cannot be seeing numerically the same datum. For the same entity cannot be at the same time both square and not square. There are, therefore, two data, one of which is perceived by *A*, the other by *B*. We express this by saying that each has his own "private" datum.

Most people hold that there is a common or public "object" to which these two data "belong." Whether the object is conceived by them as the cause of the data, or their part-cause, or source, or as being related to them in some other way, does not concern us here. The theory of cells denies that there is a public object, and holds that nothing exists except the data and the consciousness which together constitute the cell. But whether this is so or not, the privacy of the data themselves is the conclusion to be based upon the facts quoted. This conclusion does not depend upon the denial of the outside object. Even a representative theory of perception, which believes in a public object, usually holds the data to be private. Also most realists maintain the privacy of data.

The different shapes of the data for different observers lead to this conclusion. But the same kind of argument may be used as regards colour, size, taste, and other sensed characters of objects. Colour blindness affords an extreme example. I see the object as red, while a colour blind person sees it as green. A red datum and a green datum cannot be numerically identical. Nor, in the sphere of colour, is it necessary to introduce colour blindness. For two observers of normal vision will see the object as of different colours, or different shades of the same colour, as a result of their different angles of vision.

It also follows from these arguments that the spaces occupied by the data are private. *A* sees a square expanse of space as occupied by the painted board, while *B* sees an expanse of a different shape. The same piece of space cannot be both square and not square. Therefore *A* and *B* are not seeing the same spaces. Therefore their spaces, as well as the data which occupy them, are private.

[3] See, for instance, Russell, *The Problems of Philosophy*, p. 32, and H. H. Price, *Perception*, pp. 145 and 274.

But what does "private" *mean*? Evidently it means that the two observers are not seeing numerically the "same" datum. They are seeing two "different" data. The question at issue is as to the *number* of data in existence. If you assert that data are public, this means that, according to your account, there is only one datum shared by the two persons. If you say the data are private, this means that, in your view, there are two distinct data, one for each of the two observers. But what are the meanings of "the same" and "different"? And what are the meanings of "one" and "two"?

One is tempted to say that twoness is dependent upon counting and counting upon pointing. Can we point to the data and count them and so give a decisive answer? It will be clear that this cannot be done. For I can only see my own datum and not yours, and you can only see your datum and not mine. Neither of us will be able to point out two data. It might be thought to follow that the conception of privacy is baseless. But I believe that, if we follow this line of thought at all, the more proper conclusion to it will be that both the notions, privacy and publicity, are equally baseless and that the whole issue is a false one. But this would leave unsolved the problem posed by the different shapes and colours perceived by two observers viewing the "same" object. Moreover one might on the same grounds deny that the question whether the universe contains only one mind or a plurality of minds is a genuine question, since I cannot point out and count any mind except my own. We may conclude that this method of counting the data is a false trail.

But if twoness does not necessarily depend upon the ability to point out and count, it does certainly depend absolutely upon division, separation. Twoness arises from separation, and therefore, if there is twoness there must be a *principium divisionis*. In most common cases the *principium divisionis* is space or time or both. There are two billiard balls on the table. That which separates them and makes them "different" from one another is a spatial interval. If they occupied the same space, they would be one ball. A separating interval of time may also constitute twoness.

But the difference between the two data of the two observers cannot mean this. For if the *principium divisionis* as between the two data is to be space, they must both be in the *same* space. My two billiard balls are only numerically distinct because between them runs a continuous spatial line in one and the same continuous space. But we have seen that if *A's* datum is private, so is the space which it occupies. Hence we have not one and the same space to divide the two data. We have to find a *principium divisionis* which will divide, not merely the two data, but the two spaces. And this cannot be space itself. For if the two spaces were divided by space, they would continue across this space into one another, and what we should have would be one continuous public space of which our private spaces would have to be considered parts. And evidently this is not what is meant.

Shall we then give up the notion of privacy and conclude that after all the data, as well as the spaces they occupy, are public? We were led to consider them private, but on examination the notion of privacy seems to possess no intelligible meaning. It purports to mean that the data are "two." But twoness, as ordinarily understood, is constituted by spatial or temporal separation, and it is nonsense to talk of private spaces being separated by space, or of private times being separated by time. And since the notion of privacy turns out to be meaningless, we shall be invited to give it up and to conclude that we directly apprehend public data and public spaces and times.

But if so, the incompatibilities between our data remain on our hands an insoluble mystery. How *can* a red datum be numerically identical with a green datum? How *can* a square surface be numerically identical with a not-square surface? We are forced back by these considerations to the concept of privacy. And since our well-intentioned attempts to interpret this in terms of a spatio-temporal *principium divisionis* have brought us to this pass, we must try to discover some other *principium divisionis.* We must stick to the belief that the privacy of *A's* and *B's* data means their numerical twoness, and that this implies that they are in some way separated from one another. But by what are they separated, since it is not by space or time?

♦ The answer given by the theory of cells is that the *principium divisionis* is constituted by personality or by the principles of personal identity and personal difference. There is something which constitutes me at once a self-identical person and a different person from you. My consciousness and your consciousness are two distinct consciousnesses. Something divides them. This something is not time or space. But this something is also that which divides our data and our spaces and times. The privacy of our data means in the first instance simply that my data are "mine" and that your data are "yours." Thus the question what divides one cell from another is simply the question what divides one consciousness from another consciousness. This *I* is not that *I*. The principle of separation of the *I's* is the *principium divisionis* as between cells, as between private data, private spaces, and private times. ♦

8

SINCE the *principium divisionis* as between cells is that which makes one consciousness self-identical and separates it from another consciousness, we have now to investigate what this is.

Earlier attempts to discover this principle in a spiritual substance arose from the incurable materialistic bias of the human mind. An *I*, it was supposed, must be a "thing," and the example *par excellence* of the "thing" is a piece of matter. The self-identity of the material thing was supposed to be secured by the division of substance from quality. And this must be the same with the spiritual thing. The spiritual substance must remain the same while the consciousness changes. But the empirical principle forbids the notion of a material substratum, and it also forbids the notion of the spiritual substratum. There is nothing in the cell except datum and consciousness. There is consciousness, but there is no thing which *has* consciousness. Consciousness is perpetually changing, and data are perpetually changing. Wherein, then, lies the self-identity? Clearly it lies in the unity of consciousness. The items of consciousness are grasped together in a unity. But there is no thing which, like a forceps, descends on them externally and grasps them together. The self-identity lies in the unity itself, not in anything which makes the unity.

The unity of consciousness is two-dimensional, horizontal and vertical. The horizontal unity grasps together the simultaneous items of consciousness, the vertical unity grasps together the items which lie at different dates along the timeline. I hear a sound and simultaneously see a red object. The sound and the red object are together in one consciousness. Or again I see a bookcase before me and a chair to the left of it, both together in a unity of consciousness. These are examples of horizontal unity. Again I hear a sound today and I saw a face yesterday. The sound and the face have been included in a single consciousness. This is an example of vertical unity. Memory is the special name for the vertical unity. For some reason or other no name has been bestowed on the horizontal unity. But the two unities are strictly analogous. Together they constitute the unity of a person. Memory is not a unique phenomenon of mind. It is simply one out of the two aspects of mental unity. It seems to have escaped attention that the horizontal unity is identically the same thing as memory except that its direction is different.

This twofold unity is what constitutes the single self-identity of a person. What falls within it is *his* experience. What falls outside it is the experience of some other mind. This is accordingly the *principium divisionis* as between cells.

I hear an immediate outcry that this explains nothing, that it does nothing except to put before us the very mysteries which have to be explained. I have been doing nothing except to give the problem itself as the solution. Memory, for instance, is a mystery. *How* does the mind remember? What enables it to exercise this miraculous faculty of calling up the past? How can mind make this transcendent leap beyond itself over twenty or thirty years of intervening time? And when we have explained all this, we shall then be expected to turn to the horizontal unity of mind and answer the same sort of questions. How does the mind grasp together the simultaneous sight and sound?

I can only reply that all these questions are completely childish and proceed from a mind which has not as yet absorbed even the *A, B, C,* of empirical philosophy. How does the mind remember? What is the meaning of the word "how" here? Whatever happens in the universe, no one can say how it happens, nor has the question any meaning except in the sense that it may be a request for more detailed or accurate information as to *what* has happened. Nothing can be done by the intellect of man—or for that matter by the intellect of God—except to describe what happens. You can ask how the steam in an engine pushes it along the rails. Your enquiry is answered by describing the piston, connecting rods, etc. If the questions persist I may have to go on to describe the molecules of the steel, their movements, and so forth. But however far I go I can never get anything except more and more detailed descriptions of what happens. Now as to memory, it is simply a fact that mind remembers. This is just one of the characters of consciousness. And moreover it is an essential character, since consciousness is impossible without it. If the question "how?" is a request for further details, perhaps they can be given. One may look up a psychology book and find them. But beyond giving us more detailed information about memory, this will not help us to understand any better the ultimately unanalysable fact that the mind does remember. That minds remember has to be accepted as an ultimate fact about them just as that bodies are extended, heavy, impenetrable, have to be accepted as ultimate facts about bodies.

What is it that makes the mind able to remember? For what information does this question enquire? Does it suggest that some other "thing," which is not itself mind, from the outside pushes the mind into remembering or enables it to remember? And if we found this other thing, should we then be asked what third thing enables this thing to enable the mind to remember? Since memory is one of the essential characters of consciousness, these questions are like asking what it is which enables a triangle to be triangular.

But how can the mind make this transcendent leap across the years? This question is just as senseless as the others. The answer is that the mind just does make this leap, that this is part of the character which it is empirically found to have, and that whatever character a thing has we have to accept it and can do nothing more than describe it. But it is worth remarking that this particular question—and perhaps the others, too—apparently proceed from the aforementioned materialistic bias of the human mind. First of all, there is a sort of vague picture of consciousness as a kind of material thing. And as pieces of matter cannot fly across twenty miles of space without passing through the intervening space (or at least this is the common belief), and cannot go backwards in time, it is then asked how a mind can jump backwards across twenty years of time. But why should the laws of mind be the same as the laws which apply to a piece of matter? If you want to describe memory metaphorically as a "leap across time," you can. But you ought to recognize that it is merely your inveterate prejudice which causes you to suppose that a mind must necessarily behave like a lump of matter.

The solution of the problem of memory consists in seeing that there is no problem.[4]

---

[4] This remark does not apply to the question of the logical justification of knowledge by memory, a question which is not raised in the text and is irrelevant to the present discussion.

Exactly similar questions may be asked about the supposed mystery of the horizontal unity of mind. Exactly similar answers would have to be given. I forbear to weary the reader with them.

Of course, whether memory is the essence of personal identity has been doubted.[5] But none of the doubts seem to me to be very substantial. In the first place there are, of course, other elements in the popular conception of what constitutes the same person over a period of time. Obviously the self-identity of the body is most often thought of. But this does not concern us because we are enquiring what constitutes the identity of a *consciousness*. Again, continuity of disposition and character may be appealed to. But this is certainly not the vital thread. Theoretically at least two persons might have the same dispositions and character. Yet they would not thereby become one person. Memory is the vital thread.

But still doubts will be raised. What happens when there is total loss of memory? Is there then continuance of personal identity? I should answer, No. There are two successive consciousnesses. There is plainly not one consciousness. And if this reply seems to depart widely from common usage, that is because common usage in this matter is a vague mixture of many different criteria. This reply might seem mistaken to the practical man because he is thinking mostly of the sameness of the physical body. But it will be said that an infant two days old remembers only the sensation of perhaps a second ago, and beyond that all its past experience is gone? Are we to say that it has not the same consciousness over a period of minutes? I do not think that it is necessary to conclude this. If each moment is linked by memory to the *next* moment, we shall have a single continuous chain. I will explain this point further in the ensuing paragraph.

[5] See, for example, Bradley's discussion in *Appearance and Reality,* Chap. IX.

But then there are great gaps even in the memory of a normal adult person. My early life is totally forgotten. I cannot even remember most of my experience of yesterday. I forget what I ate for breakfast this morning. And what happened between noon and two p.m. this day last year is a total blank. Thus since memory is not a continuous thread how can it constitute personal identity? This, however, is not the point. Each moment of experience is linked to the next moment by memory, and the next to the next, and so on throughout life. That I forget now whole stretches of the past is nothing to the point. A being who could not remember anything beyond one minute might still have each minute of his life connected to the next by the thread of memory and so the whole would be connected. If at time t I remember the experience of the previous moment, t', and if at t' I remember the experience of the moment just before that, t'', then there is continuity from t'' to t even though when I arrive at t I have forgotten the experience of t''. But even so there may be gaps of pure unconsciousness over which such a continuity cannot run. What then? I see no difficulty. Consciousness throws a line back across the blank time and links the two disjoined ends in spite of all. Do we not remember what occurred before we went to sleep?

ᵖTo sum up. The *principium divisionis* as between cell and cell is I-ness or personality. One cell is different from another, not because they are divided by space or time, but because they possess two different consciousnesses. My data are numerically distinct from your data by virtue of the fact that they are yours and mine respectively. And the difference of one I from another I is constituted by the fact that the experiences of the first have neither horizontal nor vertical unity with the experiences of the second. And that one set of experiences are together in one unity while another set are excluded from it, but included in another unity, is a bare fact, inexplicable, not reducible or analysable into anything more simple, ultimate, forcing its acceptance upon us. And if we ask further questions, our questions will have no meaning.ᵖ

9

The Principle of Cellular Correspondence. Between the data of different cells there is in general "correspondence." But there are also important divergences from correspondence. These must be carefully noted, but it will be best to begin by elucidating the notion of correspondence in abstraction from all divergence. On the principle of cellular correspondence depend the conception of a common world, the possibility of communication, and the possibility of mutual influence between cells.

'Correspondence may be illustrated by the following case. If two observers, *A* and *B,* are simultaneously inspecting what is commonly called the "same object," for example, if both are looking at the same white sheet of paper, then in cell *A* there will be a certain squarish white datum; and in cell *B* there will also be a certain squarish white datum. These two data are said to "correspond." According to the theory of cells there is no common "object" external to the cells. Nothing exists except the data and the consciousnesses of them. But the data exhibit correspondence.'

Correspondence is structural or functional. It concerns relations. It does not concern sensuous content. It does not imply similarity of sensuous content. Thus if two cards such as the five of diamonds and the five of clubs be compared, there is correspondence between the marks on the two cards although there is a large measure of sensuous dissimilarity. The central club corresponds to the central diamond, although they are of different shapes, and although one is black, the other red. But the central club bears to the other four clubs the same relations as the central diamond bears to the other four diamonds. So it is with the corresponding data in the two cells *A* and *B.* It is not asserted that the white squarish datum in *A* is sensuously similar to the white squarish datum in *B,* either as regards colour or shape or any other sensed quality or character. For all we can tell there may also be this sensuous similarity, and if so this is a very interesting fact. But it is not affirmed by the principle of cellular correspondence. What is affirmed is that in each cell there is a certain pattern of data, and that these patterns are similar just as are the patterns of the two cards. And if datum a in A corresponds to datum b in B, this means that a bears to its context of other data in the A-pattern the same relations which b bears to its context of other data in the B-pattern. Thus it is not asserted that my sensation of white is sensuously similar to your sensation of white, although this may as a matter of fact be so.

Before going further it may be well to distinguish as clearly as possible between "similarity" and "correspondence." The relation of similarity itself is unanalysable and indefinable. But in our terminology two entities are said to be similar when the relation of similarity holds directly between these two entities. If the entities themselves are dissimilar but there is similarity between the relations of the first to its context of other entities and the relations of the second to *its* context of other entities, then the entities are said merely to "correspond." The term "entity" as used here includes relations. Thus not only may data either be similar or merely correspond but it is true of relations also that they may either be similar or merely correspond.

The exposition of the principle of cellular correspondence contained in the opening paragraphs of this section might seem to imply that, although there may be dissimilarity between the sensuous content of corresponding data in two cells, yet there must be similarity between the two sets of relations in the two cells. This would mean, for example, that the relation "to the left of" in cell A must be similar to the relation "to the left of" in cell B. It is not, however, necessary to suppose this, although it may happen to be the fact. The relations in A may not be similar to the relations in B, for they may merely correspond. This will imply in each cell a further network of relations of relations. Two relations, namely R' in cell A and R'' in cell B will, in the absence of similarity between them, correspond, if R' is related to the other relations in A by a relation similar to the relation of R'' to the other relations in B. This hierarchy of relations of relations, and of relations of relations of relations, and so on, might theoretically proceed *ad infinitum.* The theory of cells holds that there are no infinites, and that therefore the hierarchy must come to an end. But even apart from this general consideration no communication would be possible if there were an infinite regress. And since communication exists as a fact, it must be the case that somewhere the hierarchy ends. At that point mere correspondence must give place to similarity. But so far as the principle of cellular correspondence is concerned the hierarchy may be drawn out to anything short of an infinite series. There may be direct similarity holding between the data of different cells, or the similarity may be found at any higher level. This is indifferent to the principle.

For the sake of simplicity I have here been speaking solely of sensuous data and their correspondence. It must not be forgotten, however, that the principle of cellular correspondence applies to all data, or at least to all data regarding which communication is possible.

The considerations of this section show that the relation of similarity is peculiarly fundamental in the universe, and cannot be put on the same level with other relations such as "to the left of." "To the left of" may be one relation for cell A and another dissimilar relation for cell B and these two relations may merely correspond. But the relation of similarity itself must be the same for all cells. For correspondence in the end rests upon similarity and is made intelligible by it. Similarity therefore cannot be itself mere correspondence. The relation of similarity in cell A must be similar to the relation in cell B which goes by the same name and cannot merely correspond to it.

10

THERE is probably never at any given moment complete correspondence between the data of any two cells. And it is necessary to say something regarding the divergences.

In the first place we must distinguish the actual pattern of data existing in a cell at any particular moment from the complete pattern of its possible data. The former may be termed the momentary pattern for the cell. The latter may be termed the world-pattern for it. For instance, the now actually sensed data which "belong to" this piece of white paper on which I am writing are included in the momentary pattern of the cell of which "I" am an abstract element. But the data of the back of the paper are not. Nor are the data which belong to the Tower of London, since I am not now perceiving the Tower. These tower-data are, however, parts of the world-pattern of my cell, since they are known to be possible experiences for me. Of course the momentary pattern is part of the world-pattern.

Now when we compare cell with cell as regards correspondence we may be thinking either of the world-pattern or of the momentary pattern.

The connection between the momentary pattern and the rest of the world-pattern is not arbitrary, but is governed by definite laws, or sets of relations; and the laws in one cell correspond to the laws in other cells. Hence there are definite tracks of obtainable experience along which it is possible to pass from the data actually in a cell to any other given datum in the cell's world-pattern. Thus there are many definite tracks of possible experience leading from my present data to the data of the Tower of London. I pass along one of these tracks when I visit the Tower.

Of course, when we speak of there being a world-pattern for a cell consisting of possible data, we must not be supposed to mean that these data are, so to speak, waiting ready outside the cells to be taken into them. Nothing actually exists except the consciousness and its momentary data. But it has been found that certain types of data are always followed by the coming into existence in the cell of certain other types of data. In this sense datum *a,* which actually now exists, leads to datum *b* which does not yet exist at all. Datum *b* leads to datum *c* and so on till a whole track is found. It is doubtless merely a matter of faith that these tracks of experience, like other laws of nature, will continue to repeat themselves.

Now since the tracks of data in the world-pattern of one cell correspond to the tracks of data in the world-patterns of other cells, this means that there is in general correspondence of world-patterns. If this were not so, if there were merely occasional correspondence between momentary patterns, there could hardly be belief in a common world or any communication.

Nevertheless there are considerable divergences of world-pattern. Sets of data appear in a cell to which not only are there no corresponding sets in other cells, but no track of experience can be found giving passage for other cells to the corresponding sets. When this occurs we have a failure of correspondence of world-patterns and these sets of data are known as unrealities, hallucinations, and the like.

A universe is a set of cells having *inter se* a recognizable general correspondence of world-pattern. Our universe is such a set, and it includes all the private worlds of human beings and probably of all animals. The theory of cells recognizes the possibility that there may exist other universes than ours, that is, sets of cells having as between themselves a general correspondence of world-pattern but no correspondence with the cells in our universe. Since these universes would be invisible to us, it cannot be known whether they exist or not. But there might be any number. The possibility of alien universes is not open to a realistic metaphysic with its realistically conceived space and time containing all existence. The existence of single cells having no correspondence with any other cell, solipsist universes, is another unverifiable possibility.

If now we examine momentary patterns we find the following. We compare the two simultaneous momentary patterns of the cells *A* and *B*. Momentary patterns are defined as simultaneous when they contain data which correspond not only as taken in the contexts of the momentary patterns themselves but also as taken in the total contexts of the respective world-patterns. There may of course be simultaneous momentary patterns between which there is no correspondence, as happens when two observers are at the "same" moment far apart or looking in different directions. But such cases of what we may call indirect simultaneity have to be defined in terms of the direct simultaneity defined in the previous sentence. If now we compare one momentary pattern with another simultaneous momentary pattern—apart from cases of indirect simultaneity— we shall find cases of which the following may be taken as typical. Two observers, *A* and *B*, are perceiving the "same" object, say this piece of paper. In both cells there will be what each observer will call a white square datum. These data will correspond in their relations to their respective contexts. They will also partially correspond each to each as regards what each observer will call their shapes and colours. This does not, of course, necessarily mean that the shapes and colours will be similar, but that they will correspond in their relations respectively to *A's* and *B's* geometrical systems and colour scales. So far there will be correspondence. But there will also be divergence. For *A's* datum will be a true square, while *B's* datum will be of a different shape. And *A's* datum will be one shade of colour, while *B's* datum will be a slightly different shade depending on the different angle of incidence of the light. But these divergences will not be arbitrary. Just as the complete divergences previously studied are connected by tracks of experience which turn out on examination to be laws or sets of relations; so here the partial divergences will be connected by definite relations which render possible a passage from divergence to absolute correspondence. The laws of perspective are such sets of relations.

11

THE possibility of communication is based upon the principle of cellular correspondence in the following manner.

Consciousness in its aspect of valuation is an impulsion to act. That consciousness acts means that it produces alterations in some of its data. It *can* produce alterations in some data, but not in others (except indirectly). "Can" simply means "does." (Thus when you say that water *cannot* run uphill, you simply mean that it does not.) All directly controllable data are somatic data, but of course not all somatic data are controllable. Indirectly consciousness can often produce changes in non-somatic data, as when I move the paper with my hand. I alter somatic data, and these changes are, in accordance with certain laws or regular sequences of data which I have learned, followed by the desired changes in the paper-data.

This, of course, is simply the doctrine of interaction translated into the language of the theory of cells. The doctrine requires no special defence. It has the absolutely overwhelming evidence of all human experience in its favour. Its truth is attested every time a man intentionally raises his hand. Of course it is here assumed, and it is an essential part of the theory of cells, that consciousness is a definite kind of being distinguishable from its data. This has often been denied, and many philosophers have attempted to reduce consciousness to a complex of data. If this attempt succeeded, the whole question of interaction between consciousness and data would fall. That the attempt has not been, and cannot be, successful, I shall try to show in the chapter on consciousness. What I am at present saying is that, *on the basis of the definite distinction between consciousness and data,* it is impossible to dispute the overwhelming evidence in favour of interaction. It is senseless to ask *how* a material entity can interact with a non-material entity. It is simply an experienced fact that it does so. And if this conflicts with some accepted physical principle (though this is probably not the case) what this shows is that the physical principle has only a limited application. The question *how* is as senseless here as it was in the case of memory, and all that was said there applies here.' The old objection that it is "inconceivable" that a non-material entity could move a piece of matter is a mere barbarism, a relic of pre-empirical times. Nothing is inconceivable save what is logically self-contradictory.' And interaction involves no contradiction. It is no longer plausible to declare *a priori* from an armchair that something in nature is "impossible" because it outrages some prejudice of ours. No *a priori* argument against interaction has the slightest weight. Experience is the only arbiter. And experience leaves no doubt that interaction occurs. I do not discuss here the objection from the so-called principle of conservation[6] beyond observing that, if that principle really conflicts with interaction (which I do not believe) then the principle cannot be, *in the form in which it is commonly stated,* wholly true. It would have to be modified by limiting its scope. For the evidence in favour of interaction is a million times greater than the evidence in favour of conservation.

Freedom is the alteration of somatic data by the valuations of the consciousness of the cell to which the data belong. Their alteration by any other agency is unfreedom. Thus if my body is thrown out through the door by the porter I move unfreely. But if my movements are caused by the valuations of my own consciousness they are free. Freedom does not mean that my actions are uncaused. It means that they are caused by my consciousness. Nor does it mean that my immediate state of consciousness is uncaused. This may have been caused by some previous state of consciousness or by something external to it, that is, by some datum or complex of data. Consciousness is in no sense free from determination by causality. And the threads of causality run freely backwards and for-

[6] Because I have nothing to say which has not already been said. An admirable discussion will be found in Professor C. D. Broad's *Mind and Its Place in Nature,* pp. 103-9.

wards between consciousness and data—which is the meaning of interaction. Thus freedom is not an exception to causal determination, but an example of it. That I am free means simply that my actions—in so far as they are free—issue from my conscious valuations as their cause.

This is the principle. Of course the application of the principle to a complex mass of details is often very perplexing. For example, my actions may be, and doubtless usually are, the effects of many joint causes. Some of these part-causes may be states of my consciousness, while others may be data— that is, what would ordinarily be called external things or forces. In that case I feel, and am, only partly free. Freedom is a matter of degree. Or the act may have been wholly caused by consciousness, but the immediate state of consciousness may not have issued from the train of my previous mental life, but may have been itself the effect of some physical fact. This happens when my act is caused not indeed by an external physical force, but by the threat of force. In such case I am *formally* free, since the proximate cause of my act was my own consciousness—I might have refused in spite of all— but I have a low degree of freedom.

It is now possible to show how the principle of cellular correspondence renders communication possible. We are, of course, not concerned with the questions how communication historically began, or, having begun, grew up to maturity, or even how there developed that sense of the presence of another consciousness without which communication could have hardly any meaning. What we have to explain is simply the essential principle of how communication is possible, or in other words, what occurs when communication takes place. Let datum a in cell A be a datum within the immediate control of the consciousness of the A-cell. Let it correspond to datum b in cell B. The A-consciousness can now alter a to a'. Thereupon by the principle of cellular correspondence datum b in cell B changes to b'. Thus the A-consciousness can indirectly alter the data, or some of the data, in cell B. This constitutes the possibility of signals or language. How it comes about that such signals can be interpreted by one consciousness in the manner intended by the other consciousness is a matter for the historian of mind, the psychologist, or the anthropologist, rather than for the metaphysician.

12

WHEN the consciousness in cell A, by altering its own data, indirectly alters the data of the B-cell, the valuations of the consciousness in the B-cell will also be altered. For this consciousness will not value datum b', which has replaced b, in the same manner as it valued b. And since it is valuation which impels to action, this alteration of consciousness will cause alteration of action. Thus indirectly the A-consciousness can alter both the B-consciousness and the physical activities which issue from it. When this occurs the A-cell is said to "influence" the B-cell. Thus the possibility of mutual influence between the cells is, like the possibility of communication, based upon the principle of cellular correspondence.

It was sure to be objected to the theory of cells that it pictures a universe composed of little worlds completely cut off from one another and incapable of any action upon one another. This is now seen to be a mistake. Influence passes from cell to cell as easily as light from one region of space to another. It is probably the metaphor of being "cut off" which is responsible for the misunderstanding. It is certainly no more than a metaphor. Cells are not "cut off" from one another except in so far as the interior of each being private to itself constitutes being cut off. But on almost any metaphysical theory my consciousness is private to myself and is in that sense cut off from other consciousnesses. The theory of cells, of course, adds that the data as well as the consciousnesses are private. But this, or at least something very like it, would also be admitted by most theories. On any theory there must be some sense in which the green datum which the colour-blind man sees in place of the normal red datum is peculiar to himself. Certainly other people cannot see this greenness. Nor can I see that the assertion that there exist two data, and not one common datum, imposes upon the theory of cells that consequence of everlasting loneliness and aloofness which it seems to suggest to some minds. If two men are conversing across the dinner table, will they feel more lonely or cut off from one another for being told that there exist two tables and not one?

There are, however, other grounds on which it may be asserted that the doctrine of the mutual influence between cells is unacceptable. The essence of influence, according to the theory of cells, is the fact that when datum a in one cell is altered to datum a', datum b in another cell is altered to b'. This, it will be said, even if it should occur, is not *influence*. For there is no *passage* of influence *between A* and *B*. All you have is something happening in A and then something happening in B, without any *connection* between the two.

Need I say that, on the empiricist view, all that influence can possibly mean is that it is always the case that when something happens here, something else happens there? When the sun exerts influence on the wax so as to melt it, when the moon exerts influence on the tides, in all cases influence can be interpreted only in this way. If so, the fact that a change in the datum of one cell is invariably accompanied by a corresponding change in the datum of another cell is as clear an example of influence as can be found anywhere in the world.

But is this empiricist view of influence correct? This is an ancient argument, and I will not be drawn into a revamping of the issues. I will, however, add certain pertinent observations.

In the first place, in most common cases of influence there is supposed to be a passage of "energy" across a continuous space. This feature is absent in the case of influence between cells, since there is no space between them. But it is not certain that all common cases of influence are cases of energy-transference across space. This does not seem to be true of influence between mental entities, as when one idea in my mind produces another idea. But apart from this, how is the idea of energy-transference itself to be interpreted except on the lines suggested? Does it not simply mean that when something happens in one region of space, something else happens in the adjoining region of space, and then something else in the next adjoining region, and so all along the line?

Among recent writers Professor Whitehead is notable for his rejection of the empiricist theory of influence. And since to consider his arguments cannot be regarded as a mere revamping of old controversies, something may be said of them. Professor Whitehead takes the case of a flash of light *making* a man blink. He thinks that we have not only the flash followed by the blink, but also the *making*. That is, one event exerts "power," or influence, over the other. He writes: "The man will explain his experience by saying, 'The flash made me blink': and if his statement is doubted, he will reply, 'I know it, because I felt it.' . . . But Hume intervenes with another explanation. He first points out that in the mode of presentational immediacy there is no percept of the flash *making* the man blink."[7] And Professor Whitehead argues that there *is* a percept of "making" in the mode of causal efficacy. But in whatever mode, a percept is a percept. It is the perceiving of a datum. Hence if Hume made any mistake in his analysis of the complex of data, it was only that he left out one datum, that of *making*. The principle will in any case be the same. Either on Whitehead's interpretation or on Hume's what we have is a number of data following, or accompanying, one another. The flash making the man blink will be, after all, nothing but a bare succession of data.

In Professor Whitehead's own philosophy the notion of influence or "power," which is not mere succession, has a leading place. And it is therefore worth while asking whether he succeeds in making any such conception comprehensible. One actual entity, according to his philosophy, "prehends" another

[7] *Process and Reality,* Part III, Chap. VIII, Sec. 3.

actual entity. The "feeling" of this second actual entity is thereby "objectified" in the first. This constitutes a flow or transference of feeling from the second to the first, and this is equivalent to a flow of energy or power. Feeling, energy, or power flows on and on from actual entity to actual entity in long series or "historic routes." This conception is intimately connected with Professor Whitehead's belief that "reasons" can be given for things which will "explain" them. Causation, physical energy, perception, memory, are all "explained" by this flow of feeling. In fact what I must make so bold as to describe as the delusion that explanatory *reasons* can be given for things seems to me at bottom identical with the delusion that in such a flow of feeling as is here postulated there could be anything more than a bare succession. That there *is* something more he certainly supposes, just as he supposes that in causality there is something more than succession of data. It is this mysterious something more which is regarded by him as power. And it is this power which is supposed to explain things and to constitute a reason for them. But this suggestion of a something more in addition to the succession of data or feelings is incomprehensible because in the last analysis it is meaningless—meaningless for the same reason as substance in the sense of an invisible substratum is meaningless. For suppose that there is such a flow of feelings from actual entity to actual entity. What can this mean except that there is first a feeling here and then a feeling there—a mere succession of feelings? It seems quite clear that the metaphor of a *flow* of some physical fluid along a route is part of the imaginative picture which this philosophy (whether intentionally or not) suggests, and moreover that it is impossible to understand this philosophy without, perhaps unconsciously, relying on this metaphor. But if we consider an actual flow of a fluid, say water, along a route, we find that there is nothing present to our minds except a continuous succession of volumes of water. If we are entitled to make use of the metaphor in understanding the philosophy of organism—and I am suggesting that there is no other way of understanding it—then we are entitled to make use of the metaphor in criticizing it. Draw what imaginative picture you will of the flow of feelings, you will find that you have nothing there except a bare succession of feelings.

I cannot think, therefore, that either Professor Whitehead's arguments against Hume, or his own positive doctrine, give us any ground for abandoning the empiricist doctrine of influence. And if this doctrine is admitted, then we have established the existence of influence as between cells.

13

THE universe is composed of self-contained cells, each a little independent universe. But the data in each cell correspond—in ways which have, in general, been explained—to the data in all the other cells. This is a very queer universe, miraculous one might say. It seems incredible that the cells *would* correspond as it is alleged they do. Would they not, each left to itself in this manner, develop independently, each taking its own path? Even if by some miracle they started together, that is, in mutual correspondence, would they not rapidly diverge in all directions so that before long no two would be alike, and no common experience or common life would be possible? To bring this whole criticism to a point, is it not *almost infinitely improbable* that there should be the correspondence postulated by the theory of cells, unless there be introduced some special principle whose function it would be to keep the cells in unison?

The monads of Leibniz spring to mind here. They also developed independently, and yet corresponded. But Leibniz had at least the grace to postulate a preestablished harmony, the work of God. The theory of cells has suggested no principle whatever to ensure harmony. The reader may harbour the suspicion that God is to be dragged in in the last chapter to perform this office. But he need have no fear. The theory of cells postulates no principle, either godly or ungodly, to bring about correspondence. But in that case is not the correspondence completely incredible?

There is a most important logical principle involved here—important not merely for the theory of cells but for philosophy generally. It is my belief that many of the greatest philosophers in the past have been the victims of a very subtle logical fallacy, which has arisen from failure to understand the nature of probability. This fallacy vitiates some of the fundamental metaphysical concepts of Leibniz, Berkeley, the occasionalists, Spinoza, and also the twentieth century realists. It also vitiates the teleological argument for the existence of God in some of its forms. I am about to expose this fallacy and at the same time to lay down what I hold to be important propositions regarding the nature of probability. These considerations, in themselves of a perfectly general nature, will also be found to provide the key for solving the difficulty in the theory of cells stated in the first paragraph of this section.

The common criticism against Leibniz is that the preestablished harmony is an arbitrary *ad hoc* hypothesis, and that the God of his system is a mere *deus ex machina*. However, this is the wrong criticism, and misses the real point. If a principle be required, what more admirable principle than God? The proper criticism is that Leibniz's preestablished harmony is a barbarism because *he failed to realize that no principle at all is required to ensure correspondence.* The same observation applies to the occasionalists. Their fault was, not their introduction of God as the principle on which to base the correspondence of body and mind, but that they thought it necessary to introduce a principle.

The question at issue is: is it almost infinitely improbable, or is it improbable at all, that the cells (or the monads of Leibniz, or the bodies and minds of the occasionalists and Spinoza), developing independently, without mutual influence, and without any external cause to establish and maintain them in unison, should yet correspond? If it is, then some *special cause* of the alleged correspondence must be postulated. If not, no special cause is required, and the criticism of the theory of cells which we are considering falls to the ground.'

Of course, it is not quite accurate to say that there is no mutual influence between the cells. For they do influence one another. But this will hardly help. The correspondence caused by mutual influence is absolutely negligible as compared with the vast area of correspondence of general world-patterns. It is true that I can indirectly produce a sense-datum in your private world, as when I shout at you. But in general, apart from a few trivial data of this kind, your world of data is not produced by me. *I* did not produce the stars you see, the ocean you traverse, the forests you roam. Yet in general our world-patterns correspond. Thus, in spite of trifling mutual influence, it is very nearly accurate to say that cells are all independent of one another, and yet correspond. So the question recurs: is it in some very high degree improbable that the cells, without any special principle to bring about correspondence, should yet correspond?

The first thing to notice is that cellular correspondence is an example of the more general concept of *order*. We live in an orderly universe, not a chaos. The notion of order implies uniformity, regularity, repetition. If any area of experience be orderly, this means that it exhibits patterns which repeat themselves regularly over the area like the patterns of a wall-paper. Unit pattern corresponds with unit pattern. That is, the area of experience can be split up into sections such that each section contains one example of the pattern. Then if each section be taken as a unit, the units will exhibit structural correspondence each to each. It may also be possible to split the sections into subsections such that one subsection of one section corresponds with one subsection of another section; and so on. There may or may not be similarity of content as well as correspondence of structure. Thus the unit patterns of the wall-paper may be of the same colour or of different colours. But if they are of different colours, then complete orderliness will demand regularity in the colour-variations, so that the individual patterns should again fall into a pattern of patterns.

In any area of orderly experience the unit-patterns may be simultaneous, spreading themselves out laterally, though not necessarily spatially. Or they may follow each other in time, spreading themselves vertically down the time-dimension. The wall-paper is an example of the first kind. A tune, in so far as it exhibits repetitions of some unit-series of notes, is an example of the second kind. The essential point is that we should be able to detect in all different instances of order the same common character, which is the repetition of patterns or, in short, correspondence. Thus correspondence is the essence of order, and the kind of correspondence called cellular correspondence is a particular case of order.

Cellular correspondence is plainly one example of order, each cell being a unit pattern. It is of the lateral variety, since the patterns of the cells, in so far as they correspond, are simultaneous. (This follows from the *definition* of simultaneity, see Section 10 of this chapter.) But the pattern is not, of course, spread out spatially like the wall-paper, for there is no space between the cells.

The correspondence of the monads of Leibniz would be another example of order. So would Spinoza's parallelism of body and mind, to explain which Spinoza—making the same mistake as Leibniz and the occasionalists—thought it necessary to postulate a special principle of substantial identity.

Causality is the final example of order to be mentioned here. It is of the vertical kind, but its time-dimension does not affect its complete assimilation to cellular correspondence, to the Leibnizian principle, and to Spinoza's parallelism, in respect of its being an instance of order. Causality is correspondence of patterns of events. If we take a simple causal sequence *A—B,* the postulate of causality is that this keeps repeating itself all down the time-dimension of the world-pattern. (Of course, this is a grossly over-simplified picture of causality, but it serves to disentangle the essential point.) Each case of the sequence *A—B* is a unit-pattern. The units show structural correspondence each to each, the *A* of one unit corresponding to the *A* of the other, the *B* to the *B*. In this case there is also similarity of content, but that is irrelevant to the present issue.

Thus our problem really is: does order in the world require a special principle for its explanation? Or otherwise stated, is it in any degree antecedently improbable that the world should be orderly—apart from some special principle which should have the function of imposing order?

Reflection on the example of causality should shed some light on this. We are apt to take causality for granted, and to demand no special explanation of it. *This is because it is an example of order with the idea of which we are very familiar.* That which is familiar passes without our question. That which is unfamiliar, such as the idea of cellular correspondence, appears queer, and we either disbelieve it or demand that some special principle be discovered to account for it. But this granting of special dispensations to our familiar friends is irrational. Cellular correspondence and causality are in all respects parallel examples of order in the universe. They come before you demanding equal treatment as of right. It is a scandalous injustice that you should pass causality through the barrier because you know him well, while you hold up cellular correspondence simply because I have only now introduced him to you for the first time. To put it otherwise. Causality and cellular correspondence are both examples of order which—it is claimed on behalf of each—are actually found as facts in the universe, whether miraculous or not, and whether or not you think that they are *a priori* likely to be found there. If one is improbable, so is the other. If it is very improbable that cells should correspond, it is equally improbable that causal sequences should repeat themselves. Yet we do not think this improbable, nor demand any special cause to account for it. Indeed it would appear ridiculous to demand a cause for causality itself, for the demand would imply that we have already accepted causality. It is true that those who think that the existence of causal order in the world points to a divine mind as the cause of the causal order commit this very absurdity. But they cannot justify themselves. And however this may be, the point to be emphasized is that if the critic declares that cellular correspondence is very improbable, he ought to say the same thing about causality. And if he is ready to swallow causal order as a simple fact about the universe which we find to be true however miraculous it may appear, he ought to be equally ready to swallow cellular correspondence as a simple fact about the universe which we find to be true however miraculous that may appear.

Nevertheless this does not get to the bottom of the problem. We have only pointed out that *if* there is a difficulty about cellular correspondence, there is the same difficulty about causality—which nevertheless does not prevent our believing in it. We have not cleared up the supposed difficulty—in either case. And the issue—to state it once more—is this. All those who think that a special principle is required to account for order, Leibniz, the occasionalists, Spinoza, and finally the critic of cellular correspondence, are plainly basing their contention on the assumption that *there is an antecedent improbability that the world would, of itself, be orderly.* We have to examine this assumption.

The assumption is false. It depends upon a confusion as to the natures of probability and improbability. The true doctrine is as follows.* Before we can talk intelligently about probability or improbability we have to start with a belief in some general character of the world. This believed general character of the world forms an essential background by reference to which we estimate probabilities. The probability or improbability of any particular sequence of events—such as a particular throw of dice—is entirely relative to this background. What is probable relatively to one background will be improbable relatively to another background. Now the general character of the world which we have taken as a background may be true or false. That is, the world may actually have that character or it may not. This has to be decided empirically by examining the world. But whether it is true or false, it cannot be declared either antecedently probable or improbable. For probability is always relative to the assumed background. Therefore the background itself, having no further background against which it can be placed, cannot be either probable or improbable. It is simply found as a fact or not found.

The conception of the orderliness of the world is just such a general character of it as is here spoken of. The disorderliness of the world, its chaotic character, would be another such general character. Whether the world is actually orderly or disorderly is a matter to be settled by examination of it. But neither general character can be declared in themselves either probable or improbable. To talk in this manner is meaningless, since it implies a further background which is nonexistent.

Another way of putting the same point is to say that the notion of probability has application only to assertions about the characters of particular bits of the world taken in the context of the world-system. It has no application to any assertion about the general character of the world-system as a whole.

I will illustrate the principle by an example. It is very improbable that, with unloaded dice, I should throw twelve consecutive aces. Why? Because as a matter of fact the causal laws of the universe happen to be such that a run of twelve aces occurs on the average only once in about 6^{12} occasions. Our expectation that there will not be such a run is founded upon empirically discovered facts about the laws of the universe. Against this background the run of twelve is very improbable. But the universe might have been constructed on a different model. We might find ourselves living in a world in which dice almost always fell ace upwards unless there were some special cause to prevent them from doing so. In that case any irregular throw, such as 5. 3. 1. 3. 1. 6, would be extremely improbable. Thus the probability or improbability of any sequence of events is relative to the kind of universe we inhabit. *In itself* no sequence of events is either probable or improbable. If the constitution of the world is such that x very rarely happens, then at any particular moment x is very improbable *in that world*. But if the constitution of the world were such that x were of very frequent occurrence, then at any particular moment in *that* world x would be very probable.

Failure to understand these principles has vitiated many philosophical discussions. Thus the famous teleological argument for the existence of God might conceivably possess some force if it could point to some evidence of conscious purpose in the world. But sometimes the mere fact of the orderliness of the world is taken as evidence of purpose. It is argued that the universe could not exhibit these regularities of sequence, this uniformity of behaviour, this governance by laws, unless there were a divine mind to impose law and order. The argument presented in this manner is worthless. It rests upon the assumption that disorderliness is in itself more probable than order, and that therefore the actual existence of order must be the result of some special cause. And this assumption is false.

Again it is sometimes asked how, if the world were originally a "fortuitous concourse of atoms," it could ever have become what it is. Now if by the fortuitous concourse were meant a chaotic state of affairs in which there existed no law or order, the question would have some point. For starting with a disorderly chaos the arising of the present degree of order would be almost infinitely improbable. But the fortuitous concourse is presumably conceived as governed by the laws of motion, gravitation, etc. That is to say it is not conceived as disorderly. The question in that case is without point. But clearly the hidden presupposition of the question is the assumption that it is very improbable that the throng of atoms *would* exhibit order, apart from some special cause of order such as a divine mind. And we have seen that this assumption is baseless.

Another example of the same confusion is found in Professor Montague's attempt to justify the belief in the uniformity of nature by the principle of probability.[8] Any attempt to show that it is *in itself* probable that the principle of the uniformity of nature should be true is foredoomed to failure. For a general pervasive character of the universe, such as the uniformity of nature, cannot have either probability or improbability. It is manifest that all probabilities are based upon the uniformity of nature, and that therefore the uniformity of nature cannot be based upon probability. When I toss a coin, the probability of throwing heads is one-half, because the uniformity of nature results in about fifty out of every hundred throws being heads.

To sum up. The principle of cellular correspondence is simply one example of the orderliness of the world. It is therefore no more improbable than causality or any other kind of order found to exist. It only seems more improbable than causality because the conception of it is unfamiliar to the mind while the notion of causality is very familiar. Moreover it is no more inherently improbable that the world should be orderly than that it should be disorderly. Probability and its opposite are always relative to some found or assumed general character of the world, such as order or disorder. Hence such general characters of the world cannot themselves be either probable or improbable. Thus the argument that the principle of cellular correspondence is antecedently improbable falls to the ground. In consequence, no special principle, —either a god or an outside physical object as cause—is required to account for cellular correspondence and the criticism suggested in the first paragraph of this section is without any force.

[8] *The Ways of Knowing*, pp. 199 *ff*.

14

THE fallacy of supposing that order is in itself more improbable than disorder and requires a special cause is so insidious, so difficult to uproot, so widespread in the history of philosophy, that it deserves to receive a name. I will call it the Fallacy of Special Causes.

The fallacy of special causes is exemplified in the pre-established harmony of Leibniz, in the parallelism of Spinoza, in the occasionalism of Malebranche and Geulincx, and in the teleological argument for the existence of God, or at least in some forms of it.

I will now add another important example. Our private worlds correspond and are similar to one another. This is often given as a basis for the belief of realism that our data are caused by an external physical object. Thus Russell writes "It is the similarity"—of my table-data, for example, to your table-data—"which makes us accept the theory of a common origin for simultaneous perceptions."[9] But the similarity of our private worlds is an example or order. It is that variety of order which we have called cellular correspondence. The argument of realism is based upon the view that this order is in itself improbable and therefore requires a special cause. The physical object is postulated as this special cause. Thus realism, so far as it rests upon this argument, is based upon the fallacy of special causes.

[9] *Analysis of Matter*, p. 207.

CHAPTER III

The Theory of Constructions

1

IT GOES without saying that there is no way in which a metaphysical theory can be *proved* to be true (Chapter I, Section 12). This is as true of the theory of cells as of any other. But it is reasonable to enquire in what way it can be recommended for acceptance. The grounds on which a metaphysical hypothesis can be recommended will consist in showing (1) that it is internally self-consistent, (2) that it accounts for the facts of the world, and (3) that there are reasons for preferring it to other rival hypotheses which may also claim to be acceptable under heads (1) and (2).

An hypothesis is said to account for or explain the facts when it is a generalization of which every known fact within the area of experience to be explained can be exhibited as an example (Chapter I, Section 11). In the case of scientific hypotheses the area of experience to be explained is always within some selected portion of the universe. In the case of metaphysics the area is the entire universe as experienced or known.

The reasons which can be given for preferring one hypothesis to others can never, in the case of metaphysics, be conclusive. They may be strictly logical reasons tending to show the probability of the hypothesis. Or they may be pragmatic, as when we adopt an hypothesis on the ground of its greater simplicity.

In regard to the matter of self-consistency nothing can be done except to present the theory as clearly as possible, so that contradictions, if any, may be apparent; but free from such inconsistency so far as the author of it knows. Criticism and history will reveal the contradictions if there are any. And this outcome has to be awaited. But even when a contradiction has been pointed out in a theory, the theory is not necessarily thereby condemned. There will be several matters to be considered. First, is the contradiction a real or a verbal one? A verbal contradiction is one which is merely due to the idea having been faultily expressed. There may be a contradiction in what a man says but not in what he means. It is true that it is often difficult to distinguish verbal from real contradictions and that, indeed, there is no sharp line between them. For faulty expression is generally a sign of faulty thinking. But the fault in the thinking which has caused the inconsistencies of language may have been only unclearness and not actual contradiction. These points have to be weighed and good judgment exercised in regard to them. And even when it has been decided that there is a real contradiction in a theory, the whole theory is not thereby refuted. For we have next to consider whether the contradiction is vital, that is, whether it involves the central and governing principles of the theory or merely concerns some relatively unimportant and outlying details of it. If the latter, some slight modification of these details may restore consistency. Even if the contradiction is vital, it does not necessarily destroy the whole theory. For it may still be the case that a large part of the theory is true, although presumably another large part of it must be false.

Since it is not possible to show the internal self-consistency of the theory of cells except by developing it as clearly as possible, I pass on to enquire whether it can be exhibited as satisfactorily explaining the facts of the world.

2

IN one sense it is fairly obvious that it does explain the facts of the world. It accounts for all that would ordinarily be deemed directly *perceived* facts. I include under this head facts supposed to be established by the mere process of comparing the observations of two or more persons, so long as they do not go beyond the attempt to establish correct descriptions of what has been observed. Even this, it is plain, will really involve much more than mere perception. But the distinction between the world as perceived and the world as conceived in thought, which I am making, is no more than a rough and ready one. What I mean is that the theory of cells fairly obviously accounts both for the facts of the world as perceived by a single person and the same facts as perceived simultaneously by several persons, but that it does not so obviously explain the thought-of world. I will make this clearer as we proceed.

The theory of cells has no difficulty in stating in its own terms what exists when a single person is aware of a complex of data. There is the consciousness and there are the data, and that is all. It also implies an account of what happens when a single person perceives an "object," and also an account of what the object is. What is immediately before the mind (= consciousness) at the moment of perceiving is a complex of sense-data. When we "interpret" this group of sense-data as belonging to an object, what we mean (according to the theory of cells) is simply that in certain circumstances certain other complexes of sense-data will follow upon the given complex, and that this is believed, or taken for granted, by the consciousness. There are, of course, two sides to the matter of perception. There is what happens on the side of the data and what happens on the side of the consciousness. Both have to be explained by the theory of cells. The theory of consciousness will be outlined in a later chapter (Chapter V). I am here concerned only with the side of the data. Suppose then that I am perceiving an object, say a lump of granite. This means that I am now sensing an irregular-shaped visual sensum of some dullish colour. That this is a piece of granite means that if I turn it round in my hands (for shortness this is expressed here in the language of objects, not in the language of data), I shall sense a series of somewhat similar colour patches of various shapes; that when I press it, there will be the sensation of hardness; that when I break it open, there will be various characteristic data of the "inside": that if I examine it under a microscope, or even very closely with the unaided eye, there will enter into my field of vision the various data characteristic of mica, felspar, and quartz; that if I treat it with certain chemicals, certain other data will be given; and so on. Of course, not all this is believed or taken for granted in the act of perception, by the average person at any rate. But some of it must be. And in any case I am not here explaining what happens in the consciousness, but what the object *is*. And this may now be stated in abstract form. A material object is a succession of sense-data following each other in time *in an order determined by definite laws*. Not any stream of successive data is a material object. They must constitute a regular series with observable uniformities. If a set of sense-data is not followed by the other sets which are properly expectable under the laws of the object, then we have an illusion or hallucination.[*]

According to the theory of cells the expectable data are not in existence until they are actually sensed. They are not waiting ready round the corner.

How do we distinguish between causal laws, which are also laws of succession among data, and the laws of succession among data which are constitutive of material objects? For we do not usually say that the front of the book, which we are now looking at, is the cause of its back, which we may see in a moment. Now it is not necessary to show that there actually is any absolutely rigid distinction between causal series and what I will now call object-series. For it may be that the distinction is not ultimately valid, but is merely a rough classification which we make of datal series for purposes of convenience. Both series, at any rate, are simply series of data following each other according to law. In neither case is there any special relation of compulsion between one member of the series and the next. There is nothing but regularity in either case. Yet there certainly are distinctions which, whether or not they precisely delimit the boundary between the two kinds of series, are sufficient to cause us to establish a difference between them in common speech and in common thought.

For one thing causal series are not as a rule reversible whereas object series are. Lightning is the cause of thunder, but thunder is not the cause of lightning. There may possibly be cases of mutual causation, or reciprocity, which can be interpreted as the reversibility of a causal sequence. I do not know whether this is so or not. But whereas causal series are never, or practically never, reversible, object series always are. I can turn a material object round clockwise in my hands and obtain the series of data A, B, C, D. Or I can turn it anticlockwise and obtain the series D, B, C, A. It is true that if I destroy the object, as for example by dissolving it in acids, I may find it very difficult to go back from the data which I shall then obtain to the original data. But theoretically at least I suppose even this could be done by a synthetic chemical process.

Causal series and object series may also sometimes be distinguished by the fact that the causal series is independent of our actions, while the object series is not. Thus the fact that thunder follows lightning is not in any way dependent upon me. But whether the data of the front of the table will be followed by the data of the back may depend upon whether I stay where I am or move round the table. This principle of differentiation is clearly liable to the exception that a causal series may not be independent of me and my actions. It is in fact dependent in those cases in which I initiate actions and cause alterations in the external world. And it may also be objected that an object series may be independent of our actions. For example, the table-series A, B, C, D, may have been obtained by my moving round the table; but it may just as well have been brought about by the table being revolved in its place without any action on my part. Hence it does not seem that this is a very good test of the difference between the two kinds of series. Yet it probably plays its part in causing us to make the distinction.

3

THE theory of cells also fairly obviously can give a good account of the facts regarding the simultaneous perception of "the same" object by a number of observers. It is in fact more especially designed for this very purpose. It is mainly the difficulties which realism encounters in its attempt to explain simultaneous perception which lead us to reject realism and to adopt the theory of cells. Realism holds that simultaneous observers may, in a literal sense, be viewing the same object. It is then in difficulties to explain how one observer sees the object as having one shape, colour, size, etc., while other observers see it as having quite other shapes, colours, sizes. To explain this, realism has to resort to all manner of highly ingenious, elaborate, and artificial *ad hoc* hypotheses, some of which are inconsistent with others, and none of which really do the work expected of them. Some account of these hypotheses and the difficulties which they involve will have to be given in the next chapter. The theory of cells resolves the difficulties by repudiating the realistic physical object outside of our private worlds and retaining only the data within the cells. No difficulty is then created by the fact that the corresponding data in different cells are of different colours, shapes, sizes. When two persons view "the same" object, there are in fact two objects, or rather two sets of data. On the other hand the possibility of setting up the notion of a common world, and the possibility of communication, are explained by the theory of cells as being based upon the principle of cellular correspondence.

The relation of the theory of cells to realism is much like the relation of Copernican to Ptolemaic astronomy. The latter clung desperately to the common-sense belief that the earth is at rest in the centre of the world while the heavenly bodies move round it. Rather than give this up Ptolemaic astronomy invented its ingenious and complicated epicycles. Copernican astronomy swept aside all these subtilities by boldly repudiating the prejudices of common sense. It showed that although the perceived facts are *as if* the sun moves round the earth, yet this is not in fact the case. Realism clings desperately to the common-sense belief that there "really" is a common world of public objects. This involves it in unending difficulties. But rather than give up its common-sense belief it invents its complicated paraphernalia of special *ad hoc* hypotheses, which, however, only land it in fresh dilemmas (see next chapter). The theory of cells sweeps away these artificialities and enigmas by boldly repudiating the common-sense prejudice regarding a public world. It suggests that while the facts of perception are *as if* there existed a public world, this is not in fact the case. And as Copernicus substituted for Ptolemaic astronomy an infinitely simpler hypothesis (although it did not appear simpler to the people of that day, but intolerably difficult and obscure); so the theory of cells is far simpler than the theory of realism, although this is not likely to be apparent at the present moment to the many. The parallel is perfect.

4

THUS the facts of the world *in so far as we perceive them* are certainly accounted for by the theory of cells. This requires no further elaboration. But it is the facts of the world so far as we *think* about them which present some difficulty. What has to be explained is why, if the world really is what the theory of cells says it is, the vast majority of human beings persistently and obstinately think quite otherwise. If there is in fact no common world of objects, why does practically everyone believe that there is? If objects do not in fact endure during interperceptual intervals, why does everyone suppose that they do? Thus the "facts of the world" which the theory of cells has now to explain are the facts constituted by the existence in men's minds of this common-sense philosophy, this rooted belief in public objects which continue to exist when not perceived. The explanation of these facts is the special business of that part of the theory of cells which is termed the theory of constructions.

In principle the method which is adopted in regard to this problem is identical with the method adopted by the Copernican astronomy when confronted with a similar difficulty. If the sun does not really move round the earth, if it does not really "rise" in the morning and pass across the sky during the day, why does everyone think that it does these things? The Copernican astronomy replied by pointing out that the facts, though not really what the plain man supposes, are yet *as if* they were so. It is the function of the theory of constructions to show how it is that, although in reality there is no common world, it appears to common sense *as if* there were one. The only difference is that, whereas the common-sense view of sunset and sunrise is based upon an illusion of sense, the common-sense notion of a common world is based upon a mistake of thought. Copernican astronomy had to explain the illusion of sense. We have to explain the mistake of thought.

I do not use the word construction in the manner of Mr. Russell when he speaks of "logical constructions." There may be some kinship between his use of the word and mine. There probably is. The question is irrelevant to this discussion. It will only confuse the reader here to think of Mr. Russell's notion of constructions. Mr. Russell is entitled to define his words as he pleases, and I mine as I please.

The term "construct" is also used by some scientific writers. Here again it will only confuse us to consider their usage which, in general, seems to have very little in common with mine. I will accordingly proceed to the definition of the terms "construction" and "construct" as used in the theory of cells.

¶ By a construction I mean a proposition or belief which is such that (1) its truth is not empirically verifiable, (2) its truth cannot be logically inferred from anything which is empirically verifiable, (3) it is not in fact true, and (4) it is justified only by some pragmatic consideration.[1]

It will be observed that a construction is a belief or proposition. The thing or fact which is believed in will here be called a construct. Thus according to my usage the proposition "There is an entity called energy which underlies such forms of it as light and heat" is a *construction*. But energy itself is a *construct*. Of course I am not defining the scientific conception of a construct and distinguishing it from the philosophical conception of a construction. I am concerned at this point only with my own usage of words. And in this paragraph I am distinguishing the philosophical conception of a construction as it is found in the theory of cells from the philosophical conception of a construct as it is found in the theory of cells.

5

THE theory of cells holds that all essential differences between its own doctrine and that of common-sense metaphysic are to be explained as constructions of common sense, and that all entities not recognized in the theory of cells (which recognizes nothing except consciousness and data existing when perceived) are constructs. This latter will be true whether the entities are those postulated by common sense or by science or by any other form of human thinking. The truth of these statements is what this chapter has to show.

[1] In all probability this differs from the view of a construction taken in my *Theory of Knowledge and Existence*. If so, it is simply to be inferred that I have changed my opinion. No doubt it might be possible to tabulate and explain the exact differences between the earlier and the later view. But I am not myself interested in this question.

What, in the first instance at any rate, has to be accounted for is what I call common-sense metaphysic, not realism or any other sophisticated philosophy. The question is not: why do Mr. Russell, Professor Broad, Professor Price and others, believe the doctrines about public objects, public space, etc., which they do believe. The question is: why does humanity at large take a view of the world so utterly different from that expressed in the theory of cells? Therefore it is common-sense metaphysic, not realism, which has to be explained.

Realism claims to be the philosophical expression of common sense and the justification—so far as justification is possible—of its view of the world. It is extremely doubtful whether this is true (Chapter IV, Section 6). But if it is true, or in so far as it is true, this chapter may incidentally help us to understand some of the *psychological* causes which make Mr. Russell, Professor Broad, and Professor Price believe the kind of doctrines they do believe. But this is not the object of the investigation.

I shall deal in the earlier sections with the common-sense view of the world and with the constructions which it involves. In a later section I shall, but only very briefly, mention some of the constructions employed by science.

What *is* the common-sense view of the world? What are the metaphysical doctrines which are included in it? To answer this question presents a certain difficulty. For obviously common-sense views are held unanalysed and are essentially unclear. Immediately we analyse them and make them clear they cease to be the views held by common sense. The great danger is that we should over-intellectualize them. For instance, if we say that common sense holds that a material object includes not only its colour, taste, shape, smell, etc., but also a physical object which "has" these characters, we are, I think, attributing to the common-sense man far more sophisticated views than he really entertains. What he believes in are *material objects*. But the over-intellectualization of his views just mentioned consists in attributing to him a *particular analysis* of the notion of a material object, namely the analysis given by some realists. There are, of course, other analyses, such as that given by phenomenalism. It is just as fallacious to attribute to common sense one of these analyses as it is to attribute any other. The idea is held by common sense in an unanalysed form.

But in spite of these difficulties I think there are certain definite beliefs which can be attributed to common sense. The belief in physical objects, conceived as something distinct from sense-data, is not one of them. But belief in the existence of *public* objects is. That is to say, common sense believes in material objects (without analysing the idea), and it believes that these material objects are public. I will now set down the main beliefs which, it seems to me, are parts of common-sense metaphysic. It is these beliefs which we are to try to explain.

The beliefs which make up the common-sense view of the external world appear to be (1) belief in *the publicity of material objects*; (2) belief in the *interperceptual existence of material objects*; (3) belief that a material object is a *thing* which has *qualities*. This may be regarded as a very vague attempt at analysis. And in so far as there is this analysis, the previous statement that the notion of a material object is held unanalysed requires modification. But the point is that the qualities are not thought of as distinct from, much less as actually separable from, the thing. Hence it would not even occur to common sense that the qualities might cease to exist when not being perceived and yet the thing continue in existence. Common-sense metaphysic holds that the thing exists when not perceived with all its perceptual qualities intact. The next belief is in (4) *the intersensory character of material objects*. This means that the same object can be perceived by several different senses, for example, that we can both see and touch the same table. Next comes the belief in (5) *public space and public time*. And finally there is the belief in (6) *empty space, but not apparently empty time*.

The theory of cells has to show that all these beliefs are constructions. The method adopted will be to show that they all conform to the definition of a construction given in Section 4.

6

IT has to be shown that the belief in the publicity of material objects has the four characters mentioned in Section 4 as constituting the definition of a construction. The first is that the truth of the belief must not be empirically verifiable. Now it might be thought that the publicity of objects *is* empirically verifiable. For I can point to the table which I see and enquire whether it is not the very same table which you see. You will reply that it is.

The question at issue is whether there are two tables or only one. Now when the question is; how many of some kind of entity are there?, the only empirical method of deciding it is to count. And this is just what we tried to do when we pointed at the table. When we count we point at the things to be counted one after the other, and with each pointing we name the number in the number series which we have reached (or at least that is one method of counting). In this case we only had to point once. So we concluded that there was only one table.

But in order to be sure that we counted correctly we must first know that there was only one finger pointing. For if there were two, they might be pointing at two different tables. Hence if there were, antecedently to the counting, any doubt as to how many tables there were, the pointing would not settle it, because the same doubt would reflect on the question how many fingers there were. Hence the counting settled nothing. Either I already know, without counting, that objects are public, in which case there is no use in counting, since it adds nothing to my knowledge. Or I do not know that objects are public, and in that case I do not know that there is only one finger pointing, and therefore I do not know whether my counting was correct. Thus, *if* I know that objects are public, this knowledge has not been obtained through counting. And since this would be the only empirical method of settling the question, it follows that the belief which we are discussing is not empirically verifiable.

The second character of a construction is that it is not inferable from anything which is empirically verifiable. It is quite clear that nothing which is observed when two persons are looking at "the same"object can possibly give rise to a valid inference to publicity. For the only rational *arguments* which can be used point in just the opposite direction. For by comparing notes we find that the objects which we simultaneously see have simultaneously incompatible colours, shapes, sizes, and so on.

The third character of a construction is that it is actually false. This cannot as a rule be directly proved. But it can always be shown that there is no reason for believing that it is true. In fact, in the case of each construction, this has already been shown when it has been established that the truth of the construction cannot be empirically verified or inferred from anything which can be empirically verified. Thus this third point might always be ignored. The position might be taken that since we have no grounds whatever for thinking the construction true, the *hypothesis* which we choose to adopt is that it is false. I shall therefore in each case pass over this third point very quickly. Yet it may in each case call for some mention. For it is not usually the case that there are no more grounds for thinking the construction false than for thinking it true. There may be some positive grounds for thinking it false. Thus in the present case there are the various shapes, colours, and other characters perceived in "the same" object by different observers. This may be countered by postulating a physical object behind the scenes. But this leads to endless further difficulties (Chapter IV).

The fourth and most essential point is the pragmatic character of the belief. Of course we cannot trace the actual origin and primitive history of these immensely ancient ideas of common sense. Hence if we say that they were adopted because of their pragmatic advantages, we are speculating. But this seems legitimate. For if you have a belief regarding which it can be shown that it cannot ever have been based upon even the faintest suggestion of empirical evidence (as is done in all these cases when we show that it is not an inference from anything which is empirically verifiable); and if it can also be shown that the belief *does* possess pragmatic advantages; it is then a natural conclusion that the belief must have been adopted *because* of these advantages. For what other source of the belief can possibly be suggested? Not, in such cases as these, that they are known *a priori*. Hence the method which will be followed for all the constructions of common sense will consist in simply pointing to the pragmatic advantages of the belief in question.

In the present case it is surely clear that the pragmatic advantage of belief in a common world lies in the fact that it is more simple and convenient to believe in one world than in many. If ten men are sitting round a table there is no sense (except for the theoretical purposes of metaphysics) in insisting that there are really ten tables. For these ten tables are *almost* exactly alike. For practical purposes their differences can be ignored or explained away. Moreover the ten tables all behave in exactly the same way. When one gets broken, the others get broken. And their situations in the private worlds of the different observers are alike. The table in my world is on the floor and below the ceiling. So is the table in yours. Thus there is no point in distinguishing between the ten tables. It will be much simpler to talk and think of one table instead of ten. To agree that objects are public greatly simplifies the universe for each of us. Hence it is in all ways pragmatically better than a belief in private worlds. The likely conclusion is that common sense believes in one common world *because of* these obvious pragmatic advantages.

But now what does it actually mean, in this case and in the cases of the other constructions too, to say that our remote ancestors adopted them because of their pragmatic value? Does it mean that they actually *thought out* the advantages and disadvantages of believing in one common world or in many private worlds? This would be plainly ridiculous. No doubt this belief in a common world is instinctive. It was taken for granted from the beginning. No one ever doubted it until philosophers began to do so. Thus we can call it an instinctive belief if we like. But philosophers are much too prone to trace some idea to an instinctive belief and then simply to leave the matter there. In all such cases we ought to ask ourselves why we have just this instinctive belief rather than some other. There must always be some reason. And even if we cannot be quite sure what the reason is, the matter is worth enquiry to see whether some probable reason cannot be suggested.

The reason why we have any instinctive beliefs at all is a very obscure and interesting problem to which, for some reason, philosophers do not seem to have directed their attention. While not pretending to be able to explain this entirely, I shall introduce some considerations regarding it in Chapter IV, Section 7. My suggestion is that instinctive beliefs are always connected with our practical interests. They are the beliefs which are likely to be most helpful to us in our daily lives. Men have never deliberately and consciously thought them out. But men somehow *nose out* those beliefs which will be advantageous to them. Such beliefs get included in the takings-for-granted of common sense and come down to us from the remotest ages in the form of instinctive beliefs.

Thus when I say that there must be some reason why we instinctively believe in a common world; and when I suggest that this reason lies in the fact that this belief is more pragmatically advantageous than belief in a multitude of private worlds; I do not mean that any human being ever *thought* of this reason or of these advantages. I mean that if there had been no pragmatic advantages in the belief, men would not have come instinctively to believe it. I suggest that if all the practical advantages had lain in believing in a multiplicity of private worlds, then in all probability we should have come instinctively to hold that belief. I have shown in what way belief in a common world actually is more convenient and more simple, and therefore more practically advantageous, than the opposite belief. And I suggest that this is the *reason* why men hold this belief. For they have the gift of instinctively ferreting out what is advantageous to them. How they do this I do not know. But no one who has any experience of practical affairs can doubt that men, or at least some men, have an uncanny way of sensing, without explicit thought, what is to their advantage in life.

These remarks are meant to be perfectly general. They apply to all common-sense constructions. Thus in the following sections I shall point out the pragmatic advantages of the common-sense beliefs with which they deal. I shall say that common sense has come to believe them *because of* these advantages. And my meaning in all cases will be the same as that which I have explained in this section. It will not be necessary to keep on labouring the point.

7

THE next subject we have to consider is belief in the interperceptual existence of material objects. That this is not empirically verifiable is obvious. That it is not the conclusion of any legitimate inference would also by this time be generally admitted; so that one may be excused from dwelling on it at any length. The existence of x at time t is a particular fact; and the existence of x at time t' is another particular fact. You cannot infer one particular fact from another particular fact without the aid of a general principle. If from the existence of my table now and its existence before I fell asleep last night I am to infer its existence during the interval, the general principle which I require to validate this inference is that "material objects exist during interperceptual intervals." The simple syllogism involved in applying this to particular cases, such as my table, is in fact the inference we all rely on in our daily experience.

But the general principle itself is quite incapable of proof. All attempts to establish it by logical processes will be found to be circular, and to assume the principle itself in some form or other. Thus we may argue that we often find facts which can only be explained by the continuance of causal processes during interperceptual periods. The fire in my grate must have been burning during my absence from the room because I find the fire burnt out when I come in. But I can only infer that causal processes exist unobserved by first assuming that certain things, namely causes, exist unobserved.

That belief in the interperceptual existence of material objects is false is probably not capable of direct proof. But we have just shown that there is no reason to believe it true. Moreover there are some definite grounds for thinking it false. There are reasons for thinking that sense-data do not exist when they are not being perceived. For they probably depend for their existence upon our sense-organs. This matter will be discussed in Chapter IV. If this conclusion is accepted, it is then only possible to believe in the interperceptual existence of material objects if we postulate a "physical object" which is in no way empirically verifiable, which has none of the qualities, such as colour, shape, smell, which common sense attributes to objects, and which has in fact no qualities at all which are in any way intelligible to us. This supposition, though perhaps possible, leads to very grave difficulties, which will be studied in the next chapter.

It only remains to exhibit the pragmatic advantages of the belief which we are discussing, and to suppose that it is because of these advantages that we hold the belief.

I do not think that this belief has any *very great* pragmatic advantages. But it has some. It does not really make much practical difference to me whether my type-writer existed while I was out of the room or not. So long as it always exists when I am here and want to use it, this will be all that seriously matters. Still it is actually simpler to suppose a continuous universe than an intermittent one. It is simpler in the same sense as a single continuous line drawn on paper is a simpler object of contemplation than a line of the same length broken by many gaps. The latter is more complicated since it involves a multiplicity of lines and a multiplicity of ends. I think the fact that a continuous universe is in this way an easier object to think about than an intermittent one, though it seems to give only a very slight practical advantage to the former, is sufficient to have tilted the scale in its favour.

8

WE may take next the concept of thing and quality. The notion of a quality is derivable from sense-data alone. The red sensum has the quality of being red. Thus the notion of quality is not constructed, for it is empirically verifiable. It is the "thing" which "has" the qualities which is a construct.

It is exceedingly difficult to know what common sense actually means by a thing. It seems to me that the meaning is completely vague. When it is clarified by philosophical analysis it becomes the notion of substance. It is also capable of metamorphosis into the thing-in-itself, or again into the physical object. It is the undifferentiated, unarticulated, incoherent embryo of all these later ideas. It is a kind of fog which may condense into any of them. It seems to me impossible for me to handle it at all in its hazy common-sense form. I shall therefore take it in its more developed form as substance, and try to show that *this* is a construct. And I think if it can be shown that substance is a construct, it will follow that the "thing" must be a construct too. For the thing is the same idea at a lower level of development. (Incidentally it will also be natural to conclude that the thing-in-itself and the physical object are likewise constructs, since these are again variations on the same theme.)

That substance is not empirically verifiable nor capable of being inferred I shall take for granted. This has been shown long ago by Berkeley and Hume, and is the only supposition in keeping with the empirical spirit of the present work.

The pragmatic advantages of the notion of substance are very great. It is convenient to be able to say that it is the same leaf which in the summer is green and fresh and juicy and in autumn has become brown and shrivelled and dry. All the qualities may well have changed, so that empirically nothing *is* the same. We therefore invent the idea of a thing or substance which remains the same while the qualities change. If we did not do this we should have difficulty in regarding it as the same leaf. It is true that we could think of it as a continuous flow of changing data with qualitative and spatial and temporal continuity in all the changes. And this would really be quite enough for the notion of continuing identity. Still it greatly helps the imagination to picture something more solid and self-identical underlying the changes. It seems to give greater permanence to things and therefore greater stability to our thought. We feel that it gives us more solid ground on which to stand. Hence the idea is adopted.

Moreover it helps us in another way. We have already adopted, for pragmatic reasons, the belief in a common world. This means that we have decided to believe that many different people can all inspect the same object. But then we discover that their data are all different—of different shapes, colours, and so on. Then how *can* they be inspecting the same object? The notion of the thing saves the situation. The different shapes and colours which different people sense are explained as different "appearances" of the same "thing."

9

THE intersensory object is the next construct. That there is no way of observing that it is the same table which I touch and see, nor of inferring this belief, is fairly plain. For what I see is a colour and what I touch is not. Nor is visual shape the same as tactile shape. A blind person acquainted only with a tactile square cannot recognize a visual square if he be given his sight.[2]

The pragmatic advantages of the identification of the corresponding objects of different senses arise by way of simplification. When I perceive "the" table with my five senses, it is less complicated to believe in one table than in five. And the differences can be explained by introducing again the concept of the "thing." The tactile sense-data and the visual data can be thought of as different appearances of the same underlying entity.

10

IT is not necessary to discuss at length the ideas of public space and public time. Once we have accepted the belief in a single public world of objects, the ideas of public space and time follow as a matter of course.

There remains the idea of empty space. Empty space is not empirically verifiable either by sight or touch. Not by sight, since what we see is always colour-surfaces. The visual field is a *plenum* of colours. It is not necessary to determine here whether visual data are two- or three-dimensional. Let us assume for the sake of argument that they have solidity, depth, bulginess, since this is now the most common opinion. (Whether this is true or not does not matter. For the following argument will apply equally if visual data are "flat.") Although the visual data are thus three-dimensional, yet the visual field from side to side is completely full of colours. Hence if empty space is visible, it must be the space which is supposed to lie in the dimension between the eye and the coloured object. But this is not visible because it is a line of which only one end-point, that

[2] Professor Price writes: "When I lay my hand on a penny I sense a cold circular expanse; and when I look at a penny from directly above I sense a brown circular expanse. It is just obvious that the two shapes are exactly alike." (*Perception*, p. 244.) This seems to me mere dogmatism. I agree that it is "just obvious," but I believe it is also untrue. To be suspicious of the obvious is the beginning of philosophy.

which lies on the surface of the coloured object, is visible, while the other end, at the eye, is not. Hence empty space is not visible at all.

The fact that visual sensa are three-dimensional, if they are, will not imply that we see empty space. For what we see is only sensa. We cannot see the absence of sensa, which is what alone can be meant by empty visual space. The fact that the sensa we see are three-dimensional has no tendency to prove that we see the absence of sensa.

Neither can we verify empty space empirically through touch. For what we touch is always a tactile surface, never the absence of a tactile surface. Touch-space is a three-dimensional *plenum* of tactile data. When we walk towards a distant object to touch it we do not experience by touch the empty space between. We experience the touch-data of the ground along which we walk.

Neither is there any way in which empty space can be inferred from data. For the presence of sensa in one place can never imply the absence of sensa in another place.

As to the construction, it would seem that the idea of empty tactile space comes first. Certain muscular sensations have become associated with touch-space. For instance, I pass my hand over a surface and at the same time receive muscular sensations in the biceps and other muscles of the arm. But we have experiences of these muscular sensations without the tactile sensations (as when the arm is moved freely). This suggests that there is a tactile space vacant of any tactile data. This is the idea of empty tactile space. Now such empty tactile space is found between the eye and the seen object. For I have to put out my hand to touch it, receiving, during the outward movement of the arm, muscular sensations without tactile sensations. But tactile and visual space have already been identified by a previous construction. Hence it is believed that there is also empty visual space between the eye and the visual object.

11

WITH the constructions of interperceptual existence, of a public world in public space and time, of things and qualities, of intersensory objects, and of empty space, the common-sense view of the world is, I believe, complete. The whole common-sense metaphysic is pragmatically based. Its divergence from the theory of cells is thus explained. One may sum up the whole explanation by saying that while the theory of cells gives the truth about the world, yet common-sense metaphysic is that account of the world which has proved the most advantageous for practical men to adopt. It is not really true, but we can, with advantage, act *as if* it were true.

But the mind's work of mental construction does not stop with the elaboration of the common-sense view of the world. It is prolonged into the region of science. Science has taken the common-sense metaphysic *for granted*, and has proceeded to refine it, elaborate it, and build out further constructions far beyond it. The palace of knowledge may be said to have two storeys, of which the first floor is common sense and the second floor is science. The only way in which the metaphor is unsatisfactory is that there is, of course, no sharp line of division between common sense and science.

It goes without saying that the theory of cells holds all such entities as energy, the electron, the atom, the molecule, the ether of space, vibrations of ether or of space itself, space-time, curved space-time or straight space-time, finite empty space or infinite empty space, to be constructs. What alone exists is consciousness and data.[3]

The objective of science is the coordination and systematization of experience. It also seeks to "explain" all particular

[3] This, it will be said, is a highly cavalier treatment of scientific objects! I admit the charge. But I have dealt with the questions at issue as fully as I am able in the chapter entitled "Scientific Knowledge" in my book *The Theory of Knowledge and Existence* and in an article "Sir Arthur Eddington and the Physical World" in *Philosophy*, Vol. XXXI. I did not wish to repeat here what I have there written. The philosophically instructed reader will already be quite familiar with the general line of thought indicated thus briefly in the text.

phenomena in the sense of exhibiting them as examples of general principles. It is unnecessary to assert, with the pragmatist, that the motive of all this is "practical." Indeed what science *does* is what is alone of importance. The motives of particular scientists in doing this are irrelevant to anything except their biographies. And I do not know what can be meant by the motive of science itself, apart from the individual motives of particular scientists. The coordination, systematization, and explanations of science may be undertaken either for some ulterior end or for their own sakes. But the constructions of science are pragmatic, either in the sense that they are mere prolongations of the constructions of common sense, which are pragmatically based, or in the sense that they are new constructions initiated by science itself for convenience in linking together separated elements and strands of experience. Sometimes we have a mixture of both alternatives. Thus the atom is primarily a development of the common-sense notion of the thing. But most of its modern elaborate detail consists in new constructs made with the purpose of harmonizing apparently conflicting elements within itself.

It is not meant that *all* scientific ideas are constructions. This would be very far from the truth. And to think this is one of the chief mistakes of the older pragmatism.[4] It found the element of construction with its *motif* of mere convenience in science, and it jumped to the quite absurd conclusion that science is nothing else. Many scientific laws are purely factual and contain no element of construction whatever, save that which is taken over ready-made from common-sense metaphysic. Thus there is no element of construction in the law that cold of a certain degree freezes water, nor in the law that prussic acid kills, nor in most of the discoveries of such sciences as biology and geology. That there are animals of such and such species, or rocks of such and such ages and strata, are pure facts—except that they assume the common-

---

[4] I mean the pragmatism of such writers as James, Dewey, and Schiller, as distinguished from that of such a writer as C. I. Lewis.

sense view of the world. They are for the most part empirically verifiable, or else capable of being inferred from observable data. Physics and chemistry are the sciences in which constructs are most frequent. But even here there is much that is purely factual, for example, the laws of the expansion of bodies by heat.

It is a mistake to suppose that science reasons *from* data *to* its atoms, ether, space-time, or other constructs. If this were the case these entities would not be constructs at all, but inferred facts. But the direction of the reasoning is the other way. The atoms or the ether are first set up as pure assumptions or hypotheses. It is then argued that *if* the hypothesis were true, then experience would be as it actually is. The direction of inference is from hypothesis to data, not from data to hypothesis.

12

THE question may present itself why, if we think of public physical objects as constructs, we should not think of minds other than our own as constructs in the same way. For it will be said that the logical position in which we stand in regard to other minds is identical with the logical position in which we stand in regard to public physical objects. The physical object is not empirically verifiable. Neither is the other mind. The physical object is not inferable from private data. Neither is the other mind. We have no more *logical reason* for believing in other minds than we have for believing in physical objects. If on these grounds physical objects are declared to be constructs, the same conclusion should be drawn as regards other minds. The theory of cells *ought* to end in solipsism. And if it does not, this is merely because it refuses to carry its own principles to their logical conclusion.

There are two answers to this line of objection. One is that *it is untrue that our logical position as regards other minds is identical with our logical position in regard to physical objects.* The other is that even if this *were* true, the position of the theory of cells could still be successfully defended. The latter will probably be thought the weaker of the two answers—though I should deny this—and I will take it up first, leaving what may appear to be the stronger line of argument to clinch the matter at the end.

I will for the moment assume, then, for the sake of argument, that physical objects and other minds are in the same logical position. What is forgotten by the critic, however, is that the theory of cells is not set up as a philosophy which can be proved to be true. It is an *hypothesis*. All that is claimed is that this hypothesis is self-consistent, and that it accounts for the facts of the world. If these claims are admitted, then it is to that extent a good hypothesis. It is no doubt true that there may be several other hypotheses which also are self-consistent and account for the facts of the world. Solipsism is doubtless one of these. But it does not happen to be the hypothesis which I am setting up. There is no logical consideration which can compel me to prefer the hypothesis of solipsism to that of the theory of cells. If the two theories are equally self-consistent, equally incapable of proof, and in equal degree account for the facts of the world—and this is, I think, the actual position —then we have to choose between them either because one is simpler than the other, or because for some other reason we think the one we choose preferable to the one we reject. Now for various reasons I do think that the theory of cells is preferable to solipsism. And in this I believe that most other people would agree with me, including perhaps the critic who raises the present objection. It is for one thing nearer to the common-sense view, and there seems no reason to reject the beliefs of common sense out of a mere spirit of perversity.

Probably what is behind the objection is a vague idea that it is a logical inconsistency in the theory of cells to treat the physical object in one way and the foreign mind in another—if it is admitted that they are in the same logical position. But this is a mistake. We might perhaps be accused of being arbitrary or capricious in the matter. But caprice is a moral fault, not a logical inconsistency. There is no contradiction between the two propositions "other minds exist" and "physical objects do not exist." To believe that there exist many minds but no public objects is a perfectly self-consistent view of the world. And I do not see on what ground anyone could assert that it is not. If anyone does assert this, he may be invited to show what proposition in the theory of cells contradicts what other proposition. For a contradiction in an hypothesis must, in the end, consist in a contradiction between two propositions which are both parts of it.

I may be in a position in which I am unable to prove either that there is a penny in Smith's pocket, or that there is a sixpence. The penny and the sixpence will then be in the same logical position. If in these circumstances I choose to adopt the hypothesis that there is a penny but not a sixpence, I may be accused of capricious guessing, but it cannot be said that my hypothesis is in any way self-contradictory. This is shown by the fact that it may quite well turn out to be true. The parallel is in all respects perfect.

There is nothing in the theory of cells which logically implies solipsism. Plainly there cannot be, since its *hypothesis* is that there are many minds. If you start from a position containing the premiss that there is plurality of minds, you cannot possibly by any logical process, arrive at a conclusion which includes the proposition that there is only one mind. Thus the criticism cannot mean that the theory of cells leads to solipsism in this logical sense. Or if this is meant, it cannot be maintained.

13

BUT the really conclusive answer to the criticism is that it rests upon an entirely false assumption. It assumes that the logical position of the other mind is identical with that of the physical object. I have now to show that this is false. Public physical objects and other minds are in the same logical position in respect of the facts that neither is empirically verifiable and neither is capable of being inferred from data. But the difference between their positions is as follows. The assumption of physical objects leads to grave difficulties. The assumption of other minds leads to none. It is impossible to frame any idea of what a physical object is like, or what qualities it has. There is no difficulty in framing the idea of another mind or in saying, in general, what qualities it must have if it exists. This difference constitutes a perfectly good reason for the theory of cells to accept other minds and to reject physical objects, and acquits it of any kind of inconsistency or capriciousness.

I have no difficulty in framing the idea of another consciousness. It is, roughly, like my own consciousness. It has the same kind of qualities which I introspect in my own mind. The question how I know this to be true is not relevant. I do not know it. I assume it as an hypothesis. But the problem is: can we frame any idea of another mind, if such a thing exists? The answer is that we can easily do so, since we have our own minds to go upon as a model; and that this procedure leads to no difficulties.

Now consider the case of the physical object. What kind of qualities has this, and what is it like? Either it has the sense-qualities which we perceive or it has not. According to the school of realism most fashionable at the moment it has none of these qualities. But in that case we are absolutely unable to frame any idea of it at all. It is supposed to have certain intrinsic qualities which "correspond to" the perceived qualities but are in no way like them. Thus some quality corresponds to red, some other quality to green. Some character corresponds to square, some other character to round. But these intrinsic qualities are absolutely unimaginable to us. And this means that we cannot frame any idea whatever of the object.

Some realists seize the other horn of the dilemma. They say that the physical object has all the perceived qualities. But in that case they are involved in grave difficulties. For if we take any particular object, and ask what colour, shape, etc., it has, what are they to say? Has this table the colour and shape which I see from this side of it or the colour and shape which you see from that side? For these colours and shapes will be quite different. There is no reason for preferring what I see to what you see. And if it is said that the table has *all* the colours and shapes which all observers see in it, this will result in attributing to it a multitude of incompatible characters. It will have to have a vast number of incompatible shapes and incompatible colours simultaneously.

I am well aware that very ingenious solutions to these puzzles have been framed by various realist philosophers. In the next chapter I shall argue that none of these solutions is satisfactory and that realism cannot extricate itself from the difficulties which it makes for itself by assuming the existence of physical objects. For the present I shall be content with the admission that these *are* very real difficulties. And I do not think that even the candid realist himself will deny this. But this is all I undertook to show. The assumption of physical objects leads to these serious dilemmas. The assumption of other minds leads to no corresponding difficulties, indeed to no difficulties of any kind.

We have not indeed direct experience of other minds. But each of us has direct experience of one mind, namely his own. This is sufficient to enable him to frame an idea of what kind of a thing another mind will be, if one exists; just as, if we have once experienced one red object, this will be sufficient to enable us to form the idea of another red object, whether we know that such another red object exists or not. But in the case of the physical object the case is quite different. For if we assume—as is generally now done—that it has none of the perceived qualities, then this means that we have never had direct experience of even one single physical object. Hence we cannot possibly frame the idea of one. We have experienced consciousness and know what it is like. But we have never experienced a physical object. That is the root of the difference. We can avoid this by attributing all ordinary perceived qualities to physical objects. But then we land ourselves in worse dilemmas.

This then is the final justification for admitting other minds into our philosophy, while refusing to admit physical objects.

CHAPTER IV

Realism

1

THE means by which I was to try to recommend the theory of cells for acceptance were by showing (1) that it contains no internal contradictions, (2) that it accounts for the facts of the world, and (3) that it is to be preferred to other hypotheses which may also claim to be acceptable under the first two heads. I have tried to show that it accounts for the facts of the world, and that it contains no contradictions. It remains to consider its relation to other hypotheses.

It is clear that I cannot undertake an examination of all possible metaphysical systems which might be considered rivals to the one which I propose. I shall in fact confine myself to a brief treatment of realism. The reason I select this is that it has in recent years been the prevailing philosophical creed of England and America. It is the hypothesis which is the most obvious alternative to the theory of cells now on the ground.

I do not propose to try to *prove* that realism is false. I shall only attempt to show that it possesses, as an hypothesis, more disadvantages than the theory of cells, and leads to more difficulties. Although it is impossible ever to prove that a metaphysical hypothesis is true (Chapter I, Section 10), it may sometimes be possible to prove that it, or at least a large part of it, must be false. For it may be so riddled with vital contradictions that most of it must be untrue. But I do not think it is possible to show this in the case of realism.

In the nature of the case this chapter is bound to be almost entirely critical and controversial. I shall therefore make it as short as possible.

THE easiest way to make clear the essential issue between realism and the theory of cells is to consider the situation which would be described in ordinary language as "two persons looking at the same material object," say a penny. According to the theory of cells this situation is to be interpreted as follows. There are two cells, *A* and *B*. In the *A*-cell there is a certain datum, *a*—say a circular brown patch. Datum *a* exists in *A's* private space and private time. In the *B*-cell there is a corresponding datum, *b*, which exists in *B's* private space and private time. Datum *a* corresponds to datum *b* in certain respects, but there is also divergence from correspondence (Chapter II, Section 10). The divergence, however, is not merely arbitrary, but is governed by definite laws. The data come into existence when they first appear in the cells and cease to exist when they disappear from the cells. They do not persist when they are not perceived. There is no "physical object" outside the cells which is the source or cause of the data, or to which the data in any other sense belong. 'Nothing exists except the data and the consciousness.' The consciousness may, when it is perceiving and not merely sensing, expect that certain other data may in certain circumstances appear. But these other data do not yet exist.

Now with every single statement in the above description *with one exception*, a realist may agree. I do not say that all realists do agree with all these statements except one. I say that a realist *may* do so without ceasing to be a good and consistent realist. The one statement with which he cannot agree is that there exists no physical object outside the cells.

He may agree that the data are private. In *The Problems of Philosophy* Mr. Russell wrote: "But the sense-data are private to each separate person; what is immediately present to the sight of one is not immediately present to the sight of another."[1] More recently Professor Price writes: "A sense-datum,

[1] Chap. II, p. 32.

being somato-centric, is *private* to the mind which senses it."[2] (The italics are Professor Price's.) There would be no difficulty in collecting similar statements from the writings of other British realists. Now anyone who admits that sense-data are private will be compelled, if he is consistent, to admit that the spaces and times in which they appear, are also private. Mr. Russell, at the time he wrote *The Problems of Philosophy*, did admit this. After distinguishing public or physical space, which is real, from our tactile and visual spaces, which are "apparent," he says: "the real space is public, the apparent space is private to the percipient. . . . The real space must be different from the private spaces."[3] He also at that time held that sense-data do not exist except when they are perceived. They are not, of course, dependent for their existence on the mind (Berkeley's view), but they are dependent on the sense-organs, so that they do not exist when no sense-organ is making us aware of them. "Our sense-data," he says, "cannot be supposed to have an existence independent of us . . . their existence would not continue if there were no seeing or hearing or touching or smelling or tasting."[4] This is also Professor Price's view at the present day, or at least it was when he wrote his book *Perception* (1933).

So far as I can see the philosophy outlined in the first four chapters of *The Problems of Philosophy*, especially in Chapter III, is an almost perfect exposition of the theory of cells, *except* that Mr. Russell postulates the existence of a physical object outside the private worlds, and that these objects are supposed to be the causes of the sense-data and to persist during interperceptual intervals. In order to transmute Mr. Russell's philosophy (at that time) into the theory of cells, all you have to do is to amputate the physical object. What will remain after the amputation will be the theory of cells.

[2] *Perception*, p. 145. See also the longer passage on p. 274.
[3] pp. 46, 47.
[4] *ibid.*, p. 60.

The fact that Mr. Russell may have long since discarded all or any of these views is quite irrelevant. I have not quoted him in order to claim his support, but in order to show that the only issue regarding which realism and the theory of cells are compelled to disagree is that which concerns the physical object. I am simply trying to discover the most essential issue as between realism and the theory of cells. Particular realists may disagree with the theory of cells on many other matters besides the physical object. Some, e.g. Professor Alexander, have held that sense-data (or entities exactly like them), exist unperceived. And apparently Mr. Russell has sometimes held something like this view. Others, as shown by our quotations, think that they do not exist unperceived. Some realists think that sense-data and also the spaces and times in which they exist are private. Others may dispute this. These therefore are not the essential points which divide realism from the theory of cells. The vital issue is as regards the physical object. I shall therefore concentrate my fire upon that alone.

3

THE crux for realism comes when it is asked to tell us what kind of a thing the physical object is, what qualities it has. My attempt is to show that it is involved in insoluble difficulties and dilemmas as soon as it tries to give an answer to this question.

The answer of the realist will depend upon whether he adopts the generative hypothesis or the selective hypothesis. Some realists have followed one, some the other.

The generative hypothesis holds that the existence of data is physiologically conditioned. The sense-datum is the effect of two joint causes, the physical object and the sense-organ. Thus a colour is actually produced by the interaction of the physical object and the organ of sight. If this is true, there will be no colour when there is no eye. Similar conclusions follow as regards the data of the other senses. For in each case the organ and the physical object together produce the datum. Hence those who hold this theory believe that sense-data only exist when they are being perceived. Mr. Russell held this view when he wrote *The Problems of Philosophy*.[5]

The selective hypothesis holds that the sense-datum is not an effect which is produced, or part-produced, by the sense-organ, but that the function of the sense-organ is to *select* which sense-datum we perceive. Thus if I see an object as red while a colour-blind man sees it as green, the truth is that both red and green are present in the physical world; but my retina selects the red for me to see and shuts out the green, while the colour-blind man's retina selects the green for him to see and shuts out the red. And similarly as regards the other senses. The outside world actually has all the qualities which can ever be perceived in it by any organism. And those who hold this theory are enabled to maintain that sense-data exist whether they are perceived or not, and therefore that they exist during interperceptual intervals.

The selective hypothesis is not now apparently maintained by many philosophers. The first realistic philosopher to suggest it as a possibility was (so far as I know) Professor G. E. Moore,[6] and later it was championed by Professor Alexander. At present there seems to be a tendency to drop it. For though it is exceedingly ingenious, it is also very unconvincing. The

[5] According to Professor Price the way of stating the hypothesis which I have used in this paragraph is very inaccurate. Instead of saying that data are part-caused by the sense-organs we ought to say that they are somato-centric. His analysis is, I believe, a great improvement on the older statement. But I have employed the more conventional statement chiefly for the sake of brevity. For whether we adopt the generative hypothesis or Mr. Price's somato-centric hypothesis makes no difference at all to the particular results which I want to discuss. In either case data do not exist when not perceived. And Mr. Price is in exactly the same difficulty as those who hold the generative hypothesis in regard to the question of the qualities of the physical object.

[6] In an essay called "The Status of Sense-data" reprinted in *Philosophical Studies*. This article is a remarkable example of Professor Moore's genius. It contains, packed into a few pages, the germs of half a dozen different philosophies subsequently developed in detail by other men. Half the thinking of English philosophers in the twentieth century comes, or at least could have come, from this source.

natural conclusion to be drawn from it (though Alexander struggles to avoid this) is that, if it is true, then physical objects must actually have in themselves *all* the qualities which all organisms have ever perceived in them (and perhaps many others), although many of these may be incompatible with one another. For instance, the object which I see as red and which the colour-blind man sees as green should, on the selective hypothesis, be both red and green at the same time and on the same part of its surface. And I do not see how this can be the case. If it can be the case, then the whole basis upon which all modern epistemological theories are built vanishes. For they are all attempts to explain the variability and relativity of sense-data. Since the seventeenth century (at least) it has been assumed that the fact that the same thing appears one colour to one man and another to another, one shape from this position and another shape from that, warm to a cold hand and cool to a warm hand, constitutes a problem. The essence of the problem is that it does not seem possible that the same numerically identical entity should at the same time have qualities and characters which are incompatible with one another. Berkeley solved the problem by putting the different incompatible qualities in different places, i.e. in the various minds of the observers as their sensations. Modern realism (of the generative variety) explains it by denying that the incompatible qualities are in the object itself and making them relative to different sense-organs. The selective hypothesis, if it really means that the same surface can be both red and green at the same time, solves the problem by turning its back on it.

Ingenious attempts have been made to avoid this impasse. One way of evading it is to say that the red datum and the green datum are in different private spaces. But selective realism cannot say this without destroying its own basis. For it was to hold that the physical object *itself* is coloured. But the physical object must be in the one public space, not in any private spaces.

And if the physical object itself is coloured, its colour also must be in public space and not in the private spaces. The selective hypothesis cannot, of course, deny that there is a one public space and a one public object. It cannot assert that there are only private objects in private spaces, or at least if it does this it becomes identical with the theory of cells—except that it talks of objects instead of data—and ceases to be a realistic hypothesis.

Other ingenious hypotheses were invented by Alexander to evade the fatal defect of the selective hypothesis, namely that it attributes incompatible characters to the object. Thus the smaller size of an object when seen at a distance is said by him to be a *part* of the larger size of it when it is seen near at hand; and this part is selected by the mind out of the larger size. This sort of theory will not work at all in the case of the different *shapes* of the object as seen from different angles, since there is no sense in which one shape can be said to be part of another. Of course, the area of an oval can be part of the area of a circle. But the shapiness of the oval is not part of the shapiness of the circle. Illusion, as when we see a grey surface as green, owing to juxtaposition of red, is explained by Alexander on the hypothesis that the green which we see is a green which is actually somewhere in the physical world, though not in the place in which we see it. This is due to the fact that the mind squints! This green which I see here on a piece of paper in Princeton is really the green of a patch of grass in Philadelphia which has got transferred here by my squinting mind. The best one can say of such theorizing is that its ingenuity is only exceeded by its implausibility.[7]

Thus realism, if it adopts the selective theory, is in grave difficulties when it attempts to tell us what qualities the physical object really has—difficulties from which it appears impossible that it should extricate itself.

[7] S. Alexander, *Space, Time and Deity*, Book III, Chaps. VII and VIII.

FACED with the same question, will the generative type of realism fare any better?

The selective theory says that a physical object has *all* the qualities which we or any other existing or possible organism ever has or ever will perceive in it. The generative theory says that it has *none* of the qualities which any actual or possible organism ever did or ever will perceive in it. It is obvious that the secondary qualities cannot exist in the object, since the sense-organs are a part-cause of their coming into existence. If it is less obvious, it is at any rate equally true, that on the generative hypothesis, the object can have none of the primary qualities either. For this hypothesis has to hold that a colour-expanse is private. But if so, the spatial area over which the colour is expanded must be private too. Thus each organism will have its own private visual space. The same will be true of tactile space. It will follow that the physical object is not in any space which we perceive, and that it cannot have the spatial characters of perceived spaces.

May not the space in which the physical object is be *like* our perceived spaces, so that though it may not have the actual squareness, the actual bigness, the actual motion which we see or touch, it may yet have a similar squareness, bigness, and motion? The suggestion is entirely groundless. It will be in the same position as the suggestion that the object, though not having the actual colour we perceive, may have a similar colour. For the question in that case will be: which of the many colours we perceive, e.g. red or green, is the real colour like? And similarly, which of the many shapes we perceive in the table as we move round it will its real shape be like? The point is that spatial characters are in exactly the same position as colours, smells, and the like. On the generative hypothesis the primary qualities can no more be in the object than the secondary qualities can.

What, then, can the generative type of realism tell us about the qualities of the physical object? The utmost that it can do is to offer the suggestion that there is, in the object, some quality which *corresponds to* red, when we see red, some quality which *corresponds to* green when we see green, some quality which *corresponds to* sweet when we taste sweet, and so on. These qualities will be absolutely unimaginable and inconceivable to us or to any mind which perceives by means of bodily organs of any kind. And by the same logic the utmost we can say of physical space will be that it is something which corresponds to our perceived spaces, but is quite unlike them. Physical space will be unimaginable to us.

The same will be true of motion, shape, size. When we see one thing bigger than another, there must be, between the physical objects themselves, some relation which corresponds to the perceived relation "bigger than." But it is impossible for us to know, or even to imagine, what this real relation is like. If one table is round, another square, there must be in the objects themselves something corresponding to roundness and squareness, but these intrinsic characters of the object are inconceivable to us. Finally we may postulate the motion of objects, the vibration of atoms, but these will only be motion and vibration in a Pickwickian sense; for we cannot have even the faintest idea what they are really like.[8]

It seems very doubtful whether we can say that in the real world there is unity or multiplicity. Of course in a sense a plurality of characters is implied by the argument that something must correspond to the various characters of the perceived world. But real plurality will be only something which corresponds to apparent plurality, not what *we* mean by plurality. We see two books, and there must be something which corresponds to this twoness. But is there any reason to suppose that it is anything like the twoness in our world?

[8] This is clearly recognized by Russell in his earlier theory. See *The Problems of Philosophy*, p. 53.

Thus the physical object is reduced by the generative hypothesis to much the same uncomfortable position as that of the Kantian *ding-an-sich*; and the conception possesses the same kind of difficulties as the Kantian *ding-an-sich*. I will not say that the notion of it is meaningless. For the relation of correspondence attaches it, I believe, by a very thin thread to the world of our meanings. But it seems to me that the physical object attenuated to this degree is a very difficult conception to take seriously and has become a perfectly useless hypothesis. It might as well be discarded altogether.[9]

[9] Professor Price in his book *Perception* adopts the generative hypothesis (or his version of it which he calls the somato-centric hypothesis) but draws from it very different conclusions from those which I have asserted in the text to follow from it. For he holds, first, that in addition to the "intrinsic" qualities, the public physical object has shape, size, and position as perceived, and also causal characteristics. And he holds, secondly, that although each individual sense-datum is private, yet the family of sense-data is public.

I hope I am not misunderstanding Professor Price, but it seems clear to me that the first of these two conclusions depends upon a failure to see that the same arguments which prove the privacy of colour, smell, etc., also prove the privacy of shape, size, and position. Professor Price would apparently admit that in the physical object there is an intrinsic quality which corresponds to red, but is not itself red. He ought to admit on the same grounds that in the physical object there are intrinsic qualities which correspond to size, position and shape, but not these qualities themselves. Why does he not admit this? I suspect the answer has something to do with his belief that, although each sense-datum is private, yet the family of sense-data as a whole is public. I now turn to that.

How does Professor Price support the extraordinary position that though all the individual data are private, the collection of them is public? The datum, he says (pp. 273 *ff*.), is private in the sense that "only one mind can be acquainted with it." But it is public in the sense that other minds can know it by description. Hence the family is public in this sense. But this is certainly *not* what is ordinarily meant by public. It is quite obvious that what everyone means by asserting that a material object, say a chair, is public, is that we all *see* the same chair, i.e. that we are all acquainted with the same object. Publicity in the sense of being knowable by description by many minds can perfectly well be asserted of the data in the cells in the theory of cells, or in any doctrine of private worlds whatever. In the two cells, *A* and *B*, there are two corresponding data *a* and *b*. Only the *A*-consciousness can know *a* by acquaintance, but the *B*-consciousness can know it by description as "the datum in cell *A* which corresponds to, and is perhaps similar to, datum *b*." It is absurd to suggest that Professor Price has established the publicity of families of sense-data when what he has actually established is consistent with any doctrine of private worlds.

"Philosophers" writes Professor Price elsewhere (*Philosophy*, Vol. XIII, No. 52, p. 447) "have sometimes suggested that each mind lives in a private world of its own. Probably no one believes this. . . . This speculation of philosophers is nothing

Thus realism, it seems to me, is forced upon the horns of a dilemma in regard to the question of the *nature* of the physical object. It is compelled to adopt either the selective or the generative hypothesis. There seems to be no third alternative. If it adopts the selective hypothesis, this leads at once to the impossible position that an object is both green and red and perhaps many other colours at the same time and on the same part of its surface; that the same spatial area is both square and not-square; and so on. It may struggle to avoid this disaster, but can only do so by inventing unconvincing and implausible *ad hoc* hypotheses. If it adopts the generative hypothesis, it is driven to a view of the physical object which is scarcely intelligible and which is perilously near that of the unknowable thing-in-itself. I am not prepared to assert that the physical object, so viewed, is completely unknowable or completely unintelligible. But it comes unpleasantly near that state of affairs. It must be remembered that not only can the physical object never be perceived or even imagined by any human mind, but it can never be perceived or even imagined by any *embodied* mind anywhere, since presumably any such mind must be aware of the characters of the object as relative to sense-organs of some kind. Is it plausible to suggest that it might be perceived by a naked mind, wholly discarnate? But if not, it is forever cut off from all possible experience by any conceivable mind in the universe.

but a *baseless fancy*." (Italics mine.) Yet this baseless fancy follows absolutely from his own admission of the privacy of sense-data, and he himself ought on his own principles to believe in it. He only avoids doing so by the fallacious procedure of suggesting that "knowable by description to many minds" is the same as public. Once the privacy of data is admitted you are at once landed in a doctrine of private worlds. You can then save your realism by postulating a public object outside these private worlds having intrinsic qualities which are unimaginable to us. This is what Mr. Russell does in Chapter III of *The Problems of Philosophy*. And this is the only self-consistent kind of realism which can be held on the basis of the generative hypothesis. It can be regarded as the classic exposition, which cannot be bettered— although it may well be that Mr. Russell no longer agrees with it. That is why I have chosen it in the text as the proper position of generative realism.

So far we have been speaking of the *nature* of the physical object. What about its *existence?* Even if the realist cannot give any satisfactory account of its nature, can he give any reasons why we should believe that it exists? So far as I know, the only reasons which have ever been suggested are the following: (1) that it can be inferred from sense-data as their cause, (2) that it is simpler than any other hypothesis, and (3) that we have a "strong propensity" to believe it.

First, then, can it be inferred from sense-data as their cause? There is no doubt that it cannot. In the first place, such an inference will depend upon the premiss that everything which exists must have a cause. And this is a mere dogma. Within the field of my private experience I can trace causal relations. That is to say, I can trace regularities of sequence among complexes of sense-data. Thus the complex of visual data which is what I see when I observe lightning is followed by the complex of auditory data which is what I hear when I observe thunder. I express this by saying that lightning is the cause of thunder. The experiences of other people presumably exhibit similar sequences. This is really all we know about causality. We have no right to postulate causal relations outside our experience. Within our experience various items in the streams of data stand to each in such relations. We have no reason to suggest that the first datum which appeared within our private time had a cause, nor even that the first datum to appear after a period of unconsciousness had any.

If we can know that no event can ever happen without a cause, we must either know this from experience, or because there is some logical contradiction involved in supposing otherwise. As has just been shown, this knowledge cannot arise from experience. Nor is there any logical contradiction in an uncaused event. For let the event be E. Let E come uncaused into existence at time t. Then this entire transaction can be completely described in two propositions which are (1) that E

did not exist before time t, and (2) that E began to exist at time t. Proposition (1) does not contradict proposition (2). And since no other propositions are required to define completely the conception of an uncaused event, it follows that there is no contradiction in the conception.

The second point to be made is that the causal argument for the existence of physical objects is circular. The belief that all events must have causes is the belief that chains of causes and effects stretch uninterruptedly through time. But our experience is intermittent. The streams of data are interrupted by gaps. Thus the belief that everything is caused includes the belief that things, namely causes and effects, exist outside our private data. Hence we can only believe in continuous and universal causation if we already believe in entities outside our experience. Therefore we cannot base belief in entities outside experience upon belief in the universality of causation.

Finally, even if we grant for the sake of argument that every event must have a cause, and that therefore our sense-data must have causes, this will not lead to a belief in physical objects. It will lead only to a belief in the existence of unsensed complexes of data. For in every case of a causal relation which has ever actually been *observed,* the cause has been a complex of data and the effect a complex of data. The instance of the lightning and the thunder has just been given. This must be so, since all we ever observe is sense-data. If there exists any causal relation which is not a relation between data, no such case, at any rate, has ever been observed. Hence since the cause of data is always, in our experience, other data, the causal argument will lead, if anywhere, to data existing outside our private experiences. The first set of data to appear in my life, or at the beginning of a period of consciousness, must be supposed to have been caused by a set which existed unsensed before my consciousness began. Thus even if the causal argument is valid in the sense that it does prove something, what it proves is not the existence of a physical object.

It will also be seen that the hypothesis of physical objects as the causes of sense-data duplicates causality in an entirely unjustifiable way. Consider any causal sequence of which both terms are actually observed, say a flash of lightning, A, and a peal of thunder, B. In the diagram A and B are both com-

$$A$$
$$\downarrow$$
$$O \rightarrow B$$

plexes of data. The arrows represent the directions from cause to effect. Arrow AB represents the time-direction of the flow of phenomena. Arrow OB represents the direction of causality from the physical object *behind* the flow of phenomena. Now A, the seen lightning, is a *sufficient* cause for B, the heard thunder. We do not have to look for another additional cause. Why, then, postulate O, the physical object, as a *second* cause of B, and a cause which lies entirely outside the chain of ob-served causes and effects, outside the world of experience? Such a procedure is both unnecessary and unjustified. It sim-ply clutters up the universe with an unwanted entity.

It is sometimes said that the similarity of the sense-data of one person to those of another, when both are perceiving the "same" object, is a good reason for believing in physical ob-jects as their common cause. Thus Russell writes: "What rea-son, then, have we for believing that there are such public neutral objects? . . . Although different people may see the table slightly differently, still they all see more or less similar things when they look at the table . . . so that it is easy to arrive at a permanent object underlying all the different peo-ple's sense-data."[10] It is true that Russell rejects this argument. But his rejection is based upon the fact that, at the stage of his argument at which he has arrived, the existence of other minds is not to be assumed. But the argument is really to be rejected on a much deeper ground, on the ground that it is an example of the fallacy of special causes (Chapter II, Section

[10] *The Problems of Philosophy*, p. 32.

14). It assumes that the correspondence of our private worlds is improbable unless a special cause is assigned for it. And it has been shown (Chapter II, Section 13) that this assumption, either in regard to cellular correspondence or any other example of world-order, is false. Realism, so far as it is based, consciously or unconsciously, on this argument, commits the fallacy of special causes.

6

IT is stated next that belief in a physical object is *simpler* than any other hypothesis, and that this is an important recommendation of it. I am quite prepared to admit that simplicity *is* a recommendation to an hypothesis; at any rate to the extent that if there is in other ways nothing to choose between two hypotheses, we shall probably be right to accept *provisionally* the simpler of the two. But it seems to me very doubtful indeed whether realism can claim simplicity, in any desirable sense, as against the theory of cells. The question what is *meant* by simplicity in an hypothesis badly needs to be cleared up by some industrious philosopher. For there are surely many different kinds of simplicity, some of which may be recommendations to an hypothesis, but others not. I cannot attempt any complete analysis here. But I will list a few of the kinds of simplicity which occur to me and see how realism and the theory of cells stand in regard to them.

There is clearly some sense in which the metaphysic of common sense is simpler than the theory of cells. For it was precisely on this ground that common sense was seen, in the chapter on constructions, to have the pragmatic advantage. The simplicity there suggested meant, for the most part, the existence of fewer entities in the world—one common world instead of a plurality of private ones, one continuous universe instead of many punctuated by gaps, one object of the different senses instead of several.

Greater simplicity in this sense must be admitted to characterize the philosophy of common sense. I should myself be inclined to think that sufficient credit had been given for this in admitting its practical advantages without claiming also that it increases its probability of truth. But that point may be waived. It must now be pointed out that common-sense metaphysic is by no means the same thing as realism. Realism certainly claims to be the philosophical version of common sense. But for reasons which I will shortly give I doubt whether this is true. Common sense has never heard of physical objects which have none of the qualities which we perceive in things. And if this be remembered, it is very doubtful whether realism, as distinct from common-sense metaphysic, has much claim to be simpler than the theory of cells even in the sense of postulating fewer kinds of objects in the universe. The theory of cells postulates nothing except consciousness and data. Realism believes in these—except that some forms of American realism strike out consciousness—but proceeds to add an indefinite number of physical objects.

Sometimes one hypothesis is said to be simpler than another when its details are amenable to simpler mathematical treatment. It is in this sense that the heliocentric hypothesis is simpler than the geocentric. The latter required that in astronomical calculations complicated epicycles be introduced. I understand that in this sense the assumption of a non-Euclidean space-time in relativity physics is simpler than the assumption of a Euclidean space-time. This kind of simplicity has no application to the dispute between realism and the theory of cells because neither hypothesis involves any mathematical calculation.

Simplicity may be an esthetic quality. It is said that some mathematical demonstrations are more beautiful than others, because more simple, and that the more beautiful are to be preferred. Whatever this means, I cannot see that it has any application to the present case. I see no reason to admit that realism is more beautiful than the theory of cells.

The simplicity claimed for an hypothesis may refer to the ease with which it is understood. I am not sure whether it can be argued that this kind of simplicity is a recommendation. But even if it is, realism is not more simple in this sense than the theory of cells. Quite the other way. The theory of cells believes in nothing except consciousness and data. Everybody down to the lowest savage has some understanding of these entities, for he has direct acquaintance with them. But who can understand the physical object which the realist adds? Either it is an incomprehensible mass of incompatible qualities, or it is an equally incomprehensible entity which has not a single quality which anyone—even the philosophers who postulate it —can even begin to understand. To the simple outlines of the theory of cells realism adds an inaccessible and unfathomable mystery.

It is true that at first blush realism does seem easier to understand than the theory of cells. This is because it pretends to be the common-sense theory. It first arose as a protest against the paradoxes of Berkeleyan idealism—so incomprehensible to the plain man. It would take the position of common sense. It would champion the plain man's view against idealistic nonsense. This was bound to be a popular platform. It swept the English-speaking world before it. It explains the enormous popularity of realism. For, apart from the fact that the leaders of the movement might be men of outstanding intellectual calibre, every mediocre mind was sure to flock to this standard. Every moron whose profession happens to be philosophy is nowadays a realist. Now if realism lived up to its professions of being the philosophical justification of the plain man's views, it might be presumed to be simple in the sense that the plain man would find it easy to understand. But actually realism with its generative and selective hypotheses, with its objects which are both green and red at the same time, or alternatively its objects which have no known qualities whatever, with its multitudinous "families" of sense-data, with its penny existing all over the universe except in "the place where the penny is," with its private spaces, with its sense-data ceasing to exist when not perceived—with all these appanages and complexities realism is as utterly remote from common-sense views as any philosophy in the world could well be. Not that this is, in my opinion, anything against it. But it really cannot be said that it is simple in the sense that it is easy for the plain man to understand.*

On what, then, does realism base its claim to be a simple hypothesis? There is still another meaning of simplicity. There is a sense in which, in any difficulty intellectual or practical, the *simplest* thing to do is to follow the line of least resistance, to do or think what everyone does and thinks, to keep to well-tried paths, to follow the bent of old habits. Now it is alleged that there is a propensity to believe in physical objects. Everybody believes in them—that is, all sensible people. The simplest thing to do is to follow the propensity and to believe what everyone believes. It is suggested that realism does this, and that it is therefore a very simple theory. Realism is not really simple even in this sense. It does itself a grave injustice in claiming that it is. But I cannot help suspecting that this is what its claim to simplicity really means. And if the claim could be established, it would not constitute a recommendation of realism.

To sum up. I do not think the claim of realism to be preferred to the theory of cells on the ground of greater simplicity can be justified.

7

THE last reason given for believing in physical objects is that we have a strong propensity to hold this belief. In spite of what was said in the last paragraph, I am quite prepared to admit that *in some cases* a strong propensity to hold a belief may afford some evidence that very likely the belief is true. But I do not think that this is the sort of case in which this can be maintained.

It is a highly noteworthy fact that many different philosophers of many utterly different shades of opinion have agreed in placing a certain reliance upon unreasoned and more or less instinctive feelings, insights, or opinions of themselves or other men. These may be called "instinctive beliefs" or "intuitions" or "propensities to believe" or else plain "common sense." Realists have their instinctive belief in physical objects, which they freely admit carries weight with them. And they think it *should* carry weight. Idealistic ethical writers have often thought it right to bring ethical theories to the test of what they call man's "moral consciousness," by which they clearly mean some kind of instinctive moral beliefs. Professor Whitehead relies freely upon moral and esthetic "intuitions." Yet philosophers rarely enquire *why* we should put any trust in instinctive beliefs, nor in what kind of cases it is safe to do so and in what kind of cases it is not.[11] For it seems clear that it is not equally safe in all cases. Thus we may feel impressed by the claims of moral intuitions. But no one would think it safe to trust to a strong propensity to believe some particular view on a controversial question in physics or chemistry. Why? This is a very curious and interesting subject. I cannot do anything towards a thorough investigation of it, but I should like to make certain very tentative suggestions as regards it.

It is probably impossible to lay down any very definite rule as to when to attach weight to our instinctive beliefs and when not to do so. But the fact that we should practically never trust them in *science* seems to me to provide a clue. No physicist would accept as evidence against the law of gravitation the propensity of some men to believe that flame by nature mounts upward. Nor would he accept the obvious common-sense view that the sun rises and moves over the sky every day as evidence against the heliocentric hypothesis. Nor again would he regard our obstinate common-sense views about space and time as good grounds for disbelieving in relativity. Why

[11] I am not myself aware of any philosopher who has given any important consideration to this problem, or has anything to offer on the subject, except Professor Whitehead. But his views on this can hardly be accepted without accepting his whole philosophy. And even he has, so far as I know, nothing to offer on the question what *kinds* of subject are such that instinctive beliefs as regards them should be given weight.

is it that in science our propensities to believe carry so little weight? I suggest that the following either is the reason or at least has something to do with the reason. Mankind in general has sound instincts in regard to *practical* affairs, but not in regard to any question of pure theory. There seem to be two reasons for this. The first is that in regard to practical affairs their interests are involved; and this sharpens their perceptions. The other reason is that they have had hundreds of thousands of years of experience of the art of living; and that this has caused them to develop sound instincts in practical matters. On the other hand questions of pure theory do not as a rule involve important human interests directly. Nor has the human race at large any long experience in dealing with them.

For these reasons I should myself be inclined to attach considerable weight to men's "moral intuitions." If I find among men a strong feeling of moral repugnance to the theory of ethical relativity and a strong propensity to believe in some kind of universal moral rule, I should consider that this might very likely be based upon a sound instinct. Perhaps similar remarks may apply to the political sphere. That Demos has sound political instincts is one of the arguments for democracy. Possibly—though here I am much more doubtful—there is something to be said for a similar view in regard to religion and art; for in these matters too the welfare of man is involved.

It is for these reasons that I should *not* attach any weight to a propensity to believe a proposition in metaphysics. In this respect at any rate metaphysics is to be aligned with science. It is mostly pure theory. As a rule metaphysical theories have little practical importance and little connection with the art of life. This is not always true, for metaphysics sometimes gains practical significance owing to its connection with religion. But it is true in the case we are now discussing. It makes no practical difference to anyone whether physical objects exist or not. This is a pure question of theory.

Perhaps it will be said that the plain man's views about the nature of tables and chairs cannot be described as metaphysical theories, although the views of the philosopher on the same subject may be. But this would be a mistake. Taking as his example the gradual fading of the colours of a wall paper Mr. Russell once wrote: "the assumption that there is a constant entity, the wall paper, which 'has' these various colours at various times, is a gratuitous piece of metaphysics."[12] And he was plainly right. If the sophisticated views of the philosopher on the subject are metaphysics, so are the naïve views of the plain man. The only difference between the two is that the former are sophisticated metaphysics, the latter naïve metaphysics.

8

WHAT I have been saying so far is that *if* men have a strong propensity to believe in physical objects, this would not, to my mind, afford any evidence of the truth of that belief. I will now add that I do not believe that men have any such propensity. They certainly believe in tables and chairs and lumps of clay and stone. They also, I am sure, have a strong propensity to believe that these things go on existing during interperceptual intervals. This, I suggest, is the instinctive belief which realists mistake for a belief in physical objects. What men believe in is the existence of these everyday objects including their existence when no mind is aware of them. But that they have a strong propensity to believe in any particular philosophical analysis of what is meant by a table or a chair—whether realistic or phenomenalistic—this is what I should emphatically deny. And that they should have a propensity to believe in the theory of the physical object—that is, an object destitute of any properties which have ever been known to them—is to me utterly incredible. For the plain man cannot even understand this idea when it is explained to him. How then can he possibly have a propensity to believe in it?

What the plain man believes about the table is that it is a square, brown, hard object which he sees existing now and

---

[12] *Our Knowledge of the External World*, p. 113, second edition.

which goes on existing, *and being brown and square and hard,* when no one is perceiving it. If you tell him that it is nothing of the sort, that the squareness, brownness, and hardness disappear when he shuts his eyes and reappear when he opens them, that they are not parts of the real table at all, and that the real table has no colour, texture, shape, weight, but only some qualities which neither he nor even the greatest philosopher can even imagine, he will not understand you and certainly will have no strong propensity to believe what you say.

The only metaphysical view of material objects which the plain man has a strong propensity to believe—namely that they exist with all their colours, shape, smell, etc., intact during interperceptual periods—is the very one which is entirely denied by most of the current schools of realism. How then can they produce the plain man's propensities as an argument for their views?'

9

IT IS not claimed that anything in this chapter *refutes* the realistic belief in a physical object. What is claimed is that this belief gives rise to so many difficulties that the theory of cells is preferable to it as an hypothesis. The reasons for saying this can now be summarized.

First, the theory of cells includes no entities which are not empirically verifiable, whereas realism introduces, in the physical object, an entity of which in the nature of the case no single glimpse can ever be attained. Secondly, the theory of cells leads, so far as I know, to no contradictions or difficulties, whereas realism is involved, if not in downright contradictions, at least in dilemmas from which a successful issue seems improbable. Thirdly, there is no valid inference by which we can reach belief in physical objects, a fact admitted by realists themselves. Fourthly, the supposed simplicity of realism is largely chimerical. Lastly, in regard to the propensity to believe, there does not seem to be anything to choose between realism and the theory of cells. Neither of them has much resemblance to the common-sense view of the world, though realism falsely pretends to have. Men's real propensity is to believe that the objects we perceive continue to exist *as perceived* when no mind is aware of them. This is denied both by the theory of cells and by every form of realism except the selective variety which, however, contradicts common sense in other ways.

10

THERE are, of course, forms of realism which do not believe in physical objects at all, or which, at any rate, reduce physical objects to mere collections of sense-data and sensibilia. It is doubtful whether such theories ought to be called realistic. They are rather to be described as half-hearted forms of phenomenalism. Thoroughgoing phenomenalism—as it is found in the theory of cells—regards material objects as composed only of sense-data which exist only when perceived. Half-hearted phenomenalism adds the existence of unperceived sensuous entities called sensibilia.

Such theories must necessarily, if they are to be consistent, rely upon the selective theory of the function of the sense-organs. They cannot maintain *both* that a sensum is dependent for its existence on an organ of sense and also that it exists in the absence of a sense-organ. They are therefore involved in all the difficulties of the selective theory.

Whether we take the realistic or the phenomenalistic view of material objects, a candid survey of the evidence known to us at the present time seems to show that colours, smells, shapes and the like cannot exist except in the presence of sense-organs, or, if we prefer Professor Price's formulation, that they cannot exist outside somato-centric complexes. In either case they cannot exist unsensed. Hence the forms of realism or phenomenalism discussed in this section are not tenable. We are left, then, with the choice between the form of realism which believes in the physical object and the theory of cells. And reasons for preferring the latter have been given.

THERE is one point in the theory of cells which does not seem to be supported by any of the considerations so far suggested. This is the assertion that consciousness and datum are abstractions which cannot exist apart from one another, and that in this respect the relation between them may be compared to that between a colour and a visual extension. If the arguments so far used are valid, what they show is only that consciousness and datum never do as a matter of fact exist apart. For if we drop the physical object, and if we also drop the selective hypothesis and the unperceived entities called sensibilia, this is what we are left with. But it is a new point, not contained in this conclusion, to say that they *cannot* exist apart for the same sort of reasons as a colour and a visual extension cannot exist apart. How is this to be justified?

I should not be greatly concerned if this addition were to be regarded as a speculative leap in the dark, a suggestion which frankly goes beyond the evidence. Even so, it would seem to be a very plausible suggestion once it is admitted that as a matter of fact consciousness and datum do not exist apart. For this would seem to show that there is some intimate interdependence between the two factors. This has always been *suspected*. Berkeley thought that he had proved it. He supposed that the existence of anything unperceived involves a logical contradiction. I think modern writers have shown that this is false. Yet though Berkeley's reasons were bad, there continues to remain in men's minds the suspicion that in some way there is an interdependence of factors.

Yet the doctrine of the theory of cells is not a mere leap made without any reason, nor a belief held on mere suspicion. But the chief positive reason for maintaining it cannot, unfortunately, be fully explained or appreciated until our analysis of consciousness has been made. I will, however, briefly outline it here. The argument will be that, unless we accept the doctrine that consciousness and datum are abstractions related to one another as colour and visual extension are related, it is impossible to give a rational account of the status of universals. For the datum is pure particularity, while consciousness is pure universality. The cell is the sole concrete individual which, as combining consciousness and datum, is the synthesis of the universal and the particular. The status of the universal is expressed by saying that its being consists in the fact that it is a moment within the individual. The universal is neither in the datum (or object) nor in consciousness. The universal is not *in* consciousness, but it is literally to be identified with consciousness. The assertion that the universal is in the object leads to the splitting of it into parts. The assertion that it is in the mind leads to the denial that the object has any characters and to the view that the mind imposes its characters upon it. The assertion that the universal is a self-subsistent entity which transcends both the object and the mind leads to the confusion of the universal and the individual. For it makes the universal an individual. The remaining possibility—which is that adopted by the theory of cells—is that the cell is the individual within which there are found as abstract elements the universal, which is consciousness, and the particular, which is the datum. If so, the datum and the consciousness cannot exist apart for the reason that neither pure universality nor pure particularity can exist apart or be anything in themselves. It is claimed that in no other way can the status of the universal be satisfactorily explained, and hence that this is indirect proof of the doctrine of the theory of cells that datum and consciousness are inseparable abstract elements in the cell which alone is the concrete reality. The final statement of this doctrine is contained in Chapter V, Section 15.

CHAPTER V

Consciousness

1

ACCORDING to the theory of cells consciousness is a definite something which is distinguishable from the datum. Given any concrete cognitive situation consciousness may be negatively defined as that in it which is not the datum. Nor is it in any way reducible to data, nor to complexes of data, nor to relations between data. The theory of cells is here indebted to the doctrine laid down by Professor G. E. Moore at the beginning of this century.[1] That doctrine has, of course, been the subject of severe criticism. Some of the criticism will have to be examined in the earlier sections of this chapter before we can proceed to constructive work.

Consciousness is that which is not the datum. This is how the matter comes before us in the first instance. Yet there is, of course, a sense in which consciousness is later *made* a datum. For we can be conscious of our consciousness. The possibility of this again has been violently disputed, but will here be maintained. According to the empirical principle we cannot introduce into our philosophy the concept of consciousness unless consciousness or its elements are experienced. And to be experienced means to be experienced as a datum. (Chap. I, Sec. 5.)

But this making of consciousness into a datum is not destructive of the doctrine that consciousness is precisely that which is not datum and which is irreducible to any complexes

---

[1] In *The Refutation of Idealism* and in other papers collected in *Philosophical Studies*.

of data or relations between them. We start with mere consciousness and data, without self-consciousness, that is, without consciousness appearing among the data. This is the primary cognitive situation, and here consciousness is no datum. The data in this situation may be called primary data. Later there comes a consciousness of this whole cognitive situation including the consciousness. In this secondary cognitive situation consciousness has become a datum. It may be called a secondary datum. The position is then expressed by saying that consciousness is never a primary datum, but may be a secondary datum. Later we shall find that this provisional statement is an over-simplification of the facts, that the primary and secondary phases do not follow each other in time, and that self-consciousness was present from the beginning. We may begin, however, by thinking in terms of the provisional statement of this paragraph.

Professor Moore may have been indebted to Meinong and others. Yet the profound originality and importance of his contribution are perhaps not generally realized. Everyone had always talked of consciousness, and also of introspecting consciousness. It was therefore assumed that this was a mere restatement of what everyone had always taken for granted. But the truth is that consciousness had never before been clearly distinguished from data, and that the fact that consciousness is utterly distinct from all data was to all intents and purposes a new discovery. For when previous philosophers spoke of consciousness, they seem always to have meant by this term some conglomeration of data. They confused consciousness with data. Thus Berkeley seems to have had no conception whatever that there is any such thing as consciousness. Or at least he thought of it as consisting of colour sensations, smells, sounds, and the like. Hence his use of the word "idea." There was the ego, the spiritual substance, and over against this there were the colours, sounds, odours. These were the ideas which the spiritual substance "had." There was nothing else. Consciousness, as something which is neither soul-substance nor data, was not recognized at all. The popular view that dreams and images are mental phenomena tells the same tale. It confuses consciousness with data. And when James and Russell attacked Professor Moore, insisting that there exists in the mind nothing except data, they were, in effect, returning to the ancient views universally held before Moore—although they purported to represent the vanguard of advanced and revolutionary thought.

Moore published his doctrine of consciousness in 1903. In 1904 William James attacked it in his essay "Does Consciousness Exist?" Hot upon the heels of this came the work of Holt and Perry (anxious to return to the ancient view that consciousness consists in data), the neutral monism of Russell, the school of behaviouristic psychology—in all of which the repudiation of consciousness as distinct from data is a main feature. Since then antagonism to consciousness has exhibited itself as a kind of phobia in America. British philosophers did not, with the exception of Russell, join in the hue and cry.

This hatred of mind exhibited by the early decades of the twentieth century is perhaps destined to become—in the future—one of the curiosities of the history of thought. Two causes may be assigned for it. First, the despotic sway of idealism at the end of the nineteenth century was bound to call forth a violent reaction. Mind had been thought to be the foundation of the universe. It was not enough to deny it this position, to put it in its proper place. The extremists must needs hoot it off the stage of the universe altogether. And when at this juncture Moore's doctrine of consciousness made a sudden appearance, the storm, just ready to break, precipitated itself at this point.

The second cause is perhaps that "scientific materialism" which, according to Professor Whitehead, colours the whole European consciousness of the last three hundred years. The universe conceived as matter under the reign of natural law is a picture of things which is beautifully manageable. It is a neat and tidy universe, everything in its proper place. It runs like a machine. The intrusion of mind into such a world, meddling and pushing things awry, is an impertinence—as unforgivable as the appearance of a spook in the scientific laboratory. Yet mind exists in the universe, whether it disturbs our neat scheme of things or not. And when the extremists and the phobiacs have finished their shouting, it will have to be taken account of.

2

CONSCIOUSNESS *is*. It is an entity, by which I mean simply that it has being. But what kind of an entity is consciousness? The question means: under what more general concept than the concept of consciousness itself can the latter be subsumed? It is as when I ask: is "whale" to be subsumed under "fish" or under "mammal"? Historically answers have been given in terms of substance, stuff, quality, relation, function, etc. Dispute has been long and vociferous. James stoutly denies that there is any *stuff* in consciousness, much less any *substance*. Although he denies "consciousness," he has to admit the existence of "knowing." And knowing is not a stuff. It turns out to be, on his account, a *relation* or a *function*. For Alexander consciousness is neither a stuff nor a relation. It is a *quality*.

What do these disputes *mean*? They seem to me to be almost entirely verbal. Everyone—so I shall maintain—knows perfectly well what consciousness is. He knows it by being himself conscious. He knows it by direct apprehension as he knows red. He learns very little more about it by calling it a stuff, a relation, a substance, a quality. But he is fascinated by the question: what *word* shall I use to describe it?

When one applies any concept to an object, what one does —and one does nothing more—is to assert certain similarities between this object and certain other objects. Thus I have an entity before me, and I say "This is a dog." This remark means only that there exist certain similarities between this entity and various other entities which I have previously seen and which I also called "dog." Of course, between this entity

[142]

and the others there are also innumerable dissimilarities regarding which my word "dog" tells me nothing. The similarities to which I draw attention when I classify an entity may be numerous and important or they may be few and trivial. They may even be nothing save faint and far-fetched analogies. But in any case a proposition of the form "this is an x" never means anything except "this is like that."

The more general the concept I apply, the less information it gives about similarities. To call this thing here a mammal means less than to call it a dog. Hence we shall expect that whether we apply to consciousness the universal category of substance, or that of relation, or that of quality, we shall in any case be giving the minimum amount of information about the similarities of consciousness to other things.

James labours at great length to show that the proposition "consciousness is a stuff" is not true. What is he denying? I am not sure what a stuff is, that is to say, I do not know the definition of stuff. But if I am asked for examples I think I can give them. Chalk is a stuff, wood is a stuff, air is a stuff. Hence anyone who asserts that consciousness is a stuff is saying that it is something like chalk or wood or air. The truth of the comparison is what James is denying. Instead of it he proposes to say that consciousness, or rather knowing, is a relation. This means, so far as I can see, that consciousness is something like "to the left of," or again that it is like "in." There is nothing else asserted here.

I do not myself deny that consciousness may be something like chalk, or again something like "to the left of." But I think the resemblances, if any, must be very unimportant. And whichever formula I choose, I do not think I am learning anything important about consciousness which I did not know before.

According to Alexander consciousness is a quality. This means that it is something like "red" or again something like "sweet." This also I do not deny. But again I think the information not very valuable. For the resemblances, if any, between consciousness and redness are very remote, very faint indeed, and I do not see that any use can be made of them either in theory or in practice.

Perhaps nothing in the universe is absolutely unique. For if anything bore *no* resemblances to other things, I do not see how it could be in the same universe with them. Thus I do not doubt that between consciousness and other things there are certain resemblances. But I believe that consciousness is, in all important respects, so very unlike all other things, so very nearly unique, that the pointing out of these similarities is to all intents and purposes worthless. This means that the attempt to subsume consciousness under some more general concept should be abandoned. There is almost no sense in asking whether consciousness is a stuff or a quality or a relation. There is only that negligible amount of sense which we found in the disputes as to whether it is more like chalk or "to the left of." What are we to say, then, when we are asked: what *kind* of an entity is consciousness? We must answer that consciousness is its own kind of entity, and that everyone knows, by direct apprehension, what kind this is, and that there is no more to be said. Consciousness is consciousness.

And yet later I shall myself refer to the *activity* of consciousness, and shall indeed say many other things about it. Is not this inconsistent? As to activity, this, as we shall maintain, means effort. And effort is only found in consciousness itself, and not in other things. Hence to call consciousness an activity is not to trace similarities between it and anything else. Activity is not, like quality or substance, a more general concept than consciousness, under which we try to subsume it. To speak of consciousness as activity is only to pick out for notice one of the characteristics of consciousness itself and to give it a name. And the same remarks will apply in principle to everything else that I shall say about consciousness.

THE first truth about consciousness is that it is that which is *not* a primary datum. Taking the most elementary cognitive situation we can find, say mere consciousness of blue, what is asserted is that there is something present which is not the blue datum nor any other datum. Hence modern denials of consciousness always resolve themselves into attempts to reduce it to data or to some relation between data. This may be very easy if only one will confuse primary with secondary data. One points to the fact that consciousness is a datum. This is true, since it is a secondary datum. One then forgets that there is a distinction between primary and secondary data. One has thus reduced consciousness to data, and the denial of consciousness is complete, since consciousness came before us in the first instance characterized only as that which is not datum. This is what Russell does in his analysis of believing. We are conscious of believing. Therefore believing is a datum. It is easy to say then that believing is a "feeling," since any datum may be described as a feeling. This means only that it is datal, something immediately there. Then it becomes a "sensation." This means that it is like red. And no doubt it is like red, since it is datal. Hence believing, Russell concludes, is not consciousness. It is merely data.[2]

Behaviourism resolves consciousness into moving somatic data. Russell resolves it into sensations and images, that is, into data of a sensory kind. Holt also treats it as composed of data, but includes universals among data. James is ambiguous. Consciousness as distinct from knowing—if one is to continue to use the word at all—is identical with the data of which it is conscious. Thus "awareness of blue" is simply identical with blue. But "knowing" is a special relation between data, and this relation too is a kind of datum since it must be found in the area of experience and must be capable of being pointed out.

[2] Russell's argument is more fully analysed in the next section. Meanwhile if the reference is wanted, it will be found in Chap. XII of his *Analysis of Mind*.

The theory of cells holds that all such attempts to reduce consciousness to data have failed, and are foredoomed to failure from the outset. A brief discussion of James and Russell will bring out the main points.

James has important elements of truth on his side. He was, in a sense, right in denying the existence of "awareness." What he said was that awareness is not introspectable, and so not in any way empirically verifiable. Under the empirical principle, which he adopts, we are not entitled to any conception the elements of which are not exemplified among data. Therefore, since awareness is not to be found in experience, we are not entitled to the conception of it. The theory of cells holds that this is correct, and that awareness is not to be found when we look for it in consciousness, because there is in fact no such thing. This is because consciousness is not properly describable as awareness. All consciousness is conceptual thinking, and conceptual thinking is introspectable.[3]

But James, who would be a complete monist if he could, has to admit that there is a duality of some kind. Although he denies consciousness in the sense of awareness, he cannot deny that there is knowing. And knowing is a relation between data. When the data are taken in certain sets of relations they constitute physical objects. The very same data taken in some other set of relations constitute a mind. Hence the crucial question is: what is this peculiar relation, or set of relations, which is the essence of the mental as distinguished from the physical?

In attempting to answer this question James is very confused. Sometimes he points to the relation referred to in his psychology as that of "warmth and intimacy."[4] At other times certain data are said to lead continuously on into other data, as when my image of a building leads me to the percept of the same building; and then this relation of *leading into* is identi-

[3] James's teaching is to be found in his essay *Does Consciousness Exist?* reprinted in *Essays in Radical Empiricism* and in the other essays in that book.
[4] *Essays in Radical Empiricism*, pp. 128-30.

fied as knowing.[5] At yet other times the loose and wild relations which subsist between certain data (as in dreams) when they are not connected by the relations known as the laws of physics seem to be taken as the essence of the mental.[6] I do not know whether any scholarly person can introduce order into this chaos, or twist James's various statements of his doctrine into conformity with one another. For our purposes it does not matter. For the essence of the argument which follows has no dependence upon which of these various relations James in the end meant.

The essential point is that James is forced to admit that there exists *some unique relation* which is identifiable with consciousness, or with knowing, if the term is preferred. By calling it a "unique" relation I mean that the relation is peculiar to situations in which there is knowing and is not found in situations in which knowledge is not present. Thus it is not found in the bare external world. It would be nonsense to suggest that some spatial or temporal relation might fit here. For such relations are found in the external world. And what is sought is precisely a relation which will differentiate a knowing situation from a mere physical situation. Thus it is bound to be a unique relation, a relation not found in the external world, a relation peculiar to the knowing situation.

When we reach this point it is surely clear that the game is up. James has to admit that there exists in the universe a unique and peculiar relation which is the essence of mind or knowing, and which is not to be found in the external world. It is important to observe that this is not due to any slip of language on James's part, to any verbal inconsistency or failure of expression. It is forced upon James by the logic of his entire position. Once say that the duality of the mental and the physical is to be explained by the fact that we take the same data now in one set of relations, now in another, and you have admitted that there exists in the universe a unique relation

[5] *ibid.*, pp. 52 *ff.*
[6] *ibid.*, p. 139.

which is the essence of mind. Thus this is really a criticism, not of James, but of any kind of neutral monism of this type, including that of Russell.

I said that the game is up when once such a unique relation is admitted. For this unique entity *is* consciousness. You have yourself analysed it out of world. James may refuse to use the word consciousness, if he likes. But he has admitted the reality of the thing. The only remaining question will be whether this unique entity has been properly described as a relation. We are then back again in the question whether consciousness is a relation, a stuff, or what else. And regarding this I do not care to dispute for the reasons already given. This is mostly a mere matter of what word you choose to use. The reality for which I contend has been granted.

4

MR. RUSSELL's book *The Analysis of Mind* purports to show that every kind of so-called mental fact, awareness, thinking, memory, desire, emotion, will, belief, doubt, can be reduced to sensations and images, that is, to data. Mr. Russell borrows weapons from many different philosophical and psychological arsenals. There are bits of Berkeley, bits of James, bits of behaviourism, bits of introspective psychology, bits of Freudian psychoanalysis. By the aid of all these implements, the whole world of mind is at last battered down into a conglomeration of sensations and images. It is a remarkable piece of special pleading. If it is not a masterpiece, it is at any rate a *tour de force*.

I shall direct attention only to one point, Mr. Russell's treatment of the mental process of believing. If in this one case his reduction breaks down; if he is forced to admit that believing cannot be reduced to sensations and images but is a genuine mode of consciousness; then the case for consciousness is in principle established as against him.

What happens when I believe something? The first thing to notice is that believing a proposition is something more than merely apprehending or understanding it. I may place before my mind the proposition "Socrates was an American," and I may perfectly understand what it means. But this is not the same as to believe it.

The fact that believing a proposition contains more than merely understanding it has sometimes been overlooked. Thus the so-called "searchlight theory" of consciousness appears to overlook it. Error is here explained as including a false proposition in the cross-section of the world of entities to which my nervous system specifically responds. Now in the mere understanding or apprehending of a false proposition there must be this inclusion of it in the cross-section. Hence in error there is something more than this. There is the *believing* of the false proposition.

Russell's theory does not commit this mistake. The judgment *which* I believe is first reduced to a combination of sensations and images. But then there remains over the process, attitude, or act of believing. This is not merely one of the sensations and images which constitute the judgment itself. It is something additional. And it has to be explained in terms of the theory. Let us symbolize as *A, B, C,* the sensations and images which compose the judgment. And let us symbolize as *X* the believing of the judgment. Then the question is: what is *X*? It is quite clear that, on Russell's theory of mind, *X* must be some additional sensation or image. Otherwise the reduction of mind to sensations and images has not been completed.

Mr. Russell accordingly writes: "In lecture 1, we criticized the analysis of a presentation into act, content, and object. But our analysis of belief contains three very similar elements, namely, the believing, what is believed, and the objective. The objections to the act (in the case of presentations) are not valid against the believing in the case of beliefs, because *the believing is an actual experienced feeling*, not something postulated like the act.'"[7] (Italics mine.) In the first sentence of this pas-

[7] *The Analysis of Mind,* p. 233.

sage it is admitted that in addition to "what is believed," i.e. the proposition, there is the believing. The second sentence says that the objections against consciousness in the case of a mere presentation, such as "awareness of blue," do not apply to believing. The objection to consciousness in the mere awareness of a sensation was the Jamesian objection that it is not empirically verifiable. This does not apply to the believing, because that is an "actual experienced feeling." Later in the same chapter Mr. Russell writes: "There are at least three kinds of belief namely memory, expectation, and bare assent. Each of these I regard as constituted by *a certain feeling or complex of sensations*, attached to the content believed."[8] (Italics mine.)

It will be seen that although Mr. Russell denies that, in presentation, a mental act of awareness is introspectable, he admits that in belief there is something, the believing, which is actually experienced. This agrees entirely so far with the position which I would maintain. With James and Russell I deny that mere awareness is empirically verifiable, but I should hold that there is something, which Russell calls believing, which is so. The only question which remains is as to the nature of this factor. Is it something "mental" or not? What Russell says is that it is an experienced *feeling*, and again that it is "a certain feeling or complex of sensations." By using these terms regarding it he considers that he has reduced believing to sensations, i.e. to data, and so obliterated from the situation the factor of consciousness.

Now it seems to me that Mr. Russell has here thrown away his whole case, and that what remains to be discussed is almost entirely a matter of words. He has admitted that when I look at this bookcase, and believe that it *is* a bookcase, there is found in the analysis of this situation, first a number of sensuous data, A, B, C, etc., and then in addition another datum X. X is not the oblong brown sense-datum which I see. Nor does Mr. Russell mean that it is one of the sensuous data of memory or

8 *The Analysis of the Mind*, p. 250.

expectation which are (according to some writers) associated in perception with the immediate sense-datum. These would all fall into the group *A, B, C*. Thus what Mr. Russell admits is that *X* is some other sensation in addition to the sense-data immediately constituting or associated with the object itself.

I should myself agree with the whole of this, except that I think the word "sensation" is unsuitable and question-begging. For it has become a mere matter of words now. When I experience my believing there is a *something* present before me which is not part of what is believed. How to describe this something? I should attach to it the label "consciousness," and I should say that when I experience my believing I am introspecting my consciousness. But Mr. Russell, for some reason, has a prejudice against the word "consciousness." So he attaches the labels "feeling" and "sensation." Mr. Russell, in admitting the existence of believing as a factor in belief distinct from the judgment believed, has given his case away and admitted the existence of consciousness, though he obstinately refuses to call it by that name.

Whether the term sensation is suitable or not depends on how the word is defined. It may be used to cover anything whatever which is a datum. Whenever anything, of whatsoever nature, is immediately presented to consciousness I may, if I choose, call it a feeling or sensation. Thus if we suppose the mystic to have a direct intuition of God, then for him God may be in this sense an actual sensation. And we do, of course, speak of "mystical feelings." But if Mr. Russell is using the word in this wide sense, his case is worth nothing. For the stoutest believer in consciousness will admit that, when he introspects his consciousness, it is immediately presented to him and is in this sense a sensation.

But the word sensation may be used more narrowly. It may refer to the class which includes colours, sounds, smells, etc. If Mr. Russell is using the term in this narrow sense, then in calling believing a sensation what he is asserting is either that it actually *is* a colour or a smell or a taste or . . . etc., or that it is at any rate very like one of these in that it possesses in common with them the quality which makes us call them "sensuous." I do not think he is asserting the first of these alternatives. As to the second, it is very doubtful whether there actually is any quality which is common to smells, sounds, colours, etc. But if there is, I cannot myself see that believing has this quality. It seems to me very unlike a smell or a colour. I think it has nothing in common with these except this one fact, that when I introspect it, it is—like redness or a sound—immediately presented to consciousness, in short, that it is then datal. But if this is the only respect in which believing is like these other things, then we are once more using the word sensation in that wide sense which I considered in the last paragraph. And we saw that, if this is all Mr. Russell means, his case breaks down.

The criticism of Mr. Russell is ultimately the same as that of James. Both are in the same position. James was forced to admit that over and above colour patches, sounds, smells, etc., there is a unique something in the knowing situation which cannot be reduced to these data. To admit this is in reality to admit the existence of consciousness, whether you use that name or not. And whether you choose to label it a relation or a stuff does not affect this result. Likewise Russell is forced to admit that in the believing situation there is a unique element, the believing, which cannot be reduced to the colours, sounds or smells in regard to which the believing occurs. To admit this is to admit the existence of consciousness. This cannot be disguised by calling it a sensation.

Thus these attempts to deny the existence of consciousness end by admitting it, but calling it by some other name. It refuses to be suppressed.

5

WE are not concerned to combat that methodological behaviourism which, while admitting that an inward consciousness *may* exist, seeks to develop a pure science of behaviour without making use of the concept of consciousness. For this is legitimate, since it is the nature of every science to abstract and to limit itself to some more or less artificially hedged off area of experience.

On the other hand, the crude and dogmatic behaviourism which *equates* consciousness with behaviour can be dismissed in a few lines with the contempt it deserves. The following is its complete, final, and absolute refutation.

Its formula "consciousness *is* behaviour" cannot mean merely that consciousness is always accompanied by, or caused by, or otherwise intimately related to, behaviour. For this would admit that consciousness and behaviour are two *distinct* relata, and would be consistent with the very dualism which behaviourism means to deny.

Hence the formula must mean that consciousness is *identical with* behaviour, in other words that consciousness and behaviour are two words for the same thing, like motor car and automobile, or like John and Jack. Now if any *x* and *y* are in this way absolutely identical, then it is impossible to experience or even think about *x* without at the same time experiencing or thinking about *y*. For instance, you cannot see John without seeing Jack. You cannot be aware of a motor car, or think about one, without at the same time being aware of, or thinking about, an automobile. But you *can* be aware that you are conscious without being aware of any bodily movement. Therefore consciousness cannot *be* behaviour.

The reply that nevertheless bodily movement may be going on without your being aware of it of course entirely misses the point of the argument.

6

JAMES's attack upon Moore's conception of consciousness was probably in part the result of an historical accident. Moore, in writing his essay *The Refutation of Idealism*, which James had in mind when he wrote his article *Does Consciousness Exist?*, was not concerned with establishing a theory of consciousness. Though this was in fact the great contribution of his essay, it was for him a mere means to an end. The end was the criticism of idealism. It was only necessary for his immediate argument to consider *one* kind of "mental act" in order to distinguish it, as against Berkeley, from data, and so to show that data are not parts of consciousness. Unfortunately he chose as his example what he called "awareness." Worse still, he seemed to identify all consciousness with awareness. Whether he would have admitted the existence of other distinct kinds of "mental act"—such as the acts of perceiving, thinking, judging, remembering, etc., afterwards distinguished by Alexander and others—I do not know. For his purposes it was not necessary to consider the question. But the result of this procedure was that James pounced upon the awareness, showed that it is not empirically verifiable, and concluded that there is no such thing as consciousness. It would not be true to say that James never considered the so-called "higher" kinds of consciousness, or enquired whether they might not be introspectable even though awareness is not. He did. But still his attention had been concentrated—by Moore's procedure—upon awareness. It was this that he thought most about. This had been identified with consciousness. This did not exist. Search where you will in the awareness of blue and you will find nothing but the blue—no awareness. Moore himself, apparently uneasy, had admitted that it was "diaphanous," "transparent." James merely capped this by calling it "totally invisible," and awareness disappeared from the philosophical map. The rest of consciousness, if there is anything else, the thinkings, believings, rememberings, so painfully elaborated by Alexander, got scant consideration. They were explained away.

Russell, however, though himself in general agreement with the Jamesian position, perceived that this would not do. At least believing had to be taken seriously. He pointed out that though awareness is not empirically verifiable, believing is. I maintain that this position is substantially correct—at least as a starting point for a theory of consciousness.

The doctrine to be maintained here is briefly as follows. There is no such thing as awareness. Nor are there, as most British realists have believed, various different kinds of mental act, sensing, perceiving, thinking, etc. This stratification of consciousness into different layers with sharp lines of division between them—as maintained not only by Alexander but again by Professor H. H. Price in his book *Perception*—seems to me to be the great error of the British school of realism.[9] The correct doctrine is that there is only one kind of consciousness, namely *thinking*. There are, however, different grades of thinking, or rather, different *intensities* of it. The conception of the intensity of thinking will be explained in a later section (Section 15). The so-called "higher" kinds of mental act are merely higher degrees of intensity of thinking. The intensities of thinking shade off continuously into one another from the top to the bottom. There are no lines between them anywhere to be found. They do not differ in kind, but in degree. But we commonly divide this scale of intensities into convenient sections. This is what we do when we distinguish inferring from judging, judging from perceiving, perceiving from sensing. These lines are perfectly arbitrary, but they have been mistaken by most of the British realists for real divisions between kinds of mental act.

A high degree of intensity of thinking is easily introspectable. A very low degree tends to become so faint that it escapes notice altogether. When we come to merely passively being "aware" of something without thinking at all (as we say) we can find nothing to introspect. There is, in fact, some thinking going on even in such a state. For if there were not, consciousness—which is identical with thinking—would disappear altogether (as indeed happens if we drift too far). But we can only know the existence of this thinking by following thinking down the scale till it is out of sight because it has become too faint to be visible.

[9] This remark does not apply to the views of Professor Dawes Hicks.

The error of dividing consciousness into distinct kinds of mental act is avoided by Mr. Joad. According to him there is only one kind. But unfortunately he hits upon awareness as this one kind, and proceeds to interpret sensing as awareness of sensa, perception as awareness of objects, thinking as awareness of universals, etc. This is to put the emphasis on the wrong end of the scale of intensities, and to set up as the standard of consciousness the one sort of mental act which does not exist at all.[10]

According to the usual British doctrine I have first to be aware of the datum before I can think about it. Thus between the thought and the datum is interposed a kind of transparent film of awareness. According to the doctrine of cells, thought actually touches the datum and acts directly upon it. It does not rest upon a prior awareness. Awareness, in so far as it has any reality—and clearly a man who says "I am aware of the door" means something, and is referring to some real fact—is itself thinking of a very low intensity. And if a man says "I am aware of the door, but I am not thinking about it," his statement, though intelligible, is not accurate.

The rest of this chapter will be an explanation, elaboration, and defence, of the theory outlined in this section.

7

CONSCIOUSNESS is thinking, but what is thinking? I have nothing fresh to contribute in the way of analysis at this point. The traditional characterizations of thought may be accepted, so far as I am aware. The essence of thinking is the concept. To think means to apply concepts to data.

To apply concepts to a datum is also to distinguish and discriminate. For if I recognize this datum as red I thereby distinguish it from what is not red. Thus thinking is also discriminating.

[10] See his *Matter, Life, and Value*, Part I, Chap. III.

Thought is also concerned to trace similarities and dissimilarities. For this is the business of the concept. To say "this is a dog" is to trace similarities between "this" and other entities called dogs and dissimilarities between "this" and those other entities which are not dogs.

Thus thought (1) applies concepts, (2) discriminates, and (3) traces similarities and dissimilarities. But these are not three activities nor three characterizations of thought. To think is to do all these things in one undivided act which has these three aspects, each of which implies and involves the others, so that they cannot be separated.

This is the nature of the thinking which, on our theory, is identical with consciousness as such.

Concepts must be distinguished from images. Images are objective and fall under the general head of data. Concepts are subjective, in that they are the constituents of consciousness. Images may be sensuous, concepts must be entirely non-sensuous. Images may have spatial shape, size, position in imaged space. Concepts have no spatial characters of any kind (Chapter I, Section 4).

In order to comply with the customary use of words I have so far spoken of the conceptual elements of consciousness as concepts—and I shall continue to do this. However, this language is apt to give the impression that consciousness is composed of immovable and static elements—for the concept is commonly supposed to be static. Perhaps it would be better to speak of consciousness as being made up of conceptual *processes*, rather than of concepts. For the actual psychological concept is an event, a changing something. Consciousness is a stream of processes. For instance, consider what happens when a man watches a colour, say the red of the sunset, which gradually changes before his eyes. He *recognizes* various shades as they appear. And this recognition involves concepts. But the concepts are continuously changing as the colours change. And even when a man perceives a relatively unchanging object, yet his consciousness is continually changing from one aspect of it to another, and this involves a continual change of concepts.

Nor are the concepts in a man's mind at any moment divided from one another by sharp lines. They overlap and flow into one another, like the ever-changing waves on the surface of the sea.

The notion of the static concept—as when we say "the concept of man"—belongs rather to logic than to psychology. It is arrived at by taking an instantaneous cross-section of a conceptual process. The static concept is like the spatial point or the instant of time—arrived at by a kind of logical abstraction.

There would be something to be said for speaking always henceforth of conceptual processes in the mind and never of concepts. But I think the above explanation should be sufficient to guard against misunderstanding. And I shall continue to speak, as is commonly done, of concepts as actual psychological facts. It must be understood that there is no implication of the mind being composed of static thought-forms separated from one another by sharp lines of division.

8

WHAT has to be shown if we are to establish that all consciousness is thinking is (1) that in all consciousness the concept is present, and (2) that nothing else is present in any form of consciousness except the concept or the conceptual process. No one is likely to doubt that judging and inferring are thinking—though it may be urged that they are different kinds of thinking. It is, of course, contrary to the theory here to be maintained that they are different kinds of thinking, and we shall argue that the difference between them is one of degree. But since it is at any rate likely to be admitted that in some sense they are both thinking, we need not discuss this for the moment. What is likely to be doubted is that the "lower" forms of consciousness, such as sensing and perceiving, are thinking and nothing but thinking. I will therefore begin by concentrating attention upon these.

I must begin by clearing up a possible ambiguity in the word "sensing." Sensing may mean (1) a pure awareness of sensa in which there is absolutely no element of conceptualization or "interpretation." The existence of sensing in any such sense is, of course, here entirely denied. For it is merely another name for awareness. But sensing may mean (2) being conscious of a sensum as distinct from being conscious of an object. Being conscious of an object is then called perceiving. In this sense sensing certainly exists. In the first place it underlies perception. I can hardly be conscious of the table without being conscious of the brown patch which I interpret as the table. In the second place such a state of sensing may exist by itself. Thus in a dim light I see a mere patch of colour which I cannot interpret as any object at all. I have no idea what it is. And if I glimpse through a very narrow slit I may see a streak of blue and not know whether it is the sky or a blue expanse of wall or a blue anything else. I may be then merely conscious of blue. This, and not the bare conceptless awareness of a sensum, is the kind of consciousness which I call sensing.

Now it is impossible to be even thus barely conscious of blue, or of any other sensum, except by the use of concepts. For I am *recognizing* it as blue. I must discriminate blue from other colours. I must trace the similarity between this sensation and other previous blues. In short I must classify and conceptualize it. I must *think*.

To this there will be various objections made. In the first place it will be said that the concept is not consciously employed, it is not abstracted, and there is therefore no concept present in the mind. And if we attempt to speak of the concept as still submerged in sensuous material and so not yet abstracted, we shall be told that this is merely some kind of a metaphor, and that in fact there is no concept present at all, and that we have in any case no right to speak of this as thinking. I beg leave to postpone this objection till somewhat later.

It will also be said that we may *not* recognize the sensum as blue at all. I may be vaguely aware of it only as something wholly indeterminate. But this is not true. It cannot be *wholly* indeterminate, though it may perhaps be more or less so. It must have *some* character, though it may have very little. It has been suggested that we sometimes see things as coloured, but not as of any particular colour—as when we meet a man and do not notice what coloured clothes he has on. But even so, the thing is seen as coloured and so as distinguished from sound or smell. There may be these indeterminate or vague sensa. I offer no opinion on this. But even these indeterminate sensa, if they exist, must have some determinateness of character in order to be anything at all. They must be this and not that. If I am in any way aware of the something, however hazy and indefinite it may appear to me, it must, if it is to register even the faintest impression in my consciousness, have some degree of determinateness and some degree of discrimination. And if so, the concept is at work classifying, relating, discriminating. To be conscious of something without concepts it would be necessary that I should not discriminate it from anything else, that I should not perceive any character in it, that I should not trace any of its relations, even the internal relations of its parts to one another. But to be thus would simply be *not* to be conscious of it. Therefore no consciousness at all is possible without the activity of conceptualizing. Thought is present in the lowest conceivable kind of consciousness.

In order to establish that sensing is thinking what we have to show is (1) that conceptual thinking is present in it, and (2) that nothing else is present. The first point has now been made clear. The second point is easily disposed of. For what else can possibly be present in sensing other than the concepts employed in the recognition of the sensum? Of course there is the datum itself. But this is not part of the consciousness. And I am not aware what other kind of consciousness could be present unless it be "awareness." But the awareness has already been rejected as not being empirically verifiable. Hence we may conclude that there is nothing present except concepts, and that the act of employing the concepts on the datum *is* the act of sensing.

9

WE MAY now pass from sensing to perceiving. Sensing was being conscious of a sensum. Perceiving is being conscious of an object, such as a chair. What is the difference between the two? Different philosophers, of course, give different accounts of what happens when we perceive something. According to one view we pass from the immediately presented datum, or set of data, to the notion of a "physical object" to which these data belong. The physical object is apparently something other than any mere set of actual or possible data. It is a sort of substance which "has" the data. This view is entirely unempirical and foreign to the spirit of the theory of cells. The view here taken is that in perception we pass from the present datum, or set of data—which we will call A—to the belief, or the taking for granted, that in suitable circumstances certain other possible data, B, C, D, etc., will appear. To say that I perceive a chair means that I am now sensing a certain datum, say a coloured patch, and that I believe that if I move in a certain way I shall see another set of data (the back of the chair); that if I use a knife in the right way I shall see still another set of data (the inside of the chair); that if I put out my hand I shall feel a pressure patch; and so on.

We need not concern ourselves with the psychological question whether in perception we have actual images of the data B, C, D, etc. Our perception includes some sort of vague expectation that B, C, D, will or may follow. It does not matter whether there are images or not. If there are, then these images are data. And in that case one difference between sensing and perceiving is that in the latter more data are involved, i.e. not only the immediately presented datum A, but also certain additional image-data. In that case there will also be more concepts in the perceiving than in the sensing. The recognition of the sensum A involves two elements, the datum A and the concept of A—e.g. the brown patch and the concept "brown." But the perception, if there are images, will involve, first, the datum A and the concept of this datum, and secondly the image-data B, C, D, and also the concepts of B, C, D. If on the other hand it is denied that there are any actual images of B, C, D, there must at least be concepts of them. For in some sense or other we are thinking of B, C, D, in that we are anticipating that they will or may follow. In either case what we have in perception is data and concepts and nothing else. Hence perception is thinking and nothing but thinking.

To this analysis it will be objected that it is ridiculous to suppose that when I perceive a chair I have in my mind all these complicated beliefs about what will or may happen. I simply perceive and recognize a chair, and that is the end of the matter. If so, then the point I am making will be even more obvious than it was if the analysis offered in the last paragraph is accepted. For in that case what I do when I recognize the chair is simply to apply to my data the complex concept "chair." And I have then in my perception only data plus the concept "chair." Perception will then be just the same as sensing except that instead of applying some such concept as "brown" I apply this concept "chair." There will therefore be present nothing except data and concepts. So that perception will be a case of thinking.

But in my opinion this analysis is an over-simplification of the facts. In some sense or other perception does involve beliefs about possible future sense-data, even though the beliefs are not explicitly present before the mind. Their not being present before the mind means that the complex of concepts which constitutes the beliefs is not free and abstract, but is sunk or submerged in the data. In short the objection here is really the same as that which was taken against the analysis of sensing given in the last section. There it was said that in sensing red the concept "red" is not present to the mind, and that therefore there is no such concept (since where could it be if not in the mind?) and no thinking. Here it is said that since in perceiving no one is conscious of having any beliefs in his mind, there cannot be any such beliefs involved. I answer that in the one case the concepts, and in the other case the beliefs, are submerged in the data, and are not free or abstract. I shall begin the treatment of this conception of submergence in the next section.

For the moment what I claim to have shown is that, *if* the doctrine of submergence is accepted, then it is the case that both sensing and perceiving consist in conceptualizing the data, and in nothing but this; and that therefore they are both thinking.

10

THE opposite of the submergence of concepts in the data is their abstraction from the data. To abstract the concepts means to draw them out of the data, set them on one side, and make them stand by themselves naked before consciousness as pure concepts. To submerge the concepts means to let them sink back into a state of fusion with the data.

But now to this entire conception of submergence, fusion, sinking, in the data, a radical objection is taken. We shall be told either that it means nothing or is self-contradictory. In abstract thinking there are concepts present before the mind. Thus the mathematician thinks of "one" and "two." He is not thinking of red patches or pigs, but of pure numbers. No one can doubt that the thoughts of one and two are really in his mind. Such abstractions are what we mean by concepts, and nothing less than this is a concept. When I recognize a chair, what is present before my mind is a chair, that is, a particular existent, not a universal, not a concept. It is useless to say that in such a case there are concepts present but they are "submerged." If they are submerged (whatever that may mean) they are not visible to consciousness. We cannot *find* them in our minds. And if they are not visible they are not there. Or at any rate no one can possibly know that they are there, nor have any right to assert that they are. We have no right to say that thinking is going on when, if we look into our minds, we cannot find any thinking.

But we have to combine two sets of facts. First, I do not see how it can be disputed that, when we recognize or perceive, there is some sort of classification and discrimination going on. And classification and discrimination are the work of concepts. Yet on the other hand it is said that we cannot find in our minds any concepts or any process of applying them to the data. Somehow we have to harmonize these two sets of facts. The doctrine of submergence is an attempt to do so. The flat denial that in sensing and perception any concepts are at work seems to take account only of the second set of facts and conveniently to ignore the first.

Yet in the objection we are considering there would still be great force if it were the case that we can draw a sharp line between the activity of perceiving and the activity of abstract thinking. We could then say that, as we pass down the scale of consciousness from abstract thinking to mere perceiving, thinking stops entirely when we pass this line. Either we think or we don't think. And in perceiving we don't think. We do something quite different, namely, perceive.

But this is utterly untrue. Perception and abstract thinking shade off imperceptibly into one another so that it is impossible to say where one ends and the other begins. And the difference between them will be found to lie in this: that in what is called abstract thinking the degree in which the concept is drawn out and separated from the datum is very great, though the separation is not complete, while in what we call perception the degree of separation is very small, though there is still *some* separation, so that the fusion is not complete. We formerly spoke as if concepts were *either* abstract *or* submerged. What we have now to see is that here too there is no sharp line, but only different degrees. In every cognitive state there are present the two elements, concept and datum. They are never either wholly separate nor wholly fused together. The concept may be drawn out from the datum only a very little. If so we talk of perception or sensing. Or it may be drawn out to a great distance. If so we talk of abstract thought. But between the two there is a continuous series of intermediate states.

Thus it is not correct that there must be *either* abstraction *or* submergence. There are always both. But there may be more of one or more of the other. The shading off of more to less submergence is identical with the shading off of perception into abstract thought. When the concept is greatly drawn out from the datum, it stands out as it were by itself, nearly pure, so that it is *visible* as a free concept. This is what is called abstraction. When it is well nigh sunk in the datum we have perception or even some lower state of consciousness. The concept is then practically imperceptible so that when we look into our consciousness we can hardly find it. But as we descend the scale of consciousness from the highest and most abstract thinking towards perception and lower states, we can trace the concept at first standing clearly out from the datum, apart and alone, plainly visible, till it retreats further and further into the datum, fading out from view as a bird in flight away from us fades gradually out into the sky, so that there comes a time when we cannot say whether we still actually see it or not. So too there comes a time when our consciousness is of such low degree that we cannot say whether we can actually introspect any conceptual element.

According to the theory here maintained, however, the concept is never wholly drawn out from the datum. If it were we should have pure imageless thinking which—although its existence has sometimes been alleged—would be a thinking of nothing. Nor is the concept ever completely sunk in the datum. If it were, it would disappear altogether and we should be left with pure datum without any consciousness.

Neither datum nor concept (which is identical with consciousness) can exist alone.

In the following sections I will give my reasons for the doctrine here dogmatically stated.

11

PERCEPTION is supposed to be different from judgment. The kind of judgment which is nearest in the scale of consciousness to perception is the so-called judgment of perception, as when I say "this is red" or "this is a chair." It is impossible to maintain this distinction because no sharp line divides the two. They are merely slightly different degrees of one and the same process.

It is said that it is one thing to perceive a teapot, quite another to judge "this is a teapot." But consider the so-called mere perception. I see the teapot. I recognize it as a teapot. It will be admitted that this act of recognition is part of the perception. But if I recognize it as a teapot, then I *know* (or believe) that it is a teapot. But what difference is there between believing that it is a teapot and judging that it is a teapot? True, when I merely perceive the teapot I have not yet framed, with my lips or in my mind, the *words* "this is a teapot." But although I have not yet verbalized my judgment, it is still a judgment. One would surely not maintain that a thought unverbalized and the same thought verbalized constitute two different kinds of mental act. For the difference between them is not mental at all. The difference is produced by the addition of the physical act of speaking, or at most by the addition of auditory images.

Is there then no difference between a perception and a judgment of perception? I think there is. I may merely notice the teapot, recognizing it as such, but putting no particular emphasis on the recognition and the classification. They are taken for granted. This is perception. On the other hand I may underline in my consciousness that this is a *teapot*. I have then a judgment of perception whether I express it in words or not.

The fact that it is a teapot stands out as it were in high relief. It is thrust forward at me by my own act of emphasis, so that the teapotishness comes to the front leaving the other characterizations of the object, its brownness, its shininess, its shape, a mere vague mass of data in the background. Thus the concept of the teapot is separated out, or abstracted, from the data.

But clearly this process is a matter of more or less. For emphasis, on which it depends, is a matter of more or less. It is for this reason that we really do not know, in any particular case, whether we are merely perceiving or making a judgment of perception. The concept comes adrift, comes free, from the data—more or less. When it is free *enough,* we call it a judgment of perception. But it is quite arbitrary where we draw the line. Thus it is clear that judgment, which everyone will admit is thinking, shades off into perception and cannot really be distinguished from it. But if so, there is no real justification for denying that perception is thinking, though thinking of a low degree.

12

WE CAN descend lower in the scale of consciousness than perception. If we do so we shall find still the same process of shading off.

It will probably be thought that what is below perceiving is sensing. But this is a mistake. Consciousness of a sensum is not necessarily lower *in the scale of consciousness* than perceiving an object. It is the *object* of consciousness, not the consciousness itself, which is lower in sensing. For a mere sensum is more meagre than a material object. But the consciousness of a sensum may be as alert, as active, as keenly discriminative, as the consciousness of a material object. Moreover the concept may be as loose from the datum as in the case of perception. We may have a judgment of sensation corresponding to the judgment of perception. "This is red" will be such a judgment. Thus between sensing and perceiving the difference is not really in the level of consciousness. It is in the level of their objects.

When we descend in the scale of consciousness below what are ordinarily called perceiving and sensing what we reach is simply a less alert, active, and discriminative perceiving or sensing. We are then merely vaguely aware, in a more or less dreamy state, of drifting things or sensations. There is no attempt to concentrate on them, to comprehend them, to discriminate them properly, to get clear about their relations among themselves. We can pass even lower than this. We can descend into a semicomatose condition. Then there are the states of consciousness which we have when we are just going into, or coming out of, anesthesia. Finally, if we seek to press consciousness lower still, it disappears altogether.

It is quite obvious that perception shades off continuously through these dreamy states into complete unconsciousness. What then is the difference between these states? I answer that it is a difference in the degree in which the concept is drawn out from the datum. In perception the concept is more loose. As we sink lower and lower in the scale the submergence increases. In a semicomatose condition the datum is still there, and it is still vaguely recognized as the sort of datum it is. It is a colour perhaps, not a smell, though we hardly know what colour it is. We are not properly classifying nor discriminating, that is, we are hardly *thinking* at all. And because consciousness and thinking are identical, consciousness grows dim as thinking grows less. The lower we go, the more everything gets confused together, that is, the less we discriminate by means of our concepts. There is greater and greater submergence of the concept in the datum. Finally the concept sinks completely into the datum, and then consciousness disappears.

We can hypnotize ourselves by staring fixedly at a single point and shutting out all else. The reason is that by concentrating on *this*, and shutting out *that*, we cease to discriminate this from that, or even one part of this from another part. Hence the this ceases to have any definite character, even as a this. We have ceased to conceptualize even to the extent of recognizing thisness. We have ceased to think, and therefore we cease to be consciousness, proving that consciousness *is* thinking.

Where there is a continuous shading off it is arbitrary to set lines of division and to assign names for the different levels. Yet we do commonly give names to them for the sake of convenience, and to this there is no objection, provided the purely pragmatic character of the procedure is admitted. Proceeding in this way we may say that we have so far shown the continuous shading off of the following levels at the lower end of the scale of consciousness:

> Judgments of perception.
> Perception.
> Dreamy consciousness.
> Semicomatose conditions.
> Unconsciousness.

In all the levels above the unconscious the only ingredient is the concept. The differences are differences of degree in the abstraction or submergence of concepts in the datum. There is also a difference in the feeling of *activity*. The higher the consciousness the more active we feel, the lower the consciousness, the more passive we feel. This fact will be explained in a later section.

13

WE BEGAN the consideration of the scale of consciousness quite arbitrarily in the middle—at the judgment of perception. From this we worked downwards to the lowest levels. But there are also degrees of consciousness higher than judgments of perception. There is, for example, the kind of thinking which goes on in abstract scientific and mathematical reasoning. There is in general the activity of *inferring* which may be thought to be different in kind from the more simple act of judging. Hence we have now to carry the scale upwards from the judgment of perception to these higher levels. We have to show that there are no sharp lines of division but a continuous shading off, that there is nothing present in any of these cases except concept and datum, and that the difference consists always in the further and further extrusion of the concept from the datum.

First of all, perception shades off into inference in general, and it is impossible anywhere to place a sharp line of distinction between them. Perception involves a *passage* from the immediately presented datum, or the concept of it, to the concepts (or images) of other possible future data. Inference also involves a *passage* from immediately presented data to further possible data. The passage is in both cases essentially of the same character. The only difference is that in inference the concepts and the passage are more clearly extruded from the data than in perception. In perception they are still relatively embedded in the data.

In order to see how perception shades off into inference, consider the thought processes involved in the following cases. The first is a case of simple perception, with a judgment of perception. The last is a scientific inference. The second, third, and fourth, are intermediate between perception and inference, so that we scarcely know which to call them. Sometimes we may class them as perceptual judgments, sometimes as cases of reasoning. The third is "higher" in the scale of consciousness than the second, the fourth than the third. We can perceive in the whole series a gradual transition from a clear case of perception to a clear case of inference.

(1) I perceive a chair, and pass the judgment "this is a chair." That is, I perceive something and expect that it has a back, an inside, that it will resist pressure, that it will bear my weight, and so on.

(2) I perceive a chocolate box and expect to find chocolates inside it (but I may be mistaken. It may be empty).

(3) On a sunny day I see a motor car pass me with raindrops on the wind-shield. I jump to the conclusion that it must have been raining a few miles away.

(4) Being a detective, I notice that a man whom I suspect of having committed a murder at a place two hundred miles away has a speck of mud on his boots. I know from my geological studies that this particular kind of mud only exists at the locality where the murder took place. I conclude that the wearer of the boots has recently been to that place, and my suspicions are confirmed.

(5) I notice that the shadow on the moon during a lunar eclipse is curved, and I infer from this and other detailed pieces of evidence that the earth is a globe.

Where in this series does one kind of mental process called perceiving begin and quite another kind of mental process called inferring end? It seems quite clear that the cases shade off into one another. Case number 1 would be set down at once as a case of perception. Case number 4 would probably be fairly confidently set down by most people as inference, though, as I shall point out in a moment, to the skilled detective himself it might be almost a case of perception. What about cases 2 and 3? As regards case 2 we might be puzzled to say whether it is perception or inference. After some hesitation we may decide that it comes just above the level of perception and ought to be classed as reasoning. But there is absolutely no difference in principle between being led by a visual chair-datum to expect that the object will resist pressure and will have a back and being led by the chocolate box data to expect chocolates inside. If one is a case of inference so is the other. Shall we say that in the case of the chocolate box we may very likely be mistaken about the chocolates, while we cannot be mistaken in supposing that the chair has a back? It is not clear, even if we do say this, what difference it will make. We cannot differentiate between perception and reasoning by the supposed fact that perception cannot be erroneous, while reasoning can. And in any case such a differentiation would be mistaken as regards its facts, as any case of illusory perception shows. I may be wrong in my supposition that the chair has a back, for it may be a mirror image or even an hallucination.

Case number 3 is obviously the same in principle as case number 2. It may be called inference. But the realization that it is raining somewhere may come all in one flash with the perception of the car, and there may be no conscious and deliberate passage from the car-data to the idea of rain elsewhere. The whole mental process may be practically an immediate perception. In case number 4 the passage from the perceiving of the mud on the boot to the idea of the recent presence of the wearer at the locality of the murder would be for most people a tedious and hazardous piece of reasoning. But it is possible that to the experienced detective it might come in a flash as an almost immediate perception. Case number 5 would probably always be an inference with human beings. But a superhuman astronomer might regard it as a case of perception.

Thus there is no difference in principle between perception and reasoning. The one shades off into the other. The difference seems only to consist in whether the passage is made swiftly, easily, and more or less unconsciously, "in a flash," or whether it is made slowly, with deliberate effort, and in the full light of consciousness. But this comes in the end to the same as saying that the difference is in the degree of submergence or abstractness of the concepts. Where the passage is practically immediate, the concepts involved are not specifically thought of as standing out from the data. There is practically no separation between them. Concepts and data come to us in a single fused whole. We then speak of perception. This is also what is meant when it is said that a man has a "flair" for a certain kind of mental activity. What for us would be a laborious process of inference is for him an immediate intuition or perception. The facts regarding the so-called intuitive type of mathematician are to be viewed in the same way. If we remember that what to one person is a piece of reasoning to another is a direct perception, there should be no mystery about this. Thus the only difference between inference and perception is that in the former the concepts are drawn out from the datum further than in the case of the latter. And this is in any case a matter of degree, so that we find intermediate types of mental activity.

We may now perhaps complete the scale of consciousness, the lower degrees of which were indicated in the previous section. The divisions are, of course, arbitrary, but the following levels may be suggested:

> Abstract reasoning.
> Everyday common-sense inferences.
> Judgments other than perceptual.
> Perceptual judgments.
> Perception.
> Dreamy consciousness.
> Semicomatose conditions.
> Unconsciousness.

All these states, except unconsciousness, consist solely in thinking, i.e. in concepts. There is no other kind of mental act save thinking. From one end of the scale to the other the difference is only one of the degree of abstractness on the one side or fusion with the datum on the other. The antithesis between the abstracted and the unabstracted concept is also the antithesis between the active and the passive, between the more intense and the less intense consciousness. And finally it is identical with the antithesis between the universal and the particular. These further points will be explained in later sections.

14

It will be said that the notion of a "submerged" concept is nothing but a metaphor. Worse than this, it is almost a self-contradictory expression. It is like "unconscious thinking." How can there be an unconsciousness kind of consciousness? A submerged concept is a similar contradiction, or perhaps it is really the very same contradictory idea camouflaging itself now under a new lot of words. To think in concepts is to have free or abstract concepts present in my mental processes, as when I talk in geometry about circles and triangles, knowing very well that these are pure abstractions. If the concept is not present as an abstraction, it is not present in consciousness at all. How can I be using concepts if I do not know that I am using them, and if I cannot find them in my consciousness when I look for them?

Now the statement that we cannot, in such a mental process as perception, find the concepts *at all* is, I think, incorrect. What is true is that they have become only very dimly visible. But it seems to me that when I perceive a chair, the concept or concepts which are involved in this interpretation of the immediate sense-datum stand out as faintly visible above the surface of, and differentiated from, this immediate datum. The chairishness stands in relief. It ought not to be supposed that in introspection the thought introspected must either be plainly and blatantly visible or not visible at all. Why should we suppose this? Physical vision may be clear or dim. Sometimes we can scarcely be sure whether our eyes are really seeing anything or not. Should we not expect the same thing in introspective vision? And if it is true that as we descend the scale of consciousness the concept gradually sinks into the datum, this is just what we should expect to find. I have previously suggested a comparison which is helpful. We watch a bird fly away from us into the blue of the sky. It fades out gradually. There comes a time when we can hardly tell whether we still see it or not. It will be useless to say that it either is present in our visual consciousness or it is not. This "either—or" is too clear cut to fit the facts. So it is with consciousness. As we pass down the scale from abstract thinking towards unconsciousness, the concepts grow less and less visible, fading out gradually because they are sinking further and further into the datum. This is why the "higher" states of consciousness are more easily introspectable than the "lower."

But in spite of these considerations I have to admit the charges made against the doctrine of submergence. "Submerged" is certainly a metaphor. (But so, the critic should remember, is "abstract" without which perhaps it is difficult for him to get on himself. For "abstract" means "drawn out of," whereas "submerged," after all, only means "not drawn out of.") To speak of concepts as "loose," "free," "extruded," "standing out," "fused," "sunk into" the datum—all this is undoubtedly metaphorical talk. And perhaps even there is at least a verbal contradiction in speaking of submerged concepts, since this seems to imply that the concepts do not appear *as* concepts.

I can only say that if my language is metaphorical and even verbally self-contradictory, it is anyhow an attempt to describe in words experiences which we actually do have. The experience is *there*. There is *something* in conscious experience which the words "submerged concepts" attempt to express. It may be that my attempt to describe this something is vague, halting, metaphorical, even self-contradictory. That is the fault of my language, and does not show that the experience which I am trying to express in words is not a reality. If anyone can present me with a better set of terms, I will gladly adopt it. What my critic is really doing is to object to my terminology and to find purely verbal contradictions in what I say. All of which does nothing to disprove the *facts* which I am—perhaps blunderingly—trying to communicate to the reader. What the critic ought to do is to teach me a better language. If he cannot himself invent a better set of terms than mine, then he ought to be silent.

When a critic says "On page so and so I find the statement '*S* is *P*,' but when I turn over the page I read '*S* is not *P*,'" and when he supposes that by this means he has disposed of a system of philosophy, we can as a rule feel it probable that we have to do with a very shallow critic. Perhaps in the end many systems of thought are vitiated by real internal self-contradictions, but these are not as a rule to be found by pecking here and there at the words. They lie deeper, and require a deeper search before they can be laid bare. The superficial contradictions which are so easily caught at by critics anxious to find something to say are more often due to failure in the power of expression.

Thus we are often told that "unconscious thinking" is a self-contradiction, since it amounts to unconscious consciousness. Without wishing to defend all the eccentricities of those who talk about the unconscious, I would defend them against the view that this verbal inconsistency disposes of their entire conception. Undoubtedly there is contradiction in the words. But equally undoubtedly there is *something* in our experience which those who use this language are trying to point to. And if there is any contradiction in the expression "submerged concepts," I can only offer the same defence.

15

THE cell is an indivisible concrete unit tending towards two potential poles. The cognitive end of the cell is directed towards one pole, the datal end towards the other. The poles themselves, however, are only potentials. That is to say, they are limits of possibility never reached—except by the collapse of the cell into nonentity. The momentary cell—by which I mean the cell at some one moment in its own internal private time—lies always somewhere between the two poles. Its position between them varies from moment to moment. If it should actually reach the datal pole, its condition would then be pure datum without consciousness, and this is an impossible abstraction. If it should actually reach the cognitive pole, then its condition would be pure imageless thought, which is the opposite abstraction. This abstraction too cannot exist. The first abstraction is the possibility suggested by the notion of pure awareness. For since consciousness *is* thought, a pure awareness without thought would be pure mindless datum. Pure awareness without thought and pure thought without datum, that is, imageless thought, are the datal and cognitive poles respectively. They are only potential, never actual.

When the thinking within a consciousness is highly abstract the cell may be said to have moved nearer to the cognitive pole. When the thinking is of low degree, as when it is mere day-dreaming or drowsy acceptance of passing things, the cell may be said to have moved nearer to the datal pole. We know that if it reaches the datal pole, unconsciousness supervenes. (I have previously said that it cannot reach the datal pole. I mean, of course, that it cannot reach it without ceasing to exist, i.e. without consciousness and datum disappearing at the same moment.) It may be surmised that if abstract thought were strained to the pole of pure imageless thinking, i.e. if the cognitive pole were actually reached, consciousness would again disappear. I do not know whether experimental verification of this might not be possible.

It is now possible to give an account of the notion of the *activity* of consciousness; also of the related notion of its *intensity*. Consciousness is usually thought of, and rightly as we shall maintain, as an activity. Yet it is difficult to know what exactly this means. There is undoubtedly an actually experienced *feeling* of activity. And it will be noticed that this feeling increases with every increase in the abstractness of our thinking; and that it decreases as we descend the scale of consciousness. There is more sense of mental activity when we reason than when we merely perceive. When we reach such low levels as mere dreamy awareness, we feel definitely inactive. The datum itself, we should say, is pure passivity. Thus the activity of consciousness is highest as it reaches out towards the cognitive pole, lowest as it descends near the datal pole, and between the two there is a continuous shading off of the degree of activity.

But what does activity *mean*? Mere motion and mere change are not as such activities. There seems no doubt that the ex-periential source from which the notion of activity is empirically derived is the experience of *effort*.[11] Only where there is effort is there activity. And this means that activity is really confined to conscious, or at least to living, beings. If we attribute activity to the inanimate world, either we mean nothing or we are, perhaps unconsciously, adopting some sort of pan-psychistic belief that the world is really alive.

Thus to speak of consciousness as an activity is to say that being conscious involves an effort of some kind. But an effort towards what or to do what? The activity grows greater as we move towards the cognitive pole, less as we move towards the datal pole. The effort, then, is an effort to move away, or better still, to keep away, from the datal pole. If this requires an effort, this must be because the natural tendency of the cell is towards the datal pole. Consciousness tends, as it were, to slip lower and lower in the scale towards the datum, and to lapse into unconsciousness. There is, of course, no way of "explaining" this. It is simply a fact. And this fact may be expressed metaphorically by saying that the datum exerts a drag upon the cell. The activity of consciousness consists in the constant effort exerted against this drag. When a piece of elastic is pulled out, the more it is elongated the greater is the drag back and the greater the effort required to keep it at full extension. So it is with consciousness. The further the cell moves towards the cognitive pole the greater becomes the drag towards the datum, and the greater the effort to keep it in its position. It is for this reason that we feel ourselves more active in abstract thinking than in some lower state of consciousness.

The same facts may be expressed in another way. In abstract thought the concept is drawn out from the datum. It would appear as if the datum is perpetually dragging the concept back into itself. The concept draws itself out *with difficulty*. And the further it is drawn out the greater the difficulty and effort required. If effort is not exerted concept and datum fall together, the concept sinks back into the datum.

[11] See William James's essay on this subject in *Essays in Radical Empiricism*.

[178]

These expressions, of course, are metaphors. Yet they do express the actually experienced facts. They mean that we tend always to slip down the scale of consciousness towards the unconscious; and that the sense of effort which makes us speak of consciousness as an activity is the effort to counteract this tendency; and that this effort increases as we think more abstractly, decreases as we think less abstractly.

It is now possible to understand the common notion that the datum is passive. The datum is at the limit of that end of the cognitive situation which is the less active end. So long as there is consciousness at all there is activity. Even in the lowest states of our mental condition there is *some* activity. For if there were none, consciousness, which *is* this activity, would disappear. Since the datum is the limit towards which consciousness tends as its activity decreases, it is itself conceived as the zero of activity, that is, as pure passivity.

The *intensity* of consciousness means the intensity of the effort exerted against the drag of the datum. Hence the higher the consciousness, the greater is its intensity.

16

THE contrast between the cognitive pole and the datal pole is the contrast between the active and the passive. It is also the contrast between the universal and the particular. This latter contrast has now to be explained.

In itself the datum is sheer particularity. *In itself* thought is absolute universality. But in both cases the "in itself" is the mark of the non-existent. The datum in itself is literally nothing. And thought in itself is nothing. This is the reason why datum and consciousness cannot exist apart, and why the cell alone is a reality. For the cell is the *individual,* that is, a synthesis of the particularity which is the datum with the universality which is consciousness.

These statements require further elucidation. First, the datum in itself is sheer particularity. But when we try to understand this we wonder whether it is not at least an exaggeration. The datum must surely have *some* element of universality in it to start with, although it may well be true that consciousness, with its interpretations, imports into it the greater part of its universality. Thus if we take some actual sensum, say a red round patch, if we strip it of all the interpretative elements which consciousness adds to it, is not this bare sensum in itself at least red and round, and must not these universals "red" and "round" be already in it? The answer is: Yes; the red patch, *as I see it,* or when seen by me, *has* universals in it. But it is not *then* a datum in itself. It is a datum being perceived. But "datum being perceived" is a concrete situation. It is, in fact, a momentary cell at a low level of consciousness. And the universals red and round are in this concrete cell, not in the datum as such. That we cannot conceive a red round patch without these universals already in it means simply that the datum "in itself" is unthinkable, is an absolute nothing.

A parallel misunderstanding will now arise as regards consciousness. Can we really mean that consciousness *is* absolute universality? For every consciousness is a particular existent. It is *my* consciousness or *your* consciousness or some other particular consciousness. If it were said only that the universal is, in the form of concepts, *in* consciousness, this might be understood. But consciousness cannot *be* universality itself, since every consciousness is a particular existent. But the doctrine which I am maintaining is that consciousness in itself is pure universality and has no particularity in it. We find particularity in consciousness just as we find universality in the datum. The statement "but a consciousness is always a particular existent" is on all fours with the statement "but a red patch has the universal red in it" and commits precisely the same mistake. The datum *as we find it* has always an element of universality because it is then combined with consciousness. Consciousness *as we find it* is always a particular consciousness because it is then combined with the particularity of the datum. Consciousness in itself is completely universal. But this consciousness in itself has no existence, and is just as unthinkable as the datum in itself. It is a mistake to say that there exist a number of individual streams of consciousness, such as yours and mine, in the world. Consciousness is not an individual. The sole individual is the cell, which is the synthesis of universal and particular. Consciousness is merely the moment of universality in the individual cell, and is not itself an individual at all. Strictly speaking it is not true that my consciousness is distinguished from your consciousness. What we should say is that my private world as a whole is distinguished from your private world as a whole. The statement that there exist a number of individual consciousnesses should be replaced by the statement that there exist a number of individual cells.

From this point of view all the common doctrines regarding the status of the universal are to be rejected. First, there is the Platonic view that the universal is a self-subsistent entity outside the phenomenal world. This view is mistaken in that it thinks the universal to be an individual or a concrete. Platonism has struggled since its inception with the contradiction that the "form" is on the one side a pure universal and yet on the other side has always to be thought of as *this* form, distinguishable from *that* form, that is to say, as an individual entity. The only individual entity is the cell.

Next, there is the Aristotelian view that the universal is *in* the thing. By "the thing" here is meant the table or the chair. This view is correct in so far as what it asserts is that the universal is only a moment in the individual, and has no being of itself. The genuine insight of Aristotle was that what alone is real is the individual, and that the individual is the synthesis of universal and particular. But unfortunately Aristotle attributes individuality to material objects, such as chairs and tables. According to the theory of cells material objects are only complexes of data, and data are pure particulars. The universal is not in these particulars as they are in themselves. For in themselves they are nothing. Individuality cannot be attributed to anything less than the cell. Therefore since the status of the universal is correctly expressed by saying that it is *in* the individual as a moment of it, the correct doctrine is that the universal is in the cell.

A third false view is that the universal is in the mind, a mere concept which the mind, as it were, brings from the outside and applies externally to the data. In this view the mind is falsely regarded as an individual. If the mind were an individual, it could certainly have the universal in it. But the mind is not an individual; it is only the universal element in the individual cell. Hence the universal is not *in* the mind. It *is* the mind.

Another common result of the failure to understand this is that philosophers distinguish the concept from the universal. They think that the concept is the mind's idea *of* the universal. However, the concept is not an idea of the universal; it is the universal itself. Nor will it follow that, since concepts are in the mind, the universal, now identified with the concept, must be in the mind. The distinguishing of the mind from the concept is as false as the distinguishing of the concept from the universal. The mind *is* the concept. We may express the whole situation by the equation: mind = concept = universal. And if we are asked where the universal is, we must say, not that it is in the mind (since it is identical with the mind) but that it is in the cell.

The controversy whether the universal is in the object or in the mind is seen to be a pseudo-problem as soon as the point of view of the theory of cells is grasped. One side says that the universal is in the object, the other that it is in the mind. Both statements rest upon the same false assumption, namely, that mind and object are individuals. It is thought that we have here two kinds of individuals which in cognition are externally brought into contact with one another. It is then asked whether the universal is in this individual or that. Whatever answer is given there arise insoluble puzzles. If the universal is only in the mind, then how can an object be red, since red is a universal? To say that the mind imposes its universal on the object seems to mean that the mind makes the object red, and this is incredible. The same puzzle appears in another form when it is asked whether the relation of similarity between two reds is in the reds (which turns universals into particulars) or is imposed upon them by the mind (which involves the absurdity that the mind makes them similar). If on the other hand the universal is said to be only in the object, and not in the mind, then how can one and the same universal be in several different objects at once without splitting itself into parts? Is it the same identical redness which appears in two red objects? Or are there two similar rednesses? The entire assumption which gives rise to all these hair-splitting distinctions and futile questions is false. The assumption is that the mind and the object are two individuals. If this were the case, then the universal could be in them, since the universal is essentially one of the moments of individuality. We find as a fact that if we assume either that the universal is in the object or that it is in the mind, in either case we meet with insoluble enigmas. The plain conclusion is that neither the mind nor the object is an individual, since it was this assumption which led us to these absurdities. If it had been seen that both mind and object are mere abstractions, and that the cell alone is a concrete individual, these questions would never have arisen. The universal is not in the mind, because it *is* the mind. And it is not in the object, because the mind is not in the object. The universal is nowhere except in the one concrete individual, the cell.

Thus the cognitive pole is the pole of universality, the datal pole the pole of particularity. The cell may move in either direction along the line which separates them. In abstract thinking it has moved towards the pole of universality, but never reaches it. Were it to do so it would be in a state of pure imageless thinking. And since all data would have disappeared, its consciousness would be the consciousness of nothing, i.e. it would be unconsciousness. In perception the cell has moved nearer to the pole of particularity, which again it never reaches. It has already been pointed out that if it did so, it would be pure mindless datum, which would be nothing. It may now be added that it would be pure particularity, which is unthinkable.

The intuition that the universal is somehow inseparably bound up with mind has haunted human thought for the last two thousand years. Complete denial of this, as by the American neo-realists, is only made in the interests of some special theory. But the intuition has been blurred and confused by its intermixture with the contrary and erroneous belief that universals are *in* the mind as ideas of something which is an object to it. For instance, an uncertain wavering between these two conceptions explains some of the puzzling features of Hegelian Idealism. For this kind of idealism the Absolute is a system of objective universals. This is the false view. But the identification of this system of universals with the idea of a universal mind rest upon a true intuition of the identity of mind with universality. Hence the apparent self-stultification of speaking of the system of universals as mind, although it is at the same time declared to be wholly independent of consciousness.

17

No ACCOUNT has yet been given of believing, disbelieving, and doubting. They do not appear in the scale of conscious states given in Section 13 of this chapter. Can the theory of consciousness here maintained find a place for them? This question would at first sight appear to be embarrassing. For it has been admitted (Section 4) that merely to understand or contemplate a proposition is not the same as to believe it, and that some additional element is present in believing. Moreover, when we understand a proposition we are already operating with all the concepts which are concerned in the proposition. It can hardly be suggested that the additional element in believing consists in additional concepts. If then the additional element is something other than a concept, what becomes of the view that nothing is present in consciousness except concepts?

The first thing to note is that believing, disbelieving, and doubting all imply that there is some *choice* before the mind. We have a choice between perhaps several propositions. We accept one and reject the others. The one accepted is believed. Those which are rejected are disbelieved. If there is hesitation which to accept and which to reject, this state of hesitation is called doubt.

Suppose there were a man who had lived completely solitary all his life, and had thus never had the experience of finding his opinions contradicted by those of other people. Suppose further that he had never had the experience of finding himself in error; that is, his opinions had never been contradicted by other opinions of his own held at some other time. It seems probable that with such a man to understand a proposition would be the same as to believe it. For he would not be aware of the alternative possibility of accepting some other proposition. Perhaps, however, we ought not to say that he would actually believe any proposition at all. The example has the merit of bringing to our notice an ambiguity in the notion of believing. Such a man might well see the clouds and thereupon act in the expectation of rain. Could it be said that he had the *belief* that it would rain? Yes, if by believing you mean acting as if a proposition were true (a meaning which has sometimes been given to the word "believing"). But if my surmise is correct, the man would not have that peculiar feeling or attitude towards the proposition to which Mr. Russell has drawn attention, and which he thinks is a kind of sensation. Now it is believing in this latter sense which we are discussing. For it is with regard to this feeling or attitude that the question arises whether it is an additional concept or what it is.

The supposititious case of the man who had never been contradicted or found himself in error seems to show (1) that it is the experiences of error and disbelief which are prior, and not the experience of believing. We could hardly learn to believe, unless we had first learned to disbelieve. And it seems to show (2) that believing (in the sense here being discussed), like disbelieving and doubting, is a mental phenomenon which does not occur unless there is a choice between propositions, and is in some way intimately concerned with this choice. Wherever we have that emphatic feeling of believing to which Mr. Russell refers, this means that in accepting one proposition we are rejecting some other. The emphasis upon the fact that *this* is what I believe is an emphasis upon *this* as against *that*. It means that *that* is rejected.

Choice, however, is a matter of will or volition. By this I I do not mean to imply that a man can believe whatever he pleases. He may find it impossible to believe the opposite of what he does believe. But this only means that his will here is determined by causes as it is in all other cases. Nor do I mean that what determines whether a man believes or disbelieves a given proposition is merely the question of whether he likes or dislikes that proposition. What I am stating is only that in all cases of believing or disbelieving what we have is a choice of propositions and a decision by the will which proposition is to be accepted and which rejected. I am not saying anything about the *motives* which determine the will in such a case. They may as a matter of fact be various, and may or may not include mere liking or disliking for a particular belief.

Thus, what, in believing and disbelieving, is additional to the concepts involved in the proposition is a decision of the will. But we have already recognized that volition is not, as used to be supposed, a kind of mental element distinct from cognition and valuation, but rather is a matter of the valuational aspect of consciousness (Chapter II, Section 3). Valuation applies primarily to data. And to be conscious of a datum at all is *ipso facto* to value it in some way. I am not first aware of something, and then by another and distinct act of mind value it. I value it in being aware of it. Now volition is simply the predominance of one valuation over another, or the overwhelming of one by another (Chapter II, Section 3). Hence believing, which is an act of volition, contains in addition to the concept nothing save valuation. In the consideration of the scale of consciousness from abstract thought to perception and lower states we considered only the cognitive, not the valuational, aspect of consciousness. That is why believing did not appear anywhere in the scale.

But this does not so far explain how the valuation operates in this particular matter of belief and disbelief, nor in the matter of doubt. There are further details which must be made clear. In the first place, valuation attaches primarily, as already stated, to data. But it may attach also to a whole fused mass of data and concepts. When we disbelieve we disvalue the conceptual-datal complex which is the judgment we reject. Now for one reason or another we ordinarily set a positive value upon true propositions. The reason for this does not matter. They may be for us only instrumentally valuable. This will in the end mean that we value them because they may lead us to some datum or data which we value for their own sakes. Or we may value a true proposition simply for its truth-character. This truth-character of a datal-conceptual complex arouses *interest* in us. This interest is the shade of value we attach to the truth. Why we should do this is no more capable of being explained—or in need of it—than the fact that we may value a sweet datum and disvalue a bitter one. Both are alike ultimate facts of our nature. Thus to believe a proposition is in the first instance simply to value it for its truth-character. This is not inconsistent with the fact that we may dislike the truth which we nevertheless believe. For we can value it for its truth-character, while disliking it for some other reason.

18

So FAR as the positive theory of consciousness is concerned, there is only one further point to be treated. This concerns self-consciousness and the conceptions of primary and secondary data.

The possibility of introspection is, of course, essential to our view. By the empirical principle we can have no concept not rooted in some experience of data. Therefore we cannot admit the concept of consciousness into our philosophy unless consciousness is, or can be made, a datum. Hence the theory of cells, in so far as it concerns consciousness, depends upon the existence of self-consciousness and the possibility of introspection.

So far we have represented this matter to ourselves in somewhat the following way. We have distinguished between primary and secondary data. In order that we may experience consciousness, and so earn the right to introduce the concept of it into philosophy, it is necessary that it should in some way be, or become, a datum. But it cannot be a primary datum, for if so the distinction between consciousness and datum vanishes. Consciousness would then be merely one of the data— as Russell and others, who deny the existence of consciousness in the usual sense, assert that it is. On our view consciousness is first of all known to us, and is negatively defined, precisely as that which is *not* datum. Hence, since consciousness has nevertheless to become a datum, we have called it a secondary datum.

This means that we have as a first stage, or ground floor, of mind, a situation in which there is consciousness and datum, but in which consciousness itself is not a datum, i.e. there is no self-consciousness. But as a next stage we have consciousness viewing itself and so making itself a datum. Self-consciousness is thus represented as a kind of second storey of the mind. And we expressed this by saying that consciousness at this stage is a secondary datum.

It has been useful during the course of the exposition to be able to think in this way. But actually it seems to me probable that it is an over-simplification of the facts. And it must now be corrected.

It seems probable that, as a matter of fact, all consciousness from the very beginning involves self-consciousness at least in some faint degree. Certainly it is so at the adult human level of consciousness. We can hardly be angry without being at least dimly aware that we are angry, nor conscious without knowing that we are conscious. But just as consciousness has degrees of intensity, so has self-consciousness. Just as I may be either alertly perceiving and actively thinking about the objects around me or merely sleepily aware of them in a half dream, so I may be either alertly self-conscious or but hardly aware of my consciousness. The former state we call introspection, the latter we usually do not. But the difference is merely a matter of degree. It is noticeable that when our consciousness is very intense, our self-consciousness is usually very faint. When we are excitedly following the trail of some idea or concentrating with great interest on a scientific observation, we can hardly at the same time introspect the process.

I see no reason for denying that animals are self-conscious, though I think it probable that their self-consciousness is very faint. For my part I would not deny self-consciousness even to any oyster. Nevertheless there does not seem to be any reason, or any ground in the way of evidence, to be dogmatic about the matter.

If the view here suggested is correct, the metaphor of the lower and upper storeys of mind must be retracted, and the conceptions of primary and secondary data revised. Strictly speaking there is not first of all a time when consciousness is not a datum, and then later a time when it is. Consciousness and self-consciousness seem to be intertwined with one another from the beginning, and to have grown up together. Yet self-consciousness rests upon consciousness in the sense that the former is not possible without the latter, and in the sense that consciousness is prior to self-consciousness. Moreover both have degrees of intensity; and it seems likely that, in the evolution of consciousness, whether in the individual or the race, both grow in intensity at the same time. It is suggested that both begin at the same time as very faint and dim, so that they cannot really be distinguished. But when they have increased in intensity and volume to such a degree that we can make out the difference between them clearly, we begin to speak of the arrival of self-consciousness. This is perhaps why we feel inclined to deny self-consciousness to animals and very young children.

How shall we re-interpret the notions of primary and secondary data in the light of this? We shall have to say, I think, that there is a real distinction between consciousness and self-consciousness, and that although consciousness is a datum, it is not a datum for consciousness but only for self-consciousness. Thus consciousness is not a datum on the same plane with such data as colours and sounds.

19

FINALLY, I will briefly discuss some possible objections to the theory of consciousness.

To take first a very trivial objection. Our theory is that all consciousness is conceptual thinking. Animals are believed to be incapable of conceptual thinking. But they are probably conscious. Therefore consciousness cannot consist in conceptual thinking. This objection, of course, is purely verbal. By conceptual thinking the critic means abstract thinking. Of this animals are probably not capable. They do, however, perceive. But perceiving is, as we have shown, an example of thinking in the sense of that term here used. So that in this sense animals do think.

Objections to the theory of consciousness are either empirical or *a priori*. The objections of James and Russell, already considered, are empirical. They consist in saying that consciousness cannot be found in experience. There is, however, an *a priori* objection which asserts that the notion of the introspection of consciousness gives rise to an infinite regress. For if I assert that I am conscious, how can I know this? It must be because I am conscious of my consciousness. But how can I say that I have a consciousness of my consciousness?

Only, it seems, by having a consciousness of the consciousness of my consciousness. And so *ad infinitum*.

For my part I have given up being frightened when a philosopher shakes at me the bludgeon of an infinite regress. For these regresses are to be found, if we choose to look for them, in every bush. For instance, it can be argued that there cannot exist any such relation as similarity in the world. For it will involve an infinite regress. If *A* is similar to *B*, and *C* is similar to *D*, then the relation of similarity between *A* and *B* must be similar to the relation of similarity between *C* and *D*. Then this third relation of similarity will have to be similar to the previous two. This will engender a fourth similarity, and so on for ever. I do not know what the fallacy is, and I should not be much interested to learn. But I know there is similarity in the world *because it is experienced*. And no *a priori* argument whatever can possibly defeat the evidence of experience when the question is whether something exists.

I am not any more impressed by the regress of consciousnesses than I am by the regress of similarities. For it is a fact of experience that we think and also that we know we think. This might be doubted on *empirical* grounds, but we have seen that the empirical arguments of James and Russell fail. And no *a priori* argument can overthrow belief in the existence of an actual experience. When we experience a fact we ought not to conclude that it is not a fact merely because it is difficult to analyse, or because our actual attempts to analyse it have seemed to lead us into an infinite regress or some similar impasse. We ought to conclude that our analysis must be mistaken. But history shows that philosophers will nearly always deny the existence of facts which they cannot analyse. Thus space and time are facts palpably experienced. But philosophical analysis of them seemed to lead to contradictions and regresses. Philosophers promptly declared that space and time are not real entities. Now it is just as much a matter of plain experience that we are conscious and know that we are conscious as that space and time exist. And it is surely a simple reflection that it is more likely that the arguments of philosophers are mistaken than that space, time, and consciousness do not exist.

Yet it may appear unsatisfactory that this *a priori* argument should be dismissed merely because it is *a priori* and so worthless as against actual experience. It ought to be answered on its own grounds. So I will add that there are two answers to this argument. First, if this regress is a good argument against the possibility of observing consciousness, it is equally a good argument against the possibility of observing anything whatever. If a bacteriologist observes a certain bacillus under the microscope, he may be asked how he knows that it was there. He answers "because I saw it." I then say: "but how do you know that you saw it? Did you see yourself seeing it?" And then "did you see yourself seeing yourself see it?" and so on. That the dilemma in which he is placed is precisely the same as that of the observer of consciousness will perhaps be obscured by the use of the word "seeing." This may be translated into "being conscious of a visual datum." Translating in this way the conversation will run thus: "I know there was a bacillus because I was conscious of a certain visual datum." "But how do you know that you were conscious of it? Were you conscious of the consciousness of it? If not, you cannot be sure that the consciousness of the visual datum existed in you, and therefore you cannot be sure that you saw the datum."

The second answer—and this is the decisive one—will consist in pointing out that there is no objection to an infinite regress of thinkings except a purely practically one. We do think about thinking. We even think about thinking about thinking. We are doing so now when we study self-consciousness. I cannot see any reason why a man should not proceed any number of steps along this regress of thinkings except that it soon becomes tedious and futile and increasingly difficult to keep separate in one's mind the successive steps. In short the objection to an infinite regress here is the same as the objection a man might have to going on counting the cardinal numbers. Theoretically there is nothing to stop such a man going on for ever. What stops him is that he gets weary or wants his lunch or dies. We have to stop in our regress of thinkings for essentially the same kind of purely practical reasons. We may therefore admit the theoretical possibility of the infinite regress of thinkings, but deny that it constitutes any objection to our views.

Finally, an attempt may perhaps be made to use the weapon of the infinite regress against the doctrine of the theory of cells that consciousness and datum are abstract elements of the cell, each of which is impossible without the other, so that if one disappears the other must disappear also. It will be suggested that if this is so, then, on our own showing, consciousness cannot exist except when we are conscious of it. If red patches disappear when we cease to be aware of them, consciousness must disappear when we cease to introspect it. It will require self-consciousness to keep it in existence. And this self-consciousness will require another consciousness, and so on.

But this is a complete misapprehension of what the theory of cells actually holds. It maintains that consciousness and datum cannot exist without *each other*. What it says is that datum cannot exist without consciousness, and *consciousness cannot exist without datum*. It does not say that consciousness cannot exist without another consciousness. What consciousness requires to keep it in existence is not another consciousness but a datum.

Of course it is true that consciousness cannot exist *as a datum* without there being a consciousness of this datum. For no datum can exist without a consciousness of it. But this only means that for consciousness to be a datum there must be self-consciousness. And this is obviously true.

CHAPTER VI

*Value*¹

1

VALUE is the product of valuation, and valuation is an inseparable aspect of consciousness (Chapter II, Section 3). Thus value is produced by consciousness. What is valued is always the datum, or some complex of data, or some relation between data. But the data which are valued may include secondary data. That is, we may value our own conscious states. Indeed in so far as our conscious states become data, we do and must value them, since the consciousness of consciousness must include the valuation of it. For valuation is inseparable from consciousness.

Valuation is to consciousness as the colour of a beam of light is to the light. And the value of the datum is as the colour shed upon an object by the light. And as the colour of an object changes when the light changes its colour, so the value of the datum changes when the valuation of consciousness changes. Hence the same datum (or corresponding data) may have different values to different consciousnesses and to the same consciousness at different times. Indeed the value of a datum for the same consciousness does not remain constant for a single instant. It alters and flickers. What interests me at this moment interests me less or more or not at all or in some other way at the next moment. It is to this that the constant

---

¹ In my book *The Concept of Morals* I considered moral value, and in *The Meaning of Beauty* esthetic value. But neither book contained any treatment of the nature of value in general nor its place in the metaphysical scheme. The present chapter is intended to supply a brief treatment of these themes.

shifting of attention is due. I attend now to this now to that according to the way in which I am valuing the data.

This is of course to be classed as a "subjective" view of value. But it does not imply the relativity of value in the usual sense in which the term relativity is understood. The belief that the subjectivity of value implies its complete variability; and the consequent belief that, if we are to avoid chaotic relativity, the only way to do this is to make value "objective," is the fundamental mistake of modern value-theory. It is a presupposition which underlies the work of all schools alike, whether relativist or anti-relativist. I know of no modern work on value which is not vitiated by this disastrous delusion. The main work of this chapter will consist in correcting this mistake.

The problem will be to show how the subjective and shifting character of all valuation is consistent with, and can moreover give rise to, the kind of permanence and universality which our esthetic and moral natures undoubtedly demand.

Meanwhile it may be noted that those philosophers are right who assert that value is pervasive in the universe, and that nothing either does or could exist of which value is not an ingredient. For every datum in every cell in the universe possesses value at every moment of its existence in virtue of the mere fact of its being an object of consciousness. For to be conscious is *ipso facto* to reflect value on the datum. Nor is a valueless datum even a possibility. For if the valuation of the datum disappears, the consciousness disappears and with it the datum.

Not only every datum has value, but the consciousness of it also has value. For there is no consciousness without at least some degree of self-consciousness (Chapter V, Section 17). Thus since consciousness is always a datum, it must as a datum have value.

Thus nothing exists in the universe which is indifferent to value. The universe is full of value. Moreover the insight of those is correct who say that the very existence of the universe is dependent on value. Value is the dynamic force which keeps the world in being. For without it consciousness and datum—that is, the whole world—would collapse. For consciousness is inseparable from valuation. A valueless datum is an abstraction from the concreteness of the cell. Nothing less than a cell can be. And every cell is filled with value.

But these considerations do nothing of themselves in any way to secure that permanence and universality of particular values which, as we have seen, is demanded by our natures. For every consciousness and every datum might well have value in the manner explained, and yet, owing to the shifting character of valuation, the position might be as completely chaotic as the most extreme relativist affirms that it actually is. Thus some other basis than the mere fact that everything in the universe has value has to be found if the requisite stability is to be discovered.

2

ALL movement and behaviour of men and animals is the product of valuation. If I make even the slightest movement, if I raise my hand, if I flicker my eyelid, it is valuation which produces the movement. The attraction of a possible datum to which I attach a certain value draws me to pass along the track of experience in my world-pattern which I believe will bring the desired datum within my cell. Or I seek to expel from the cell a datum which I disvalue as repellant. For the movements of somatic data are followed by changes in other data. The motivation of all action and voluntary behaviour lies in the desire to alter the datal content of the cell.

Valuation is thus the dynamic force of life. Change of valuation also plays its part. I shift my position in the chair because the immediate datum has ceased to be pleasant to me and has become wearisome. Even of those things which we most consistently value highly the valuation still changes momentarily, so that we alter our course to suit the new valuation. Even of the sweetest music the musical soul tires—at least for a time. And we desire a change from the company even of those whom we love most.

3

It is probable that there are as many shades of value and valuation as there are of colour. It is very insufficient to divide all values into the pleasant and the unpleasant and to say that our actions are motivated only by the desires to seek pleasure and avoid pain. No doubt we can roughly divide our valuations into positive and negative, attractive and repulsive. But this only accounts for the direction in which we move in regard to the datum—towards it or away from it. And for many practical purposes this is perhaps all we want to know. But this is to miss the qualitative character of our valuations with its infinite varieties of shades and subtle nuances.

Perhaps the field of esthetic value is that in which the finer shades have received most notice. So that here, in consequence, we find more names for our feelings than elsewhere—though never the infinitude of names which would be required to mark all different shades. We have the graceful, the pretty, the sublime, the magnificent, the beautiful, the tragic, the comic, the funny, the ludicrous, the witty, the solemn, the grand, the grotesque, the hideous, the idyllic, the pathetic, and many others. These are in reality the names of different subjective feelings, though we project the feeling upon the datum and call *it* by these names. Great artists create new feelings and thereby new worlds of value.

Of course there must be in the data themselves some character or characters which lend themselves to the valuations we impose upon them. That valuation is the product of consciousness does not mean that we can value any datum in any manner we please. I like sugar. The quality of "niceness" is subjective, and is caused by my valuation of it. But of course there is a character in the sugar, namely the sweetness, which is what is the referent of my valuation. And I cannot like or dislike sweetness at my pleasure. I cannot attach a positive value to what is inherently painful, nor a negative value to a datum which is inherently pleasant. But this seems only to mean that the valuations of consciousness are subject to certain regularities or laws. We are so constituted that we tend always to value certain things in roughly the same way, although even then there will be a shifting, changing, ebbing and flowing of the valuational feelings. Yet it is still the valuation which makes things painful or otherwise. It does not seem to me that pain is objective in the datum—as some philosophers have held—in the same way in which colour is objective. Something is objective, some character of the sensation, say its sharp pricking character. But this is painful because we dislike it extremely. Those philosophers who have held pain to be objective seem to me to have been misled by the invariability with which all consciousness values certain data in one and the same way.

There is something in the graceful object which causes most of us to have the feeling of gracefulness, something in the sombre object which causes us to think it sombre. For the most part these objective elements will be certain colours, certain formal arrangements of parts, etc. But the feeling itself is a feeling, that is, it is subjective. It is possible that some non-human minds might feel as sombre what we feel as joyous and vice versa. Indeed variations of this kind, though perhaps not so extreme as that just mentioned, do occur in human beings. But if a majority of human beings find a certain type of data-complex pleasant or unpleasant, graceful, humorous, etc., this is because their consciousnesses all follow roughly the same regularities of valuational patterns.

4

VALUES may be instrumental or intrinsic. But this distinction is of no importance to us here. It is mentioned only to ensure that it is not thought inconsistent with the doctrine that what is valued is always the datum. Of course I may value a datum which is before me in a certain way simply because I believe it will lead to some other datum in my world-pattern which I value for its own sake. This is what is called instrumental value. Obviously it is derivative from intrinsic value, which is the fundamental concept of value theory. Hence it is only intrinsic value which is considered here.

The important distinction is between those valuations which are thought to be purely matters of personal taste and those which are not. If I dislike pepper and say "pepper is nasty," no one is likely to suggest that I am making a false judgment, and that if I knew the truth I should like pepper and say "pepper is nice." It is admitted that this is a matter of personal taste, and that here the saying *de gustibus non est disputandum* is fully applicable. But it is otherwise with moral and esthetic values. If I judge "cruelty is good" it will be claimed by most people—though not by some philosophers—that this is a false moral judgment. And if I admire cruelty it will be felt by most that I *ought* rather to abhor it. Again in matters esthetic it is believed that some works of art are really better than others, and therefore that we may make false esthetic judgments if we fail to see this "really better" character. And it is felt that we *ought* to admire such and such a painter, and that if we do not do so we exhibit "bad" or false taste. There are believed to be both moral and esthetic norms.

It will be convenient to have terms by which to express this distinction, or alleged distinction—for we have not yet decided whether it is a genuine distinction or not. I will call those kinds of value in regard to which we think there can be true and false value-judgments, and that we "ought" to value certain things in certain ways, *normative* values. And I will call all other values, those which are admitted to be matters of mere personal taste, non-normative or optional values. The normative values will be those which are moral and esthetic. Truth is sometimes given as a third normative value. But this will be found to rest upon a mistake.

There are those—an apparently increasing number—who deny the validity of the distinction. They will no doubt admit that people believe in norms, even that there are norms in the sense that rules are accepted. But these norms for them have no foundation in the nature of things. They are set up by mere custom, or even by arbitrary convention as "postulates." And they will not admit that a value judgment can be true or false.

From a practical point of view this is the most important philosophical issue now being debated in the world. It may decide the fate of civilizations. For instance, the issue between the so-called "dictator states" and the democratic states is at bottom the issue whether there are any moral norms (other than those sham ones which are merely set up by convention, custom, or what not) or not. It is not really that the dictator states have *different* norms, though an effort is made to make out that this is their true position. The truth is that they deny that norms are really binding in places where they are not set up as postulates, or where they are not the content of the customs. In short their real position is precisely that of the ethical relativist. The ethical basis upon which alone democracy can be built is the belief in the validity of moral norms and in the truth-falsity value of moral judgments. This is what the jurists call the rule of law in international affairs. It is not for nothing that Mussolini claimed to be the inventor of "political relativity."

It is almost universally believed by philosophers of all schools that the question at issue depends upon whether value is "subjective" or "objective." If value is created by the valuation of consciousness, that is by the subject, then it is thought that we must necessarily fall a prey to sheer relativism. For all values will then be like those which we attach to the tastes of sugar, pepper, or what not. One man likes sugar and another does not. And that is an end of the matter. There is no norm here because each man's private taste is the only rule for him. And this is so precisely because the values involved are admittedly subjective. No one pretends that the "niceness" is an objective quality of the sugar.

Hence those who wish to defend the distinction between normative and non-normative values almost always try to do so by asserting that the normative values are "objective." There are different views as to the nature of this objectivity according to the different metaphysical views taken of the nature of the objective world generally. According to one view, normative values are objective in the sense that they are characters of the datum. A datum is beautiful and good in the same sense as it is red and round. According to another view, value is a "subsistent" universal, or at any rate a subsistent entity, which is objective because it is in no sense a part of consciousness and would still continue to "be" even if there were no consciousnesses. According to a third view, value is rooted in the Absolute, which is considered to be the only true and genuine object.

I will not stop to criticize these various opinions. It goes without saying that each has its difficulties. The view here to be maintained is that the entire presupposition of *all* these schools, as well as of their opponents the relativists, is false. This presupposition is that if value is subjective it cannot be normative, but must in the end be optional. Or it may be stated in the form that only by making value objective can we avoid relativism. The doctrine of the philosophy of cells, on the contrary, is that all value is subjective, including normative values, but that the distinction between normative and non-normative values is yet to be maintained—with all that it implies regarding the possibility of true and false value-judgments. We have now to see how this view can be upheld.

5

THE important thing is, not that normative values should be shown to be objective, but that they should be shown to be normative. It is profoundly important to believe that when moral judgments such as "you ought to be unselfish" or "cruelty is evil" are passed, these judgments are *true*, not in any Pickwickian sense, but in the same sense as other judgments are true. It is useless to show that they are true in the sense merely that people believe them to be true; or in the sense that they correspond to some norm established by mere convention, or by custom, or by postulation; or in the sense that they truly express the emotions of those who utter them. For these things may be said of any falsehood or superstition. It may be the custom of the tribe to believe the superstition; it may express some emotion of theirs; it might even be set up as a postulate of belief. But none of these things will make it anything but a falsehood. That moral and esthetic values should be normative means—in my language at any rate—not merely that they should be in accordance with a rule or norm, but that this rule or norm should itself be a *true* principle.

Thus it is the truth of the norms which is the real point at issue. What is *not* important is the question of the *locus*—whether subject or object—in which norms have their source. *It does not matter at all whether these values are objective or subjective so long as the value-judgments to which they give rise are true.* It must be really true that men ought to be moral, and that they ought to be moved by what is great and noble in art. If it is really true that men ought to be unselfish, then this precept is not confined to those peoples who happen to believe it or who have happened to have accepted this ideal as a custom. If it is true, then it is—like any other truth—obligatory upon all men, whether they know it or not, whether they believe it or not, whatever they think or feel about it.

The supreme mistake of all theorists of value of all schools has been to suppose that the only way in which the normative character of moral and esthetic values can be validated is by showing that they are objective. This is the root fallacy of all axiology to date. It is presupposed by the relativists, who think they have only to show that value is subjective to win their case. Values must then vary with the personal tastes of the valuing subjects. And it is presupposed by all those who oppose relativism, whether they be idealists or realists; so that they spend their whole energies in trying to prove either that value is a character of the datum, or that it is a subsistent entity, or that it is part of the essential nature of the Absolute. I hold that the fundamental presupposition of all this is false, and that all this energy is misdirected. Even these idealist and realist writers themselves do not really care whether value is subjective or objective. What they *want* to prove is its normative character with the implication of the truth of value-judgments. But they think that in order to do this they must show that value is objective.

This is not only false, but it is also profoundly unfortunate. For it becomes every day more evident that all value *is* subjective. Not, I mean, that any new facts or arguments in support of this view are being discovered. The truth that a thing cannot have value unless it be *for* someone, and that this value for someone must in the end consist in the satisfaction of that someone's feelings, so that the value a thing has for a man will depend on what feelings that man has—this truth has always stared everyone in the face. It is rejected, not because there are really any facts or reasons against it, but because it is thought that to admit it would be to open the gates to relativism and to the destruction of belief in the reality of values. But an attitude of this kind always in the end gets beaten down, as the long history of religion, with its series of defeats at the hands of science, shows. That is why I say that the presupposition that values can only be normative if they are objective is not only false but very unfortunate. For it results in the appearance that the anti-relativists—since they persist in rejecting the palpable subjectivity of value—are fighting a losing battle, are the last upholders of a lost cause.

I hold that the only hope of saving this situation is to cut loose from the mistaken presuppositions of the past, to admit the subjective character of all value, but to point out that there is an alternative way in which belief in the normative character of value can be supported. How is this to be done?

6

THE answer to this question cannot be brought before the mind at a stroke. We have to pass from point to point, perhaps not at first seeing the way ahead.

The first point to notice is that although the valuations of each consciousness are constantly shifting, yet they possess a certain stability and regularity of performance. Each of us tends to recur constantly to the same valuations. This regularity of pattern gives rise to valuational dispositions. Thus although my valuation of a sweet taste is reversed if the taste "palls," yet after a while I revert to it. It is then commonly said that I "like" sugar. Another individual may have a special liking for a certain shade of purple. This does not mean that he wishes always to have this purple before his eyes. His desire for it is intermittent and variable in strength. But it recurs. He then has a valuational disposition. This disposition is not, of course, an entity. It is a law of regular recurrence. It is simply a fact that some special valuation keeps on repeating itself in an individual consciousness. It is a pattern of feeling. The disposition is not something which goes on existing in the intervals when the valuation is absent. Much less is it something which causes the valuations. It is simply a name for their periodic recurrence.

The next point to notice is that human minds are built upon a common psychological plan. In all normal human minds there must be certain common characters, and certain characters in regard to which individuals vary. This is the case, so far as I know, with all *classes*. Thus triangles have in common those elements which are included in their definition, and also some others. But they differ in respect of size, and in many other ways. The same would be true of the zoological class of leopards. Also the class of human bodies must presumably have anatomical features in common. But human

[204]

minds are a class. Presumably, therefore, they exhibit a common psychological ground-plan as well as many individual differences between themselves. Certainly this has always been believed. For instance, the possession of reason, of emotions, of the power of abstract thinking, would appear to be common characters of all normal men.

That moral and esthetic values are subjective implies that they are relative to human nature. But why does it imply that they are relative to the *differences* between human beings? Quite clearly it does not imply this. If values are based upon psychological elements in respect of which men differ, then these values will be variable. But if they are based upon elements of psychological structure which are common to the human species, then they will be invariable. The position in regard to psychological structure will be identical with the position in regard to physical structure. There is a dietetic norm which says that it is a bad thing to eat sugar. But this is based upon the diabetic condition of some men, which is not a part of the common physical structure of man as such. Therefore this rule will apply only to diabetics. It will not be universal. On the other hand there is a norm to the effect that men should eat some organic matter as food. This is based upon the common structure of all human bodies. Therefore this rule is applicable to all men in all ages and countries.

It will be the same with value-norms. I shall hold that some values are based upon mere personal or racial or other local peculiarities of psychology. These will be the non-normative or optional values. Preferences for a particular taste or a particular colour fall here. But other values are founded upon elements of human nature which are permanent and universal (I mean in the history of man so far as it has extended to date). The norms to which these values give rise will be, like the rule of diet that we must eat a certain quantity of organic matter, applicable to all men and not variable as between individuals, societies, or times. Moral and esthetic values will fall here.

Thus that values are subjective means only that they are founded upon man's psychological structure. This does not imply that they must be variable. Whether they are or not will depend upon whether the elements of structure on which they rest are a part of man's essential mental nature or are mere personal, individual, racial, or other accidental peculiarities. From this consideration alone we can see that the belief that the subjectivity of values implies their relativity to time, place, and circumstance, is much too rash and hasty.

7

YET this consideration alone does little to help us reach a satisfactory theory of normative value. It is not merely that we have still to state upon *what* essential elements of human psychology normative values are founded. The difficulty is that even if we did discover these essential elements and show that they are the bases of moral and esthetic values, this would not of itself be enough to make these values fully normative, nor to show how value-judgments can be true or false. I will postpone the question of what the actual bases of these values are in order first to consider this difficulty.

The difficulty may be made plain in the following way. If anyone thinks the taste of sugar pleasant, this arises from his valuational disposition. It means in the end simply that he *likes* sugar. But a liking for sugar is a personal peculiarity, not shared by all men. Now it is suggested that if we could find a valuational disposition which, instead of being personal to some individuals, should be common to all normal men, then we should have a value not variable but universal to all men. So we should. But unfortunately this is not what we want.

Suppose the universal valuational disposition is b. Then we shall have based upon this the universal value β. But there will be two ways in which this will differ from what we understand by a normative value. In the first place, the result will be that all men will value β in the same way. But this is not the case with moral and esthetic values. Men differ widely in regard to both. In the second place it will be a mere matter of fact that all men will value in the same way. But this again is not what we mean by a normative value. What we mean is that they *ought* to value in the same way, not that they do. But the element of "ought," essential to both moral and esthetic values, is here simply left out. What we want is a norm in the sense of a rule of how we ought to value. But what we have got is a norm in the sense of a mere regularity.

We place a high value upon Shakespearean drama. And while we would admit that even in these matters personal taste does and should count for something, yet we think this is not the whole story. We believe that Shakespeare is really in some way great, and that this *ought* to be admitted, and that any mind which simply cannot see this at all—who thinks, for example, that Shakespeare was a minor poetaster—is guilty of a *mistaken* value-judgment. But the kind of norm which has so far been suggested as based upon common valuational dispositions would not lead us to this sort of result at all. It would lead us to expect that everyone in the world would actually enjoy Shakespeare without, however, any sense that there was any right or wrong in the matter. If someone in such a world should think Shakespeare a poor poetaster, none would suggest that this was a mistaken critical judgment; or at least, if they did suggest it, they would have no right to.

8

THE key to the solution of this difficulty lies in the fact that upon a man's valuations depends his general *welfare*. I will in this section take the notion of welfare for granted as a common-sense notion, and will ask more precisely what is meant by it in the next section.

I return to the statement that a man's general welfare depends upon his valuations. It is for this reason that *his valuations may be mistaken*. The valuer always supposes that the valuation which he is making will increase his welfare. This is not an additional fact over and above the valuation. It is not a mere opinion added externally and accidentally onto the valuation. It is *part* of the valuation, and is inseparable from it. If I desire *x*, this desire includes the implicit belief that *x* will increase my welfare. But this supposal or belief may be erroneous. That which I desire may *not* increase my welfare. In that case my valuation was erroneous.

This is simply Socratic doctrine. It means what Socrates meant when he said that all men desire the good, but that they are ignorant as to what the good is. This doctrine has never been properly understood. The *words* have been understood, but not their true inwardness. It has been thought to be a paradox.

To illustrate. The sot places upon excessive drinking the highest valuation. This means, in the first place, that he has an intense physical desire for drink. But it means, secondly, that he thinks he will achieve happiness, or welfare, by his drinking. This, of course, will be disputed. He *may*, of course, think this—it will be said. But the chances are that he does not. He may think nothing about it. Or he may think the exact opposite of the belief that he will increase his welfare. You have his own evidence. May he not protest that he knows very well he is destroying his own happiness? This may be quite sincere. It may truthfully represent his settled view. He may *know* that drink brings him no happiness. But does he know this *when* he is drinking—I mean at the actual moment in which he is lifting his glass to his mouth? Or has he forgotten it then? Is he not, at that moment, really believing something else? It may be that his mind is clouded by desire so that he forgets. Or, for the moment, he deceives himself into thinking something else. This *one* extra drink, it will not make any difference to his state of happiness or misery. It cannot make matters any worse. And meanwhile it is a pleasure. So that it is really to be regarded as an asset. In one way or another the truth is obliterated from his mind, so that in the actual instant of drinking he thinks that he will add to his welfare.

The common view is that we do not do evil because we think it good. We know quite well that it is evil, and we nevertheless do it because our knowledge is overborne by the strength of our desires. Now it may be the case that it is because of our desires that we become blind to the evil of what we are doing and come to think it good. But it is because we think it good that we do it. And *when* we do it, we think it good—always and without exception.

The essence of normative value is that I ought to value a certain thing even if I actually do not do so. Why ought I? The reason is that this certain thing will contribute to my welfare. Hence if I do not value it, I am wrong and am making a mistake. For I am supposing that it will not contribute to my welfare. Again, I ought not to desire something, say the misery of an innocent fellow being. If I do desire it, the desire is evil. Why ought I not to entertain this desire, and why is it wrong? Because to desire it includes the supposal that it will increase my welfare. But this supposal is false. It may give me satisfaction, or pleasure—indeed the achievement of any desire must do so. But this satisfaction and this pleasure will not increase my welfare. All wickedness arises from mistake as to what ends will or will not achieve my good. The bad man thinks that his bad ends will yield him happiness. But they will not. This again is Socratic doctrine. Likewise the esthetically coarse man thinks that indulgence in his bad taste (which he thinks good) will add to his welfare more than possession of good taste. He is mistaken. For good art yields more return to its devotees than inferior art to its devotees. It is true that the coarse man has not at present the capacity for enjoying high art. But he has it potentially, since he is a man and since high art appeals only to that which is universally human. Therefore he could, if he would, achieve this highest enjoyment which is but latent within him. And if he did this he would achieve a higher welfare than he does at present. And because he misjudges all this, his taste is inferior. His value-judgments are erroneous. For they contain implicitly the belief that his inferior art is that which yields the better welfare.

How then are moral and esthetic values normative? First, value-judgments are true or false. For without exception they contain, deeply buried within their affective content, a proposition. The proposition is: "this, which I value, will advance my welfare"; or perhaps "this, which I value, will advance my welfare more than that." Now these propositions may be true or false. Therefore the value-judgments, of which they are the essence, will be true or false. Secondly, for this reason I *ought* to value aright. For I seek my welfare. "I ought to do thus and thus" *means* "to do thus and thus would increase my welfare." Let it not be asked whether there is any obligation on a man to seek his welfare. The question is meaningless. "All men seek the good," that is, they seek their welfares. Nor is this a mere fact. It is a necessity. It is the law of life. For every action of every man and of every beast has but this one end. And this is true if a man commits suicide, or if he burns himself to death. For all men seek the good, but they are ignorant what the good is. If a man burns himself to death he—at the instant when he commits this act—does it because he believes that therein lies his best welfare.

9

THE concept of welfare is one which is entertained by all men. Sometimes it is called the good, sometimes happiness, sometimes self-realization. Happiness is the term most used by simple unphilosophical men. It is really the best term, because it is the nearest to the soil of experience. But it has been ruined by philosophers.

It may seem surprising to suggest that all these terms mean the same thing. Are they not plainly different ideas, and do not philosophers dispute as to which is the true end? Thus if one says "it is happiness," another says, "no, it is self-realization." How then can they be the same?

I mean that the *denotation* of them all is identical. I do not say that they have the same connotation. They are all talking about the same thing, but they are saying different things about it. There is this one thing which all men seek and which all men know. Simple unphilosophical men do not analyse it at all. But when philosophers come with their analysis, their attempts to make it clear, they give different accounts of it. One then calls it self-realization, another something else.

At this point in the chapter it seems plainly my duty as a philosopher to perform an analysis. I am not going to do so, because I am not competent to do so. I cannot analyse this concept, which is the key concept of all value-theory, and on which all else depends. At this point I fail utterly. But I will add that all other philosophers have also proved incompetent, and all have utterly failed. I take comfort also from the fact that the Socrates of the *Republic,* being asked to analyse this concept, could do no more than weave it around with mystery and compare it to the sun. The notion seems to defy analysis. And one is led to wonder whether it is not after all an unanalysable ultimate which simply has to be known by direct experience like redness.

There is at least one famous modern analysis of this notion regarding which one can say with almost complete assurance that it is radically false. This is the analysis of it as an aggregate, or sum, of pleasures. That this is false can easily be demonstrated. For if it were true, the happiest man would be he with the most pleasures, and the least happy man would be he with the least pleasures. (Of course, one would have to take into account the pains also.) But this is proved false by the almost universal experience of men. The happiest men may have few and small pleasures; the unhappy man may have many and great.

On the other hand, it cannot be said that pleasures have nothing to do with happiness. They are not simply irrelevant to it. It makes a difference to a man's welfare whether he has or lacks the things and satisfactions which he wants. And yet when we add up his satisfactions, they do not make his happiness.

Perhaps the language of the emergent theory might help us here. Let us say that satisfactions or pleasures are among the conditions upon which happiness depends. (That they are its only conditions is not for a moment suggested.) Then it might be the case that happiness is an emergent from these conditions, and that like other emergents it is unanalysable. One can give the conditions on which a colour depends, for instance, the ether waves. But the colour itself is an emergent from its conditions and cannot be analysed either into them or into anything else. Or one can give the physiological conditions of life, but life is said by some to be an emergent from these conditions and not to be reducible to them. Perhaps the relation of pleasures to welfare is like this. The welfare is an emergent from the satisfactions and other conditions upon which it depends, but is unanalysable into them or into anything else. If so, then Mill and his followers made the same mistake as those who suppose that a colour can be analyzed into etheric vibrations.

If this were the case we could perhaps understand, or at least give analogies for, some of the paradoxes of the relation between pleasure and happiness. The two main paradoxes are that a large number of pleasures may result in a small happiness; and that the more intense pleasures (e.g. sex) often tend to contribute less to happiness than the fainter more elusive pleasures (e.g. many esthetic and intellectual pleasures). Do not facts of the same kind make their appearance in the physical world whenever we have to do with emergents? This will at least be true to the extent that the character and size of the emergent product seem to have no relations to the characters of its conditions. They are not an aggregate of what went before. There is no accounting for what colour will supervene upon what vibrations, nor what elements will arise out of what atomic structures. And if two vivid and intensely coloured elements give rise to a dull-coloured compound, we should perhaps have the analogue of the disappearance of intense pleasures in a drab kind of happiness.

Welfare being the end of life, all valuations are in the end judged by it as the final standard. So are all pleasures. Pleasures are "higher" or "lower" according as they contribute more or less to welfare. This is their qualitative scale. Their quantity is their intensity. Thus it comes about that a very intense pleasure, such as sex, is low in the qualitative scale. In general bodily satisfactions are comparatively "low" because, in spite of their intensity and vividness, they contribute little to happiness.

The judgment of valuations by the standard of welfare is what provides the criterion for deciding between true and false value-judgments, and is therefore the solution of the problem of norms. That a value-judgment is true means that it correctly estimates the contribution of that which is valued to welfare. This applies both to moral and esthetic judgments. In its application to esthetic values it gives rise to the expression "art for life's sake." The aim of art is to enrich life, that is, to increase welfare. And in the end if it is said "this work of art is better than that," this means that it contributes more to welfare than that does. And this judgment may be true or false. The truth or falsity of moral judgments must be treated in the same way.

It may be asked how the notion of welfare fits into the theory of cells. How does any such thing as "welfare" arise in a cell? The question needs little answer. There is consciousness and valuation in the cell. And welfare is a modification of consciousness on its feeling or valuation side. As to how such a modification arises, the question does not mean anything. We simply describe what we find.[2]

[2] A fuller discussion of the matter of this section will be found in *The Concept of Morals*, Chap. VI. But I have not there suggested that the notion of emergence applies.

WE NOW see that the normative value β is not based upon the fact that all men possess the valuation. b. For as a rule, they do not. Not all men value Beethoven or Shakespeare highly. And even if they did, this would be a mere fact, just as if it happened to be the case that all men without exception liked honey. There would be no feeling of "ought," nor of right or wrong. There would be no normative element.

The common element in human nature on which the normative value β is founded is not the valuation b. It is *the fact that human nature is universally so constructed that if men cultivated the potentiality of* b *which is in them, and achieved the value β, they would thereby contribute more to their own welfare than by not doing so.*

To give an example. If sobriety is an obligation, why is it so? The obligation does not rest upon the fact that all men value sobriety, β. The drunkard, when he is drinking, does not value it. And apart from the influence of temptation men may sincerely hold different opinions about it. The obligation rests upon the fact that, whatever men think, human beings are as a matter of fact universally so constructed that sobriety advances their welfare, while habitual drunkenness tends to destroy it. For this reason men *ought* to value sobriety and pursue it, whether they do value it or not. The truth of the moral rule is perfectly independent of what anyone thinks. And if a man, either habitually or momentarily, values drunkenness, he is mistaken. He *ought* to think otherwise. If a man passes the ethical judgment "drunkenness is a good thing," this is a false moral judgment, for it means "drunkenness contributes to welfare," and this is not the case. If there is a tribe in which habitual sottishness is generally approved, and is a custom of the tribe, this does not make it good or right for the members of that tribe—as the ethical relativist will be compelled to maintain. Not if every single man on the planet approved sottishness would it thereby become a good thing.

For in that case every single member of the human race would be deceived and would be involved in a false judgment.

Thus when the old-fashioned idealist urged that values are inherent in the nature of things, he was quite right. It is part of the nature of things that sottishness destroys human welfare. This does not mean that this value is "objective." It is subjective. For welfare is a state of the subject, not of the object. But it is nonetheless true that this subjective law is part of the nature of things. It is the fact that it is a *law* which is important. For men have to bow to the laws of the world. It is perfectly irrelevant whether they are laws of the object or laws of the subject. Not to have seen this is the great error which writers on ethics and value theory have made.

In regard to esthetic value the fundamental principle is exactly the same. Works of art are superior or inferior because they enrich life, that is, contribute to welfare, more or less. They do so, of course, in their own special way—in the esthetic, not in the moral mode—which has yet to be studied. Welfare, or the enrichment of life, is the final end by which all values, whether moral or esthetic or purely optional, are judged. But this does not prevent each from having its own kind. The esthetic and the moral, as also the merely pleasant, are subspecies of the good.

In esthetic matters, as in moral, there is a certain feeling of obligation. We feel that other people ought to agree with us in our esthetic judgments. But the feeling is far less strong in the esthetic than in the moral sphere. We indignantly condemn the bad man and demand his punishment, but we only mildly censure the man of bad taste as a philistine. The reason for the difference is that we feel that all men *can* do what is morally right, while not all men have it in their power to appreciate great art. Lack of cultivation or inherent defects of nature stand in the way. As a matter of fact this difference is merely one of degree. True, it is hardly practical to say to the esthetically coarse and uncultured man "you ought to appreciate Beethoven." But it is also not very practical to say to the morally coarse or the naturally cruel man "you ought to be a saint." Defects of education and of inborn nature stand in the way here too. But in both cases the feelings of "ought" and of condemnation, whether strong or weak, stand on the same basis and have the same kind of justification. The philistine could not *now,* in his present state, enjoy the highest art. Neither could the criminal, in his present condition of moral coarseness, enjoy the happiness which comes from the most sensitive moral feeling. Yet in both cases there is the potentiality of improvement. There is the germ which can be cultivated and made to grow. This is what justifies the word "ought," used to such men, and the condemnation we pass on them. The man ought to cultivate the germ of better things which is in him, because by doing so he will achieve greater welfare and conceivably even the highest blessedness, if not now at once, then at some later time. To say to the philistine "you ought to enjoy Beethoven" has the same sort of meaning and the same sort of justification as when one says to a man who is so muscularly weak that he cannot walk five miles "you ought to develop your muscles until you can enjoy a twenty mile walk."

The difficulty will be raised that different races have very different types of art. Indian music is very unlike European music. Yet it cannot be said that there is no bridge from one to the other. A European can learn to perceive the beauty of Indian music, and an Indian the beauty of European music. All that it is necessary to maintain is that music is, in some sense and in spite of local differences, a universal language founded upon a common element of human psychological structure. The common element is not that all men do actually value what is great in music, but that they are so constructed that for all of them it is true that from great music great joy is to be obtained, if the capacity for this joy is developed. It is for this reason that an esthetic judgment may be mistaken. To value a pot-house tune above a symphony of Beethoven involves the judgment that there is greater enrichment of life, greater joy, greater welfare, to be obtained from the former than from the latter. And this is false. It is not denied that the man who makes this judgment may *now* obtain more pleasure from the former than from the latter. But it is denied that the pleasure which he receives is really equal to that joy and enrichment of life which could be his if he would but develop his esthetic capacities. Of course, if his preference is merely the assertion that at the moment, or in some passing mood, he would enjoy the pot-house tune and not the other, this is not false and is justifiable. The best musician may himself feel this at times. It is only if his preference contains the judgment that the pot-house tune is really the better art that he commits an error.

The notion of common psychological elements must not be exaggerated. If we say that *x* is such an element, we ought not to attempt to mean that every single being born of a woman possesses this element. For there are freaks born into the world. To possess a face, hands, feet, belongs to the common anatomical structure of men. Yet there are men born without them. So there may be men born utterly destitute of those common psychological elements on which the obligatory nature of moral and esthetic values is founded. Undoubtedly the obligation to these values cannot extend to these men. A deaf man, or a tone-deaf man, cannot have an obligation to appreciate fine music. A man utterly destitute of normal human feelings cannot be expected to be moral. He can only be segregated. We must be content with the justification of the *general* validity of our values, and not expect their justification as literally universal in the logical sense. Only a pedant will want to press his case thus far.

11

THE essence of morality is summed up in the precept that we should consider the welfare of others as our own, that we should do unto them as we would that they do unto us. It would seem that every strictly *moral* obligation can be deduced from this, and that the virtue which falls entirely outside it belongs to some species of value other than the ethical. This is perhaps a mere matter of definition which need not detain us. For even if some wider definition be preferred, it will be admitted that selflessness is the root of nearly all that is really morally noble, that it is the essence of the highest morality. Hence I shall confine myself to it here.

Selflessness is a normative value, valid for all human beings as human, and not confined to Christian peoples or to any special time, race, or set of social conditions. It is the source of all that is morally great in all civilizations. It is not necessary for the value theory here being propounded that it should be *recognized* by all men as binding upon them. What has to be shown is that it actually *is* binding whether they think so or not. Thus our view would be quite compatible with a state of affairs in the world in which many societies, and perhaps a majority of humanity, failed to recognize this.

Nevertheless it seems to be true that all the great moral systems do emphasize the duty of selflessness and of having regard to the welfare of others. This moral idea is found at least, in germ, everywhere. It is the essence of Christian ethics. It is emphasized, though not so effectually, in eastern religio-moral systems. Indeed it must necessarily be recognized everywhere, at least in a minimal degree, even among savages. For human beings simply cannot live together at all if they have no regard whatever for each other. The war of all against all, pictured by Hobbes, has never been either the ideal or the fact, in any human society. It is true that some of the highest civilizations seem at the moment to have repudiated the ideal of selflessness and to be following the Nietzschean ideal of ruthless power. Yet even here in actual daily life selflessness cannot be repudiated altogether. At any rate, what the present theory is concerned to show is that those civilizations which repudiate it are, in so far as they repudiate it, mistaken in their moral valuation. And we will hazard the guess that they will some day discover that they are mistaken.

The theory of normative value is not that all men do actually have the same valuation in any matter, but that there is, in certain matters, only one *true* valuation, which therefore men ought to accept; and that in so far as they fail to accept it, they are valuing wrongly.

Regard for the welfare of others is the only true moral valuation because men—all men, except perhaps some psychological freaks—are so constituted that this alone is what leads to their own highest welfare. If anyone would attain his own highest welfare he will find it, not in selfishness and the disregard of the welfare of others, but in unselfishly caring for the welfare of others. This is not an ideal, but an empirical fact, a psychological law of our natures. It is true that it is not capable of the kind of rigorous verification and proof which we apply in the case of physical laws. But this does not make it less true. It only makes it more difficult to prove its truth. And it seems to have been verified, so far as verification is possible, by the long experience of humanity in the art of life, as focused and expressed in its greatest men, in those who may be accounted moral geniuses. It is the meaning of the concept of "dying to live" and also of the saying "seek ye first the kingdom of God and all these things shall be added unto you." That is, make the welfare of others your end, and your own welfare will be achieved. If one wants to talk in the language of self-realization, one will say that a self finds its fullest realization in the forgetting of self and in the service of others. It is open to anyone to say that such expressions are mere high-sounding phrases. It is open to anyone to disbelieve their truth. But the hypothesis here being presented is that they are as literal a statement of a psychological law of our natures as Boyle's law is a literal statement about the behaviour of gasses.

If this is so, we can see the basis of the normative character of moral value. If I accept the moral ideal of selflessness I am valuing rightly. But if I repudiate it, I am valuing wrongly. For what I then think is that by ignoring the rights

[219]

of others, by grasping whatever I can get for myself, I shall best realize myself and attain my own happiness. And in this I am making a psychological mistake. The way to my own welfare lies rather through selflessness. Thus I ought to accept the ideal of selflessness for the same reason as a man ought to accept the truth of the multiplication table or of Boyle's law. To admit this ideal is to make a judgment which is true. To deny it is to make a judgment which is false.

12

THUS if it be asked what are the common elements of human psychological structure on which the moral ideal is founded, the answer in the most general terms is that all men are so constructed that they can achieve their own highest happiness only by seeking the happiness of others. But if this be thought to be too mysterious and paradoxical a psychological law to be accepted on the mere say-so of even the greatest moral geniuses, one may tentatively offer the following further suggestions and elucidations, designed to show how this can be the case.

We can perhaps discern at least two common elements of human nature on which this law seems to be based. (And there may well be others as yet undiscerned.) The first is the character of sociality. It is simply a fact regarding the structure of human personality that the society of our fellows is necessary to our happiness. A man cannot live alone. The affection, friendship, or at least acquaintanceship of other persons is as necessary to him as is food. But this necessitates at least the minimum of morality which consists in an elementary regard by each for the welfare of the others. And it is soon discovered that this minimum of morality is not enough for the best happiness. Sociality can be cultivated. And when it is cultivated it increases welfare. In its finer shades and nuances are discovered well-springs of happiness. Thus I increase my own welfare by granting to others, not merely their bare rights, but much more also. Friendship cannot be based upon a niggardly and grudging spirit. It demands generosity. Thus by cultivating this generosity I increase the sources of my own happiness in the friendship and affection of others. A higher and higher development of sociality means a higher and higher morality and equally a greater and greater enrichment of life. And he who develops sociality in himself, who makes it a practice to benefit others, finds therein an increasing source of his own self-realization and happiness. And the man who fails to do this, who grasps whatever he can from others, is in fact missing his own happiness. He may himself think otherwise. But he is mistaken about himself. He is therefore involved in a false value-judgment. For he thinks that his selfishness is the best way to seek his own welfare, and is thereby in error. Even to the coarsest man, even to the savage, one can say this. He has failed to develop the best instrumentality of his own happiness. And if it be said that this coarse and brutal man would not in fact be happier for acting unselfishly, for his very coarseness prevents him from achieving happiness by that means, the answer is that since he is after all human, he has in him the potentiality of a higher happiness than that of which he is at present actually capable; and that if he would achieve his own welfare, he ought to develop the potentialities of his own happiness.

The second common element on which morality seems to be founded is the psychological fact that men, through sympathy, are normally made happier by the happiness of others. I do not mean merely that for benefits given they receive a return in kind. Of course this is true. But this is the basis of policy, not of morality. I am pointing to the fact that men tend to receive happiness from the happiness of others *apart from any such commercial return*. This is the basis of most acts of pure generosity, of which after all civilized life holds many. The point I am making is that the disinterested interest in the welfare of others is, or can be if developed, a supreme source of the welfare of those who practise it. It is a better road to happiness than the opposite road of selfishness. The selfish man fails to see this truth and the value-judgments implied in his selfish actions are therefore erroneous.

Here again one must repeat the usual warning. It is not alleged that all men would actually now, in their present state, increase their own happiness by this means. It is meant only that they could increase their happiness if they would develop this source of happiness.

13

THE essential nature of artistic value is incapable of being comprehended except in terms of the doctrine of the submergence of concepts in data (Chapter V, Sections 10-14).

The work of art differs in only one respect from the normal perceptual object. Esthetic experience differs in only one respect from ordinary sense-perception. Sense-perception is the relative submergence of concepts in data (Chapter V, Sections 10-13). Esthetic experience is also a case of the submergence of concepts in data. The difference between sense-perception and esthetic experience lies in the fact that in the two cases two different kinds of concept are submerged in the data.

When I sense red the concept involved is the concept "red." When I perceive a chair the concepts which are sunk in the data are such concepts as "back," "inside," "hard," "square," "brown," "heavy," "shiny," and many others of like kind. What is common to all such concepts is the fact that they are fully exemplified within an exceedingly small area of experience. Usually this area is small enough to constitute a single sense-object, or a single sense-field, or at most a few contiguous sense-fields, such as we have when we sweep our eye over a panorama of things. Thus the concept "red" is exemplified in any single red object. So are "hard," "inside," "shiny," exemplified in single objects. Concepts which are exemplified in very small areas of experience in this way may be called *perceptual concepts*. And these are the only concepts which are, in the case of sense-perception, submerged in the sensuous data.

[222]

But there are other concepts which, although they have been abstracted from experience, are abstractions from areas of experience far too large to be included in any single act of perception. They cannot be abstracted from these small areas because they are not exemplified in them. They are exemplified only in areas which far exceed that which can be included in any single specious present or any small series of such presents. They can never be found in the immediately presented data now before consciousness. To find them exemplified requires a sweep of the mind's eye over great tracts of experience spread over days, months, years, centuries, or millennia.

To take only a single example. Consider the concept of "progress." This cannot be found exemplified in any single experience, certainly not in any single act of sense-perception. It is not like "red," the exemplification of which is there now immediately in front of my eyes. To discover progress requires reflection upon experience spread out over a long period of history.

Concepts which are such that they can never be found illustrated in sense-perception may be called *cultural* or *human concepts*. For they are possible only to human beings. They arise from the reflective examination of past, present, and expected future taken together in a single view. They can only be discerned by a being who "looks before and after." The animal, though it must possess a minimal power of memory, has a consciousness which is practically tied to the immediate objects now before it. It cannot survey the whole course of its own past experience. Much less can it synthesize in a single view its own experience and the experiences of other conscious beings made known to it by testimony. Hence in animal consciousness there can be present only perceptual concepts. These others to which attention has just been drawn are possible only for human beings. Moreover they include all those thoughts about life and about the world which are the substance of civilization and culture. For that reason I call them cultural concepts.

It follows from what has been said that cultural concepts are never among those which are submerged in data in any act of normal sense-perception. Hence their normal status in human consciousness is that of abstractions.

Now the special function and activity of the artist consists in the fact that he takes these cultural concepts, plunges them into a sensuous field, and submerges them in a complex of data. *They thereupon become for the first time perceptible, visible to the eye or audible to the ear.* What was previously merely thought, merely a pale abstraction, now becomes sensuously present to us.

Of course it is not meant that the way in which the artist works is to begin with an abstraction and then deliberately to sink it in data. It is conceivable that a work of art might be produced in this way. Indeed this is perhaps what actually happens in propagandist art. The artist there begins with the idea which he wishes to communicate. And he then casts about for the sensuous material in which to encase it. But this is not, one imagines, the normal procedure of the artist. For him as a rule ideas tend always to exist from the beginning in sensuous forms. He does not put abstraction and sense together in an external way. He thinks sensuously, in pictures, in stone, in sounds, from the first. What is here being described is not the artistic procedure, but the artistic product, the work of art, however it may be produced. The work of art *is* the fusion or sinking of cultural concepts in data in such manner that they are exemplified in an immediate object in the same way as perceptual concepts are exemplified in ordinary perception.

For instance, the rock statues of the Buddha found in Ceylon and elsewhere in the East exhibit in their facial expressions a character which, if one word is sought to describe it, may be called serenity. But serenity is of two kinds. There is that kind which is below the struggle of life and that kind which is above it, because it has transcended and overcome it.

The facial expression of a cow exhibits serenity, but it is the serenity of a consciousness which has never known struggle, difficulty, disaster, sorrow. The serenity of the Buddha is that of the man who, having known all struggle, having plumbed every depth of sorrow and disaster, has conquered them. For him they are no more because they are overwhelmed by the inner light. There is here the religious and moral ideal of a whole culture. This serenity which is depicted in stone is not a single unitary concept. It is a vast conceptual complex covering an entire cultural attitude to human experience. It is the essence of an entire civilization. The sculptor has sunk this entire concept-mass into the stone. Almost a whole philosophy has now become *visible*. It has been robbed of its abstract character as a philosophy and has been turned into an object of perception.

It is in this way too that the music of an epoch contains the social consciousness of the epoch. The concepts which constitute that consciousness are sunk into the sounds and become audible there.

The delight of art lies in the fact that the abstraction is made concrete. The pale has become vivid, the invisible visible. So long as the ideas, ideals, and values of civilization remain as mere ghostly presences in the intellect, they do not fully satisfy. For men desire to see and to handle the things of which their life is made.

14

THE normative character of esthetic value rests upon two facts.

First, the capacity to submerge ideas in sensuous data is a common character of the human mind as such. It is not the peculiar possession of any age, race, or tribe.

Secondly, the ideas which the artist submerges in the sensuous medium, are invariably ideas of universal human value. They are general cultural ideas. They differ, of course, from race to race and from age to age. They constitute the reactions of man to his world in different times and places. But because man is everywhere man, and the world is everywhere the world, these reactions are of permanent meaning and value. The differences between them are differences of emphasis. Now one aspect of the truth about life is emphasized, now another. But life has all these aspects. Thus the fundamental ideas about life held in different civilizations will differ. But all will possess their own truth, and all lie open to any man in any age or place if he have but the vision for them. They are not private to the peoples or times which produced them. There are different facets of a universal truth. There never existed a civilization whose ideas of life were radically and inherently false—which is not to say that they may not have been mixed with falsehoods and superstitions. For a civilization based upon utterly false ideas would perish out of hand. Even the cultural ideas of the savage, which he embodies in his art, possess some truth, and therefore his art possesses some permanent value. Much more will this be the case with civilizations on a high level, however much they are unlike that to which we happen to belong. The Greek view of life was a true view—true then and true now. So also was the view of the Puritans. So also is the Chinese view, gracefully depicted for us of late by Mr. Lin Yu Tang. So also was any view of life ever held by any considerable body of human beings over any considerable period of time. Each view has its limitations, whereby it requires the others as its complements. There is room for all. Each adds to the world's store of riches its own special contribution. For these reasons the embodiment of human cultural ideas in art is of universal and permanent value—for all races at all times. Hence the man who is blind to these esthetic values is as much in error as any other man who makes a mistake regarding truth.

Art is superior or inferior in respect of these two criteria. The more perfect is the fusion the more perfect the art. The greater the value and truth of the conceptual complex, the greater the art. Superior art is really superior. It is not a matter of personal taste.

TRUTH is commonly placed in a class along with moral and esthetic value. It appears to me, for reasons to be given, that this is a mistake. Truth is not in itself a value at all. For this reason I shall not enter into a discussion of the nature of truth, for in my opinion this is not a part of the theory of value.

Of course we value truth. And it is indeed a precious thing. It is, however, an instrumental and not an intrinsic value. And this puts the difference between it and moral and esthetic values.

The above is *not* a statement of adherence to pragmatism or instrumentalism. I maintain a correspondence theory of truth. And I hold that pragmatism—though it has contributed important insights to modern philosophy—is as a theory of the nature of truth fundamentally false. But the question with which we are now concerned is not that of the *nature* of truth, but that of its *value*. And I hold that truth, which is the correspondence of concepts with data, is not anything which is valuable in itself or for itself, but is valuable only in that it leads to other values.

Of course, the only absolute and final value is welfare. And in a sense beauty and morality are alike only instrumental values as leading to welfare. Yet that which contributes directly and immediately to welfare may be regarded as having intrinsic value. For we may define intrinsic value as that which satisfies (i.e. yields welfare) *of itself*. Now beauty and morality do this. Man obtains enrichment of life directly from a work of art or from an unselfish act. But man does not obtain enrichment of life directly from mere truth as truth. Let us examine the sort of cases in which it is said that the value of truth for its own sake is revealed. This is usually said when no obvious utilitarian or "practical" advantage is sought. We think it valuable that a man should know history, philosophy, science, mathematics, quite apart from the help they may give in building bridges or in earning a living. And this is what we call valuing knowledge for its own sake. But in reality we are valuing the knowledge because it enlarges the mind, destroys prejudice, gets rid of arrogance and egotism. In other words it has a *moral* value. It is not the value of truth as truth which is being stressed. It is the value of truth as a means for the production of better citizens and better men. Knowledge so regarded is instrumental to ends essentially moral. Thus we think it valuable that a man should know of the vast spaces, nebulae, stellar systems, with which astronomy acquaints us. This is much better than that he should think that the earth is at the centre, and that the sun, moon, and stars are lamps revolving round it to give him light. But the reason this is valuable is that it destroys petty views and self-conceit. It makes for humility. It tends to liberate the mind from narrow views which hem it in and make it small. It aids detachment from selfish personal ends. It prevents men from attaching too great importance to small things. It makes more valuable human beings.

That it is not really the truth of the truth which we value, but something ulterior, will be made plain by the following consideration. Value in the moral and esthetic spheres admits of degrees. One thing is more beautiful than another, one act more morally good than another. And the more good or beautiful anything is the more valuable. But the situation is quite different in regard to truth. One truth is not more true than another. A proposition is either true or not true. It cannot be more or less true. (A complex of propositions may be called more or less true. But this means only that it contains a greater number of true propositions or a less number of true propositions.) If there are 2,530,704 blades of grass in my lawn, this truth is fully as true as the law of gravitation. And yet we should say that knowledge of the former truth is worthless while knowledge of the latter is of great value. This shows that what we value in the truth of the law of gravitation is not its mere truth. For the proposition "there are 2,530,704 blades of grass in my lawn" is equally true. And if it is truth *as such* that is valued, then the latter truth is as valuable as the former. The mere fact that an object is beautiful is its esthetic value. The mere fact that an act is morally good is its moral value. But the mere fact that a proposition is true does not as such make it valuable at all. It merely makes it true. Thus truth is not a value in the same sense as beauty and morality are values. The proposition about the blades of grass surely shows that one may have perfectly valueless truths. And if truth were *in itself* a value, one could not have a valueless truth.

There is, however, one kind of situation in which truth is genuinely valued for its own sake and so becomes an intrinsic value. This is the case when its value lies in the fact that it satisfies pure curiosity. If I happen to be curious to know how many blades of grass there are in my lawn, without any ulterior motive at all, then I am valuing this knowledge for its own sake. But then the value conferred upon a truth by curiosity is not a normative value. It is a mere personal value like that conferred upon sugar by the fact that I happen to like it. It is no doubt important that everyone should possess curiosity, just as it is important that everyone should enjoy some food or other. But there is no kind of obligation to be curious about any particular thing, just as there is no obligation to like any particular taste. The curiosity-value of truth is in every way on a par with preferences in foods, smells, colours and the like. These too import intrinsic values. A man wants a sweet taste for the sake of the sweet taste and not as a means to anything else. That a value is intrinsic does not place it along with beauty and morality. It is the normative character of esthetic and moral value which place them in a sub-class by themselves within the class of intrinsic values. The intrinsic value of truth as satisfaction of curiosity is not normative. And when truth appears to have a normative value—as the value of science, history, philosophy—this normative character is borrowed by it from some other source, usually a moral source.

What is the cause of the confusion which makes philosophers suppose that truth is one of the values of the same kind as beauty and morality? This seems to be due to the fact that truth is coercive. And is not coercive the same as normative? But there is a great difference. If "*S* is *P*" is true, it is obligatory to admit that it is true. But it is not obligatory to hold it of any value. As in the case of the blades of grass I may admit that it is true but regard the truth as valueless. But when we say that morality and beauty are normative what we mean is that there is an obligation to value them. This latter is what we mean by a normative value. And truth is not such.

Thus the consideration of truth does not belong to the theory of value.

CHAPTER VII

God

1

THE metaphysic of cells is not incompatible with the survival of consciousness after bodily death, though it does not in itself imply any such survival. The question is entirely one of empirical evidence, and does not fall within the purview of metaphysics. For it is not the function of metaphysics to decide upon particular matters of fact. I shall confine myself to showing that there is nothing in the theory of cells which is inconsistent with survival, and that therefore the question is open for the hearing of evidence.

The sole metaphysical condition upon which the existence and continuance of consciousness depends is the existence of data. Consciousness is not dependent upon a body, but upon data. Hence an unembodied spirit having data is a perfectly possible conception.

For the philosophy of cells the body is resolvable into a complex of data. Following Professor Price we may call these data somatic. Now somatic data stand *before* consciousness in exactly the same manner and relation as do non-somatic data. We may revert to the image of the cell as the interior of a hollow sphere (Chapter II, Section 4). The interior walls, illuminated by consciousness, are a kaleidoscope of colours. These colours are the data. They include both the somatic and the non-somatic data all of which lie side by side on the interior wall of the sphere. The essential relation of consciousness to somatic data is not any different from its relation to non-somatic data. What is essential to the existence of consciousness is the existence of *some* data, but not of data of any particular kind, such as those of the body. Thus a consciousness having before it nothing except non-somatic data, that is, an unembodied consciousness, is a perfectly possible metaphysical conception. Whether any such consciousness actually exists or not is, of course, a matter of evidence.

These statements may appear to contradict the plain evidences of physiology that consciousness is dependent upon the body. This, however, is not really the case. For the evidence of physiology is readily translatable into the language of the theory of cells, and when it is so translated it becomes plain that there is no inconsistency. What physiology establishes is not any relation between consciousness and body, but a relation between data and data. That this must be so is evident from the fact that consciousness does not appear among the objects which physiology examines. And if it does not appear in the evidence, it cannot appear in the conclusions. If it is shown that a red patch never appears except to an eye, this has no bearing upon consciousness. For the red patch is not a part of consciousness. It is a datum. The conclusion to be drawn, therefore, must concern the relation of data to the body, not the relation of consciousness to it. The contrary idea is a relic of the ancient confusion of data with consciousness, the notion that red patches and the like are parts of consciousness (Chapter V, Section 1).

We cannot see without eyes, hear without ears, smell without noses. Hence it is said that all sense-data come to us *through* the body. Thus data depend upon the body, and as consciousness depends upon data, it is argued that consciousness depends upon the body. Even if this were a correct statement, it would not follow that there can be no consciousness without a body, unless it is assumed that there are no non-sensuous data. For it is only sense-data which depends upon sense-organs. But that there are no non-sensuous data is a very big and unsafe assumption. On the other side it might be urged that even non-sensuous data are likely to be dependent for their existence upon interior states of the brain, even though not upon exterior sense-organs. This dependence of non-sensuous data upon states of the brain cannot be proved and may reasonably be doubted. For instance, Bergson has attempted to show that memory cannot be wholly dependent upon the brain. Yet all this is mere scientific speculation, and we shall be well advised to leave it alone and not rely upon it. We will therefore admit, for the sake of argument, that non-sensuous data, if any exist, have the same sort of relations to our bodies as do sensuous data. The real question is: what sort of a relation is this?

The essential thing to observe is that the relation established by physiology is not a relation between consciousness and data; it is a relation between one kind of data and another kind. What physiology establishes is that there is a constant relation in our experience between somatic and non-somatic data. It is very difficult to state this relation with any degree of accuracy. It is tempting to say simply that we never have non-somatic data without somatic data; or that non-somatic data always follow upon somatic data. But the actual relation is far less simple than this. Take for instance the correlation of colour vision with the eye. How is this to be stated in terms of data? One would like to say that the consciousness of a red non-somatic datum is always preceded by the consciousness of an eye-datum. But this is not the case. When I see the red patch, I do not see my eye, nor is there any necessity to think that I must necessarily have any kind of eye-datum at all. It would appear much more correct to say that whenever I see a colour there is the possibility that an eye-datum may appear in my cell (for instance, I may touch my eye with my finger) or in some other cell (for instance you may see my eye). This is only a constant possibility, not necessarily an actuality. For when I see the red colour it may be the case that neither I nor anyone else is perceiving my eye. But there will be an eye-datum of my eye in the world-pattern of my cell and therefore also in the world-patterns of other cells. Likewise the alleged relation of my non-sensuous data to my brain states is a relation between my non-sensuous data and certain brain data in the world pattern of the surgeon.

What all this shows is that in our experience non-somatic data are always correlated with somatic data or the possibility of them. That is, non-somatic data never occur unless there are certain body-data either in the same cell as the non-somatic data, or in some other cell, or in the world-patterns of the community of cells.

This, however, does not show that non-somatic data are universally dependent upon somatic data. It only shows that this is the case so long as we are embodied. It shows that so long as somatic data continue to appear to us, our non-somatic data stand in a constant relation to them. It does not show what would happen if somatic data disappeared from our cells altogether. When all swans which had ever been actually experienced were white, the hypothesis that there might exist black swans could not be adversely affected by pointing to the whiteness of all the swans within our experience. For the hypothesis was not that there are black swans within our experience but outside it. So here, if there is an hypothesis that there exist consciousnesses in which there is no correlation between somatic and non-somatic data, it is no argument to point to the correlation between the two kinds of data in all the consciousnesses of which we have so far had experience. We may perhaps think it reasonable to conjecture that the constant relation which we find in our experience is likely to be absolutely universal in all possible experience. But this is not a certain conclusion. It is a very unsafe generalization. And it is liable to be overthrown by any empirical evidence to the contrary.

It is a complete mistake to say that we see *with* our eyes or *through* our eyes, that we hear *with* our ears or *through* our ears. There is neither withness nor throughness. There is no physiological evidence of any such relations. To the contrary, we see and hear *with* our minds. And the seeing and hearing is not *through* anything at all. It is direct. Data are presented directly to consciousness. Nothing stands between consciousness and datum, nothing through which consciousness has to look to perceive the datum. The truth about eyes and ears which is attested by physiology is, not that we perceive objects with or through them, but that our minds only perceive objects at the same time as our minds, or some other minds, do or could perceive our eyes or ears. My mind can never be conscious of a red patch except when it, or some other mind, does or could perceive an eye.

It would seem that the common misunderstanding as to what happens when we perceive an object is something like this. Outside the body is the object. This, through light rays, causes changes in the eye. These are followed by changes in the optic nerve, which are followed by changes in the brain, which are followed by changes in the mind. Thus the mind is something sitting waiting behind the eye, behind the optic nerve, behind the brain itself. And it looks *through* all these at the remote object. It looks out of the eye as a man looks out of a window, except that in the case of perception there are more entities besides the eye, such as an optic nerve and a brain, through which it has to look. No wonder, if such a picture is drawn, we get into complete confusion about the theory of perception, and even become sceptical about the existence of a mind at all. For in the first place, although the account here given as to the series of physical changes between object and brain is doubtless correct, the last step of the series is completely misstated. The change in the brain does not cause a change in the consciousness. It causes a change in the *data* of consciousness. For instance, it may cause the existence of a red patch. But a red patch is not consciousness. This is the old confusion between consciousness and its data which Professor Moore laboured to remove (Chapter V, Section 1). In the second place the mind does not look through the optic nerve and the eye. Nor does any of the physiological evidence even suggest that it does so. It looks direct at the object, or rather, at the datum. But alongside this datum there lie other data, or there is the possibility that there may lie other data, namely the body-data of the eye, ear, brain, etc., which are equally directly presented, or presentable, to the mind.

So long as it is supposed that we only see through an eye, it is likely to be concluded that visual data are only possible by *means of* an eye. And the conception of an unembodied spirit having visual data then appears an impossibility. But the presupposition of all this—that we see through an eye—is false. There is, of course, still the fact that we never have visual data without the possibility of having eye-data. This is the case when we have bodies. But it does not follow that it would still be the case if we had no bodies.

Thus the possibility of survival after death is open. Also there is the possibility that not only non-sensuous but sense-data as well may be possible without bodies. And the same line of argument shows that there may exist minds which have never had bodies at all. Whether there is any actual evidence of all this is, of course, quite another matter.

2

To the majority of metaphysicians it has appeared an absolute necessity to make God the foundation stone of the metaphysical scheme. So that a metaphysics without God appears incomplete. It may be that this is true. But I propose to examine the proper relation of metaphysics to the idea of God.

What function has the concept of God fulfilled in the metaphysical systems of the past? There appear to me to have been three possible functions. God appeared in metaphysical systems either (1) as a satisfaction to the religious consciousness of men, or (2) as the ultimate explanation of the universe, or (3) to fill in some gap in the metaphysical system.

The suggestion that the metaphysical concept of God has as its function the satisfaction of the religious consciousness may mean either one of two things. It may mean that the religious consciousness is in any case a fact, and that metaphysics must take account of this fact and give it a place within its scheme. This is true, in so far as it is true that all facts must be exhibited as examples of metaphysical principles. No fact can be left standing in contradiction to the metaphysical hypothesis. Every fact must be at least capable of being accounted for. But it does not follow that the religious consciousness must be accounted for by introducing the concept of God. It might be explained in other ways, for example as a delusion. This might be the wrong explanation, but it would be *an* explanation. It could not then be said that the religious consciousness had been ignored, or not taken account of, or that it remained outstanding as a fact for which the metaphysical hypothesis could not account. Hence the necessity of God for metaphysics does not follow from the mere fact of the existence of the religious consciousness in the world.

The suggestion that God is necessary to metaphysics as a satisfaction of the religious consciousness may have another meaning. It may mean that it is one of the functions of metaphysics to *satisfy* religious feeling, and that this can only be done by introducing the idea of God. But this suggestion is entirely illegitimate. It is not the business of metaphysics to satisfy feelings of any kind. Its function is purely theoretical and cognitive. For instance, a complete philosophy will no doubt include an esthetic theory. It must give an account of esthetic experience. But this will be a *theory*. And it will be intended to satisfy the intellect. It will not be, or should not be, intended to satisfy artistic feelings. That is the function of art itself, not of philosophy. Likewise a metaphysical system ought not to aim at satisfying religious feelings. That is the function of religion itself. The business of philosophy is to account for religious feelings, not to satisfy them. The purpose of metaphysics is to give a theoretical account of the nature of the universe. And if the universe includes God, this fact will of course be of tremendous importance to metaphysics, and must be included in its view of the world. Hence if God is to be introduced into metaphysics, the reason must be that it is impossible to complete the metaphysical theory without Him. That is, the motive must be theoretic, not religious. Thus this first supposed necessity for the idea of God in metaphysics carries no weight. We have to consider the other two.

Both the other suggested functions of the idea of God in a philosophical system are legitimate at least in the sense that they are theoretic. Examination will show that they have none the less been misconceived. But this will not show that God must be excluded from metaphysics. On the contrary, I shall maintain that the idea of Him ought to be included, although all the reasons historically given for this in the different systems are false. That is, the relation of God to metaphysics has to be put on an entirely new basis.

3

THE second suggestion, namely that God must be introduced in order to provide an ultimate explanation of the universe, arose from very simple causes. It depended upon treating the whole universe as if it were only a part of itself. Of every part of the universe we can say that it is the effect of some other part. Will not this causal relation which we find to hold between the parts of the universe *inter se* also extend beyond the universe? As we demand to know the cause of every part of the world, ought we not likewise to demand to know the cause of the world as a whole? Is it not conceivable that there might have been no universe at all—that nothing might have existed? If so, what cause brought the universe into existence? God was suggested as the answer.

This motive influenced the theistic or one-layer philosophies, such as those of Berkeley and Leibniz.

Elementary reflection shows that the universe cannot be explained in this way. It is not that God as a first cause is open to criticism. It is that the notion of a first cause of any kind is valueless. It is illegitimate to treat the universe as part of itself. This is the final criticism. The child's question, "if God made the world, who made God?" really expresses the difficulty. To assign a cause for the world explains nothing. For the cause assigned will then be as much a mystery as that which it is supposed to explain.

Philosophers, seeing this, sought next a principle of explanation which should be self-explanatory. The process of explanations *ad infinitum* must be brought to a stop. This would be achieved if we could conceive a principle which, instead of resting upon some further principle beyond, should rest upon itself. Hence Spinoza's substance *sui causa*. Hence also Hegel's world-reason which is its own reason.

But the result of this procedure is to thrust the principle of explanation outside the world of any possible experience, and so to infringe the empirical principle. From this have arisen all two-layer systems of philosophy. For the dilemma which is created by the demand for an explanation of the whole world is plain. The principle of explanation may be in the stream of time, along with other facts. This will give rise to a one-layer philosophy. But in that case the principle of explanation will be itself merely another contingent fact demanding explanation. It will therefore be useless for explaining the world. Or else we must thrust the principle outside the world of experience altogether. This will give us a two-layer system. But the principle of explanation will be incomprehensible. For we cannot formulate an idea except in terms of experience. The objections to all two-layer systems have already been discussed (Chapter I, Section 2).

The solution of the problem lies in the abandonment of barbarous notions of explanation and the substitution of a rational view of it (Chapter I, Section 11). So long as we suppose that explanation means giving *reasons* for things we shall continue to find ourselves in these difficulties. For if we go back to a cause hoping to find in it a reason we are disappointed, since every cause is a mere fact. It is useless to hurry on to further causes hoping that at last we shall find one which is a reason. Or else abandoning this vain hope, we take refuge in something which is not a fact at all, something outside the whole world of facts. We have to realize that one part of the world may be the explanation (in the true sense) of another part, but that it is senseless to ask for the explanation of the world as a whole. We are bound to strike somewhere the "ultimate irrationality."

Explanation is not the finding of reasons. It consists merely in generalizing from the facts. It means showing that every fact is an example of some general principle (Chapter I, Section 11). These principles may sometimes be exhibited as examples of principles yet more general. But however far the process might go, even if all principles could be subsumed under one final principle, the universe in the end has to be conceived as contingent. This one principle would itself be a bare fact, incapable of further explanation. The law of gravitation is just as contingent as the particular falling of this particular stone.

The conclusion is that the demand for a final and ultimate explanation of the universe is nonsense. Not that we could not comprehend the explanation if given; but there cannot be any such explanation. This whole circle of ideas rests upon a false conception of explanation. God, therefore, cannot perform in metaphysics the function of being an ultimate explanation of things. Hence this second motive for including the concept of Him in metaphysics must be eliminated.

4

THE third motive for making metaphysics include a theory of God is that He may fill in gaps in an otherwise incomplete system. This is called bringing in God as a *deus ex machina*. This motive has operated with Berkeley, Leibniz, and many other philosophers.

It is usually considered that the introduction of God as a *deus ex machina* into a philosophy is a defect in it. This criticism is entirely wide of the mark. To the contrary, this is the only respectable reason for considering God a metaphysical necessity. For it means that there is some fact or facts about the world which render the hypothesis of God necessary. And what other motive can anyone ever have for introducing any hypothesis into philosophy, or into science either for the matter of that? For instance, *if* Berkeley had been right in supposing (1) that material objects can only be ideas in minds, and (2) that they nevertheless exist when neither men nor animals perceive them, then the existence of an undying, unsleeping mind would have followed as an absolute necessity of logic. How Berkeley could possibly be criticized for this is past comprehension. He can be criticized for introducing the above two assumptions. But *if* these are once admitted, it is ridiculous to criticize him for introducing here the idea of God.

The procedure to which objection is here mistakenly taken —that of "dragging in" an hypothesis to fill a gap in the system—is precisely the procedure of science. For instance, at one period the known facts about light left a gap in the physical world. Light was thought to be dependent on waves in space. But the air does not extend from here to the sun, and hence there was nothing to undulate. So the ether was brought in as an hypothesis to stop up the gap. This ether was a *deus ex machina*. It will be found that every hypothesis in science or even in common sense follows this procedure. I hear a noise in my ceiling. There is nothing to explain this. For the nature of ceilings as such is not noisy. So I suggest the idea of a rat. I do not directly perceive the rat, any more than we directly perceived God or the ether. The rat is "dragged in." It is a *deus ex machina*.

The criticism that it is not legitimate to introduce God to fill up a gap in a system is based either upon an anti-religious bias or upon a misapplication to philosophy of one of the methodological maxims of science. And in neither case is it justified. Evidently the objection is not to setting up an hypothesis to fill in a gap. For this is what happens whenever any hypothesis is set up about anything under the sun. Hence the objection must be to the fact that it is *God* who is used as an hypothesis. What is the objection to God? Either the critic is proceeding upon the basis of an anti-religious prejudice. Or else the criticism arises from the application to philosophy of the scientific rule that for physical facts physical causes must be sought. No doubt this maxim is justified in its proper place. We ought not to introduce God to explain a clap of thunder. We should look for electrical charges. We ought to seek out the proximate and immediate causes of things. But in science this is merely a methodological rule. It is not intended to exclude the reality of God and His causality from the universe altogether. Or if the scientist so understands it, he is far exceeding his function and his rights. Science intentionally limits its scope. It is the function of physics to deal exclusively with physical things, *and nothing else*. If there is a cause which lies outside the physical world, this is automatically excluded from the domain of physics. The methodological maxim which we are discussing is correct for science because it is not the function of science to give a complete picture of the universe. But to give such a complete picture is the very function of metaphysics. Therefore it cannot exclude the mind of God from among its hypothesis, if there is such a mind, and if that mind makes a difference to the facts of the world which metaphysics has to explain. The upshot is that this maxim of science has no application to philosophy. The supposition that a philosopher has no right to bring in God as an hypothesis is one more example of the stupid aping of science by philosophy which infects our generation; and of the unintelligent application of scientific principles to matters outside the scope of science.

5

THE proper criticism of Berkeley and Leibniz is not that they used God to stop up gaps in their systems; but that they were mistaken in supposing that there were any gaps to be stopped up. The monads of Leibniz all moved in unison, although there was no connecting link between them. Hence Leibniz thought there was a gap to be filled up here. Some principle must be introduced to explain the unison. So God was used for this purpose. This procedure would have been perfectly legitimate, *if* there had existed the gap in the system which Leibniz believed was there. But there was no such gap. It has been shown (Chapter II, Section 13) that this idea rests upon a mistaken notion of probability. The assumption behind it is that it is antecedently improbable that the monads would march in time unless there existed some special cause to ensure this effect. But there is no such antecedent improbability. This unison would be merely an instance of the orderliness of the world, comparable in all respects with causality. That the world should be of itself orderly, in this or any other way, is neither antecedently probable nor improbable. For probability and improbability are relative to some assumed or empirically discovered general background of world-character. The orderliness or disorderliness of the world are themselves such general characters of the world, whether discovered or assumed. They cannot themselves be placed against any more general world-background. Therefore they have in themselves neither probability nor improbability. Therefore there was no necessity for Leibniz to introduce a special cause—whether God or any other—to account for the unison of the monads.

In Berkeley's philosophy the gap which it was supposed to be necessary to fill up consisted in interperceptual intervals. Since material objects must exist—so he supposed—during these intervals, God must be introduced as the mind which is to support them; precisely as the ether was to support waves. This reasoning was perfectly logical once you grant Berkeley's premises. The mistake, or perhaps I should say one of the mistakes, lay in the assumption that objects must exist during interperceptual intervals. This was a mere concession to popular prejudice. If this is abandoned, there is no gap to be filled up.

Thus the correct position as regards this third motive for thinking a theory of God necessary to a system of metaphysics is this: if the system necessitates the idea of God to make it complete and self-consistent, it is legitimate, and indeed necessary, to introduce this idea. Hence the question for us is: is there any gap in the theory of cells which it is thus necessary to fill up by the hypothesis of God? And this is the same as the question: is God a necessary hypothesis for the metaphysic of cells? The answer is that He is not. There is no gap to be stopped up.

The position of the theory of cells is in all respects analogous to that of the philosophy of Leibniz. The principle of cellular correspondence is for us exactly what the harmony of the monads was for him. The only question is: is it necessary to introduce a special hypothesis to account for cellular correspondence? Now this will only be necessary if cellular correspondence is antecedently improbable. But this, as we have seen, is not the case.

But the conclusion which follows, namely that God is not a *necessary* hypothesis for the theory of cells does not at all show that God is not a perfectly *legitimate* hypothesis for it. And it is now possible to explain what I conceive to be the proper basis for the introduction of the concept of God into metaphysics. God is not a necessary concept of metaphysics in the sense that (1) He must be assumed as the foundation of the world and as ultimate principle of explanation; nor in the sense that (2) the system of metaphysics logically implies or requires His existence to complete it. But God, though not a necessary concept, may be a legitimate contingent concept. His existence cannot be *deduced* from the character of the world, as metaphysicians have usually mistakenly supposed. Nevertheless His existence may be a fact. If so, it is obvious that this tremendous fact cannot possibly be left out of the metaphysical system, if it is to give not merely a self-consistent but also an adequate picture of the world. The concept of God is necessitated—if at all—by the demand for adequacy and completeness, not by any considerations of logic or self-consistency.

All this comes to the same as saying that God is a contingent, and not a necessary, being. In this respect His nature is not different from that of this river or that mountain. The existence of the river and the mountain cannot be deduced from the nature of things. They are contingent. They exist, but they might not have existed. And if they exist, they have to be discovered empirically. It is the same with the existence of God. Hence the proper basis for the introduction of the concept of God into metaphysics is simply empirical evidence of His existence, if there is any. This can only mean the evidence of what is called religious or—what is really the same thing—mystical experience. We have accordingly to face the issue of the nature and value of this evidence.

6

KNOWLEDGE of God, if it is to be had at all, must come through direct mystical experience of God. For there is no logic by which His existence can be "proved." But the mistake is to suppose that in this respect God's existence is in a position different from that of other beings. Other people's minds, physical objects, other people's data, are all in exactly the same position as God. The existence of anything other than the immediate data of one's own personal experience is pure hypothesis, incapable of proof.

In the light of what has been said it cannot be necessary for us to examine the three famous proofs of God's existence. Yet I think it will be of some interest to glance briefly at the so-called argument from design. For this has always exercised a certain fascination for many minds. This is the only one of the three which nowadays is likely to make any appeal. Hence it may be worth while to examine it. But it should be understood that the present section is a mere digression, which can be left out without prejudice to the argument of the chapter, if the reader so desires. Properly speaking, the next step in the argument will consist in the consideration of the empirical, that is mystical, evidence for God's existence. And this will be taken up in the next section.

In discussing the teleological argument for the existence of God it is exceedingly important to distinguish the concept of "order" from that of "design." Order means regular repetition of pattern (Chapter II, Section 13). Design means adaptation of means to ends. The teleological argument is based upon the latter, not the former. But it seems that many minds confuse the two and hence suppose that the mere existence of order in the world is evidence of an ordering mind.[1] This is based upon the fallacious assumption that disorderliness is antecedently more probable than orderliness. It is then argued that since the world is orderly, this fact requires a special cause to explain it. God is postulated as the cause. This is the fallacy of special causes. The whole of this argument falls to the ground as soon as it is realized that its fundamental premiss, the antecedent improbability of an orderly world, is false.

Hence we have to ask whether there is any evidence of the existence of design in the world as distinguished from order. I propose to base my remarks upon Bergson's argument regarding the *direction* of evolution. It is true that Bergson himself does not conclude to teleology. He objects to teleology as much as to mechanism. But whatever conclusion he himself draws, his instances are actually by far the most powerful and persuasive argument for design to be found in modern philosophical literature. And I shall treat it here as such.

Mere random zig-zag motion or change, Bergson argues, can perfectly well be explained by mere "chance," which word in this context means the operation of blind mechanical laws. But where the change shows persistent direction, something more than chance has to be postulated.

There are two ways in which evolution shows direction. First, there is the definite upward trend from the lowest forms through the long line of the vertebrates to man. This inevitably suggests that nature was *aiming* at man. But a far more impressive example of direction is to be found if one examines the evolution of some bodily organ such as the eye. The eye is an enormously complex piece of mechanism. All its thousands of parts cooperate towards the one end of vision. Each of these parts must be adapted to all the others. Any slight maladjustment of one to another would ruin vision. And how has

[1] For an explicit example of the confusion of order with design see McTaggart, *The Nature of Existence*, Vol. II, Sec 499.

this been brought about? Consider four of the main parts of the optical apparatus, namely the retina, lens, cornea, and optic nerve. Adjacent parts of the animal's integument must have advanced and developed *pari passu* to form them. Thus we have four independent lines of evolution. One part has developed by a multitude of steps till it became a retina; another part became a lens; and so on. Each of these four lines taken by itself shows direction, as if it were moving towards its end. But what is most marvellous is that each of these four independent lines of development should have kept pace with the others and have cooperated with them to form the single instrument of vision. And this, of course, is a great over-simplification of the facts. What we really have is not four paths of evolution converging on one end, but many thousands. It is quite impossible to explain all this by chance. Surely it shows purpose.[2]

Undoubtedly this argument is very persuasive. It is almost impossible not to be impressed. And yet it is entirely illogical.

Consider the alleged "cooperation." In any universe whatsoever, good, bad, or indifferent, things can be considered as cooperating to reach the results which actually are reached. Suppose that a volcanic vent opens in the ground and that a mountain of a certain specific shape is piled up where formerly there was a level plain. Here is a result produced by certain forces of nature. Now every one of the atoms and molecules of which the mountain is composed must have cooperated to produce just this exact result. For if any single atom had failed to do what it did, the result would have been different. Again, even in a completely chaotic world, consisting in a blind whirl of atoms, all the atoms must cooperate to produce whatever chaotic result they do produce. Again, all the molecules of air in a whirlwind must cooperate to produce the exact state of ruin of a city that is produced.

If these examples do not prove purpose—and no one would suggest that they do—why does the cooperation of the parts to produce an eye prove it?

[2] See Bergson, *Creative Evolution*, translated by A. Mitchell, pp. 60 *ff.*

The question is unanswerable. None of the examples prove anything. But it is quite evident why we tend to *think* that the case of the eye is different from the others. It is because we think vision a *good* and *desirable* thing. When something is produced which we admire or think valuable we suppose design. Thus the cooperation of the bee and the flower to produce more flowers seems to us a case of the adaptation of means to ends because we find flowers—and perhaps bees—beautiful or desirable. We do not argue thus in the case of the volcano, the chaos, or the whirlwind which ruins our homes, because we do not think these things admirable.

Thus the whole of that part of the argument which depends upon the facts of cooperation, working together, adjustment of one thing to another, is worthless. What is really in our minds is that the existence of *good* things in the world can only be explained by supposing that they have been produced by a good mind. But this argument is only valid if we already know that things of any kind must have been produced by a mind of some kind. If we knew this, then we could argue that good things must have been made by a good mind. Thus the argument from design only has any force if we *start* from the belief that a mind has created the world. Thus it assumes its conclusion.

7

THE conclusion that the existence of God cannot be proved by any logic but only, if at all, by direct mystical evidence, is certainly in accord with the best religious thinking of the day. Religious men themselves no longer place reliance on the compulsion of external proofs. Such arguments as those used by Descartes no longer carry any weight, and the analysis of them has become an academic exercise for professors. Religious men feel that the knowledge of God must come from the witness of the spirit, that is, from direct religious experience. We must now consider, therefore, what this religious experience must be.

The answer to this question will depend upon what view we take of the nature of God. The philosophy of cells takes the view that God is a conscious personal being. And this is to be understood in an entirely literal sense. This statement will be explained in the next section. Meanwhile I take it for granted.

It has already been shown that religious experience can mean nothing except the direct consciousness of God-data, the direct apprehension of God Himself. Either the religious man is directly aware of God or there is no such thing as religious experience at all (Chapter I, Section 6). But since God is a consciousness, this experience must be the direct apprehension of God's consciousness.

There is no difference between religious experience and mystical experience except one of degree. The great mystic's vision of God—assuming that it is a reality—is self-convincing and almost blindingly vivid. The religious experience of ordinary men is wavering and dim. Yet if it is genuine religious experience at all, it must be an actual contact with the same transcendent object. For if it is not an experience of God-data, it must be an experience of introspective data or even sense-data. And in that case it is a sham religious experience (Chapter I, Section 6). The difference must lie on the side of the subject, in his clearness or dimness of apprehension, not on the side of the object.

The conclusion that mystic experience must consist in a direct apprehension of God's consciousness is by no means impossible. But if it is true, it does involve a very peculiar fact. It necessitates that although we cannot as a rule directly apprehend other minds, for instance the minds of men and animals, we can directly apprehend the mind of God. It implies that we must be able, so to speak, to introspect God's consciousness as well as our own.

So far as I can see, there is nothing impossible in this. It appears to be a mere fact that we cannot directly inspect the minds of our neighbours. And if so, the question whether we can come into direct contact with the mind of God is simply a matter of evidence. We have the evidence of the mystics that they can. If we believe their word, there is nothing more to be said.

Moreover, if telepathy is a fact, it would seem that we can sometimes inspect the thoughts of other men directly. Telepathy would then be a faint analogue of the mystic's experience of God's mind.

A difficulty may be raised that the thoughts so inspected, whether in the mind of God or in that of a neighbour, will after all be, when I inspect them, *mine* and therefore private. For privacy of data simply means being included within the personal identity of the consciousness of some cell (Chapter II, Section 7). If so, we ought to say, not that the God-data of the mystic are God's own thoughts, but that they are private data of the mystic which *correspond* to God's introspective data. The difference between the two views is, however, in practice negligible. For there is no reason to suppose that the perception of other minds will suffer from the same kind of colour and spatial perspective distortion as we find in the case of the perception of material objects. One person sees the table-top as of one shape and colour, another another. This is what, in the case of sense-perception, makes the concept of privacy of importance. There is no reason to think that the God-data of different cells will vary from one another in any such way. Hence it makes no difference whether they are conceived as private or not.

What we have so far been discussing is the *nature* of the empirical evidence for the existence of God. A decision on the *value* of this evidence can hardly be made without an elaborate examination of the literature of mysticism. And such an examination cannot be made here. But I cannot myself see any reason for discrediting the mystic's evidence except prejudice. After all the logical principles involved are entirely simple. The evidence for the existence of God is of the same *kind* as the evidence for the existence of rivers and mountains. It is simply the evidence of direct perception. It is true that mystical evidence is very inferior in certain respects to that which convinces us of the existence of material objects. For sense-data are plainly accessible to all men, and their observations upon them are easily checked and counter-checked. But God-data are only clearly apprehensible by a very few exceptional men. Nor can even these men observe and check upon their observations with one another in the same easy way as is possible between ordinary men as regards sense-data.

Shall we turn for confirmation to the normal religious experience of normal men? I see no reason to doubt that we can find some measure of confirmation here. The easiest way to explain normal religious experience is to take it at its face value, and to suppose that it is the same thing as the mystic's experience at a much lower level of development. The religious experience of normal men taken thus in bulk will lead to this conclusion. But any particular religious experience of any particular normal man is gravely open to doubt. The experiences are so dim and fragmentary that they may easily be the subject of mistake. The man may mistake his own introspective data for God-data (Chapter I, Section 6).

For these reasons it seems to me that the evidence of the great mystics, few in number, far outweighs in evidentiary value the evidence of the masses of men. They claim to possess an absolutely clear vision of an object which they plainly distinguish from their own introspective data. They feel certain of this vision. Why should we not believe what they say? After all, how do I know for certain that when I think I am seeing red I am not really seeing blue? A man of very obscure vision, half blind, seeing even sense-data vaguely and confusedly, might feel sceptical of my claims clearly to distinguish the two. I only know that the red which I see is not blue, because I am inwardly sure of the clearness of my vision, and of the immediately sensed distinctions between different data. And the mystic claims to have a similar assurance regarding his data. I cannot see any reason for discrediting what he says. I am convinced that the common tendency to be contemptuous of it is the product of a supercilious materialism and of the prejudice, stupidity, and lack of imagination which are characteristic of commonplace minds.

It is often said that the evidence on which science is based, namely sense-data, is public, whereas mystical experience is private. The distinction is falsely drawn. All experience is equally private. This same mistake has led to the extravagances of behaviouristic psychology. Introspective data are supposed to be private in a way in which sense-data are not. The only real distinction is between the kind of data which many people experience and the kinds which are experienced only by one person or a few. Now there is no inherent virtue in mere multitude. The evidence of one good witness may be worth more than that of a hundred bad ones.

If we accept the view that the mystic directly apprehends God's consciousness, we do not of course mean that he apprehends the whole of this consciousness. Presumably even the greatest mystic would lay claim only to the intuition of an infinitesimal fraction of the content of the divine mind.

And we may perhaps hazard a further guess. Is it not likely that it is mainly God's feelings or valuations which the mystic receives into his own consciousness? Feelings cannot, of course, be severed from concepts (Chapter II, Section 3). But the feeling side may overwhelmingly predominate. This might account for the sense of illumination and the tremendous emotional surge which the mystic experiences. And that it is primarily God's feelings or valuations which flow into the mystic's mind will explain the conviction that the essential nature of God is love.

8

THERE remains the question what, if the theory of cells is accepted, must be the nature of God. There is only one answer which is consistent with the metaphysic of cells. God is a cell, or a super-cell. And by a super-cell I mean only a cell of great magnitude in regard both to its data and its consciousness. But the structure of God is the same as that of any other cell. He is composed of consciousness and private data. His omniscience will mean that to every actual datum in every other cell in the universe, and to every possible datum in its world-pattern, there corresponds in His cell an actual datum.

But He is not infinite. This word, applied either to His consciousness or His data, has no meaning. He is conscious of everything in the universe. But the number of things in the universe is finite (Chapter II, Section 5). And the number of God's thoughts and feelings about the things in the universe must be finite. There are no infinite beings in the universe (Chapter II, Section 5). And God is no exception to this rule.

Neither is God's time infinite. His relation to time is that His private time overlaps all other private times. He was before all the worlds, that is before all other cells, and will be after them. Hence there was no time when God was not. For His was the first time, and there was no time before Him. Neither will there be any time after Him. Thus as there was never a time when God was not, so there will never be a time when God will not be. He is alpha and omega yet His time must be finite. But His eternality may well mean that for Him His entire private time constitutes but a single specious present. So that past, present, and future, are spread out before Him at once.

That God is wholly a spirit means that all data are to Him non-somatic. In our cells there are two kinds of data, somatic and non-somatic. My somatic data include all the data of *my* body. They do not include those of my data which correspond to your data of your body. These latter are somatic data for you, but the corresponding data are non-somatic for me. Now in God's cell there are data corresponding to all the data in the universe, somatic and non-somatic. But for God those of His data which correspond to our somatic data are non-somatic. And He has no somatic data of His own. It is for this reason that God is invisible to us, or indeed to any being, except in the sense that His consciousness is visible to the mystic. God is invisible because in our cells there are no data corresponding to God's somatic data. For God has no somatic data.

That God is pure spirit does not of course mean that He is a naked consciousness without data. This is meaningless and impossible. The data of a cell do not constitute the body of its mind. The body is only the somatic data.

God is not all-powerful, nor is He the creator of the world. The world has no creator and no first cause. It *is*. The view that God is the creator is an offshoot of the vicious attempt to discover an ultimate explanation of the world, and of the cosmological argument. It was thought metaphysically necessary that the world must have a first cause. This first cause was then identified with the God of religion. Belief in God is the product of religious experience. Belief in a first cause is the product of bad metaphysics. It is in no sense necessary to religion, nor required by the religious consciousness. When the bad metaphysics is cut away, the conception of God as creator disappears. By this religion loses nothing. God is still the helper of men and their father, not in the sense that He created them, but in the sense that He cares for them as a father. And it is this which is the essence of the most enlightened religious belief.

God is not all-powerful. Or at least there is no reason to think that He is. And it is better not to think so. For if He is all-powerful, the problem created by the existence of evil is insoluble. If God is good and all-powerful, then His permission of the continuance of evil in the world is inexplicable. The belief that God is all-powerful is the product of two causes. First, it follows from the opinion that He is the creator. For if He could create the world, presumably He could destroy it or alter it in any way whatsoever. And secondly it arose from the habit of plastering God with flattering epithets as if He were an oriental potentate.

But God influences the world. This is possible through the principle of cellular correspondence. He controls and alters His own data or some of them. There occur corresponding changes in the data of the other cells in the universe. Thereupon the world changes. That He is not all-powerful means that not all the data of His cell are subject to the complete control of His consciousness. But His power is incalculably great. That He is good means that the changes which He imposes upon the world are motivated by His love for other beings. That there exist beautiful and good things in the world is not a proof of God's existence. But if we have independent knowledge of God's existence, we may then perhaps surmise that these beautiful and good things are His handiwork. We may believe that He battles for the right, that He fights along with us as our captain against evil, that He is the helper, lover, and refuge of men.

INDEX

INDEX

A

Absolute, The, 4, 5, 184, 201
Abstraction; as distinguished from concrete, 8; as a mental process, 163, 165
Activity, of consciousness, 144, 169, 173, 177-9
Alexander, S., v, 117, 118, 119, 120, 142, 143, 154, 155
American Realists, 184
Appearance, 3, 4
A priori, 13
Aristotle, 9, 181
Atoms, 34, 35, 106, 107
Attention, 43
Awareness, 146, 154, 155, 156, 161, 176

B

Behaviourism, 141, 145, 148, 152-3
Believing, 184-7; Russell on, 148-52
Bergson, 233, 246-7
Berkeley, Bishop, vi, 7, 8, 9, 11, 12, 28, 38-40, 76, 103, 116, 119, 130, 136, 140, 148, 154, 238, 240, 241, 242, 243
Bradley, F. H., 3, 4, 7, 60 n.
Bridgman, Professor, 20
Broad, Professor C. D., v, 69 n., 94
Buddha, The, 224

C

Causal Argument, for physical objects, 125-7
Causality, 12, 13, 78-80
Causal Series, distinguished from object series, 88-90
Cellular Correspondence, Principle of, 62 *et seq.*; alleged improbability of, 75 *et seq.*; as basis of communication, 68-71; as basis of mutual influence, 71-5
Christianity, 6
Common Sense View of the World, 92, 93, 94, 95 *et seq.*, 106, 127
Common World, 62, 66, 90, 91

Communication, 62, 66, 68-71, 90
Concepts, 10-13; cultural, 223, 224; distinguished from images, 157; not static, 157-8; perceptual, 222; submergence of, 159, 162, 163 *et seq.*, 222
Concrete, The, 3, 4, 5, 8, 35
Consciousness, 22-3, 139 *et seq.*; as activity, 144, 169, 173, 177-9; behaviourism on, 152-3; Holt on, 141, 145; infinite regress in, 190-3; intensity of, 36, 37, 155, 173, 177, 179; James on, 146-8; Russell on, 148-52; searchlight theory of, 149; unity of, 57-61; universality of, 138, 179, 180
Construct, 92, 93
Constructions, 92; definition of, 93; of empty space, 104-5; of interperceptual existence, 100-2; of intersensory objects, 103-4; of public objects, 96-100; of public space and time, 104; of things and qualities, 102-3; pragmatic character of, 97-100
Contradictions, effect of in philosophy, 86
Copernican hypothesis, 91, 92
Correspondence, The relation of, 63, 64; *see also* Cellular Correspondence

D

Datum, data, 13; different kinds of, 19-20, 36; emotional, 17; God, 18, 19, 20, 44, 249; introspective, 17, 18, 19, 28; non-sensuous, 20, 36, 233; particularity of, 138, 179, 180; passivity of, 177, 179; primary and secondary, 140, 145, 187, 188, 189, 190; value, 44
Death, 46
Democritus, 34
Descartes, 7, 9, 28, 248
Design, distinguished from order, 245-6; argument from, 76, 82, 84, 245-8
Ding-an-sich, 123
Doubting, 184, 187
Duration-spread, 45

[259]

146, 148, 154, 185, 186, 188, 190, 191;
on believing, 145, 148-52; on consciousness, 148-52

S

Santayana, 32
Schelling, 7
Schopenhauer, 7
Science, 106-8
Scientific Objects, 106 n.
Scientific Materialism, 141
Secondary Qualities, 8
Selective Theory, of sensa, 117, 118-20,
136, 137
Self-consciousness, 187
Self-hypnotism, 168
Selflessness, 218
Sensibilia, 136, 137
Sensing, 159-61, 165, 166-7
Serenity, 224-5
Shakespeare, 207
Similarity, 63, 64, 191
Simplicity, in hypotheses, 128-31
Simultaneity, 20-1, 67
Sobriety, 214, 215
Socrates, 208, 209, 211
Sociality, 220
Solipsism, 32, 52, 108, 110
Solipsist Universes, 66
Sottishness, 208, 214
Space, 44, 45, 48, 50; empty, 50, 95,
104-5; relation of to cells, 44 et seq.
Space-time, 106
Special Causes, Fallacy of, 84, 127, 128,
246
Spinoza, 7, 76, 78, 80, 84, 238
Subjectivism, 38, 40
Submergence, of concepts, 159, 162, 163
et seq., 222
Substance, 9, 23, 28, 56, 102
Survival, 231-6
Sympathy, 221

T

Teleological Argument, 76, 82, 84, 245-8
Telepathy, 250
Thing and Quality, 95, 102-3
Thing in itself, 102
Thinking, nature of, 156-7
Time, 4, 5, 44, 45, 48; empty, 50, 51;
relation of to cells, 44 et seq.

U

Ultraviolet colour, 14, 15
Unconscious Thinking, 173, 176
Uniformity of Nature, 83
Unity, of consciousness, 57-61
Unrealities, 66
Universals, status of, 138, 181-4

V

Valuation, 36, 40-4, 186, 187, 194, 196,
252
Valuational Dispositions, 204, 206
Value, 41, 44; esthetic, 197, 199, 205,
210, 213, 215, 216, 217, 222 et seq.;
instrumental, 41, 198-9; intrinsic, 41,
198-9; moral, 199, 205, 210, 213, 217
et seq.; normative, 199, 201 et seq.;
optional, 199, 205; whether subjective,
195, 200, 215; whether objective, 200,
201 et seq., 215
Verificational Theory of Meaning, 21-2
Volition, 43, 186

W

Welfare, 207 et seq.
Will, 43, 186
Whitehead, A. N., 3, 37, 132, 141; on
empiricism, 24-7; on explanation, 29-
31; on induction, 30-1; on influence,
72-5
World-patterns, 65, 67